Politics of Uncertainty

OXFORD STUDIES IN INTERNATIONAL HISTORY

James J. Sheehan, series advisor

POLITICS OF UNCERTAINTY

The United States, the Baltic Question, and the Collapse of the Soviet Union

Una Bergmane

Library of Congress Cataloging-in-Publication Data
Names: Bergmane, Una, author.
Title: Politics of uncertainty : the United States, the Baltic question,
and the collapse of the Soviet Union / Una Bergmane.
Description: New York, NY : Oxford University Press, [2023] |
Series: Oxford studies in international history |
Includes bibliographical references and index.
Identifiers: LCCN 2022053641 (print) | LCCN 2022053642 (ebook) |
ISBN 9780197578346 (hardback) | ISBN 9780197578360 (epub) |
ISBN 9780197578377 (oso)
Subjects: LCSH: Baltic States—Foreign relations. | United States—
Foreign relations—Baltic States. | Baltic States—Foreign relations—
United States. | Soviet Union—Foreign relations—United States. |
United States—Foreign relations—Soviet Union. | Baltic States—History—1940–1991.
Classification: LCC DK502.715 .B47 2023 (print) | LCC DK502.715 (ebook) |
DDC 947.9084—dc23/eng/20221109
LC record available at https://lccn.loc.gov/2022053641
LC ebook record available at https://lccn.loc.gov/2022053642

DOI: 10.1093/oso/9780197578346.001.0001

Printed by Integrated Books International, United States of America

To Ukrainian scholars and students
who became soldiers,
who became refugees,
who continued to work and study
despite the war that Russia waged against their country.

CONTENTS

CONTENTS

ACKNOWLEDGMENTS

First and foremost, I want to thank Mario del Pero for his long-term mentorship, his interest in my work, and his support for my academic career.

This book originates from a doctoral dissertation that I wrote at Sciences Po under the supervision of Maurice Vaïsse and Anne de Tinguy. I'm thankful to both of them for agreeing to supervise my thesis and for their feedback on my work. I'm also grateful to the Fondation nationale des sciences politiques for funding the first three years of my doctoral studies.

Over the past ten years I benefited from the support of the Association for the Advancement of Baltic Studies. Aina Birnitis Dissertation-Completion Fellowship, Mudīte I. Zīlīte Saltups Fellowship, and AABS Emerging Scholars Grant have allowed me to conduct crucial research in the American archives and finish my dissertation. In 2020, Oxford University Press received the AABS Book Publication Subvention for the publication of this book. Beyond financial assistance, AABS has also provided a framework for exchanges with the vibrant community of Baltic Studies scholars worldwide. I'm especially grateful to Andres Kasekamp for being part of my thesis committee and for his ongoing interest in my work.

One of the highlights of my doctoral studies was the year I spent at Yale University as a Fox International Fellow. I'm very thankful to late Joseph Carrère Fox, whose commitment to international knowledge exchange made this experience possible. Julia Adams, who served as director of the Fox International Fellowship, continued to support my academic endeavors long after I left New Haven. I appreciate her kindness more than I have had a chance to express.

After defending my PhD, I left Paris and spent a wonderful year as a postdoc at the Mario Einaudi Center at Cornell University. My biggest thanks go to Matthew Evangelista not only for his comments on my work but also for his unwavering support for my career.

Large parts of this book were written during my two-year teaching fellowship at LSE. I would like to thank Matthew Jones and Piers Ludlow for creating a work setting that was truly enjoyable and productive. Kristina Spohr was on a sabbatical year during my time at LSE, but as I was teaching her courses, those two years felt like a long intellectual exchange with her. As one of the very few scholars who has worked on the Baltic question at the end of the Cold War before me and has served as a member of my thesis committee, she has a special place in my academic trajectory. I also had a chance to teach the Soviet history course of Vladislav Zubok and to discuss our perspectives on Soviet history during long lunch and coffee breaks and I'm thankful for these exchanges. A special thanks go to my fellow LSE teaching fellows Pete Millwood, Tom Ellis, and Anna Cant, as their support and friendship were crucial in fighting the workload and as well as the angst of the first London lockdown. Pete and Tom, Anita Prazmowska, Dina Gusejnova, Molly Avery, Marral Shamshiri-Fard, and Tom Wilkinson kindly read one of the last drafts of this book and/or my book proposal, and I am forever grateful for their insightful comments. A heartfelt thanks go to Alexandra Medzibrodszky not only for being a fantastic teaching assistant but also for becoming such a good friend.

This book would have been impossible to write without the support and feedback of my Estonian, Latvian, and Lithuanian colleagues Daina Bleiere, Violeta Davoliūtė, Mārtiņš Kaprāns, Mart Kuldkepp, Gustavs Strenga, and Kaspars Zellis. As I finish this book, my thoughts are with Vilius Ivanauskas, the young, brilliant Lithuanian historian who tragically passed away in 2018. During the early years of this project in Paris I greatly benefited from the support of Philippe Perchoc, Céline Bayou, Eric Le Bourhis, Sabine Dullin, Katerina Kesa, Emilija Pundziūtė-Gallois, and Eglė Rindzevičiūtė. Special thanks go to Kaarel Piirimäe, my Estonian comrade in so many academic adventures. I am very thankful to Diana T. Kudaibergenova, Botakoz Kassymbekova, and Anna Whittington for our exchanges on Central Asian and Soviet history.

I have to thank my current academic home Helsinki University, the Academy of Finland, Juhana Aunesluoma, and all my colleagues at the Political History Department and Aleksanteri Institute, for the opportunity to continue building my academic career in an intellectually stimulating, productive, and welcoming work environment.

The long road between the dissertation and the book was traveled in the company of my friends. My time at Sciences Po wouldn't have been the same without the inhabitants of the *salle des doctorants 224 boulevard Saint-Germain*, especially Sibylle Duhautois, Anna Konieczna, Charles Lenoir, and Paul Lenormand. I thank them for our many coffee breaks and their years-long support. The often-daunting task of navigating doctoral and postdoctoral academic life has been made easier by the comradeship of Gaetano Di Tommaso, Michele Di Donato, Andreas Mørkved Hellenes, and Bruno Settis. Marine Guillaume, Silvia Sorescu, and Camilo Umana Dajud, whom I met during my MA studies at Sciences Po, were the ones who made Paris feel like home, and they were the ones who make me long for it. In 2011 I met Cecilia Asperti, Katharina Gnath, and Charu Singh during our Fox Fellowship at Yale. Since then, we have kept being by each other's side despite often living on opposite sides of the world. The writing of this book has regularly been interrupted, made bearable, and relativized in its importance by the sound of an incoming group chat message. The never-ending conversation that started in the corridors of the Riga French Lycée has become the background rhythm of my life, and I thank Ilze Dalbiņa, Zanda Gajevska, Marta Elīna Martinsone, Anastasija Mežecka, Daina Pravorne, Elīza Simsone, and Sigita Zosule for that and so much more.

I'm deeply grateful to my editor at the Oxford University Press, Susan Ferber, for believing in this project, for her advice and guidance, and for the careful edits of this book. I thank the two anonymous reviewers for their constructive and stimulating feedback.

Last but not least, I have to thank my family. My parents-in-law Sandra and Simi, my *belles-soeurs* Marie and Nora, my goddaughter Paula, and my godmother Ināra for all the kindness, joy and encouragements they bring to my life. To my best friend Zuzanna, for what I can describe only by paraphrasing what Montaigne said about his friendship with Etienne de La Boétie: "because it is her, because it is me." To my siblings Marta and Toms, for being my friends and my teachers, my partners in crime, and my soulmates. To my mother Ieva for raising three kids through the tumultuous years of Soviet collapse and post-independence transition, for always beliving in me and for always being my true North. To my husband Lucas for being my love and my rock. For his immense support and help. For the life we have built together.

And finally, to those who have left us—my beloved grandparents Arnis and Jana—for having been with us.

Politics of Uncertainty

Introduction

"We are unknown men from an unknown country."
> —Kaarel Robert Pusta, head of the Estonian delegation
> to the Paris Peace Conference, 1919

"After all, if we make a mistake, we will destroy the state."
> —Nikolai Ryzhkov, Soviet prime minister during a Politburo
> meeting, July 14, 1989

"Who's the enemy? I keep getting asked . . . it's the inability to predict accurately; it's a dramatic change that can't be foreseen, and its events that can't be predicted."
> —George Bush, diary entry on February 24, 1990

"You have chosen the Baltics over me and let's leave it at that," an angry Mikhail Gorbachev said to George Bush on June 1, 1990.[1]

Three months earlier, on March 11, Lithuania had become the first Soviet republic to declare its independence. On March 30 and May 4, the two other Baltic states, Estonia and Latvia, announced the beginning of a transition period toward full sovereignty. The USSR, which considered the Baltic declarations illegal, harshly condemned them and imposed an economic blockade against Lithuania. Fearing an outbreak of violence in the region, the United States tried to de-escalate the crisis, pressuring all sides to engage in dialogue. When the Soviet and American presidents met during the Washington summit in June, Gorbachev, to his great surprise, realized that Bush was seriously considering not signing the newly negotiated Soviet American trade treaty because of the Baltic situation.

Politics of Uncertainty. Una Bergmane, Oxford University Press. © Oxford University Press 2023.
DOI: 10.1093/oso/9780197578346.003.0001

The idea that the United States could refuse to support the Perestroika effort because of events in the Soviet periphery outraged Gorbachev. To him, Estonia, Latvia, and Lithuania were an integral part of the USSR, and their secessionist tendencies were a distraction from what actually mattered—the monumental opportunity for change that the Perestroika project offered to his country and the world.

The Soviet president was not the only one whose hierarchies of importance were challenged by the sudden re-emergence of the Baltic question on the international agenda. George Bush, France's François Mitterrand, and Germany's Helmut Kohl were equally exasperated by the events at the margins of the Soviet empire that risked destabilizing Gorbachev and souring East-West relations at the time of German Reunification. Yet, for various reasons, the big powers were unable to keep the Baltic question out of international politics.

First and foremost, most Western states had not recognized the 1940 Soviet annexation of the Baltic countries as legal, and thus from 1989 to 1991, the White House had to perform a highly challenging balancing act: affirming their full support for the reformer Mikhail Gorbachev while claiming that in principle the three Baltic states deserved their independence. Furthermore, the Baltic question was not just an American foreign policy issue; domestic and transnational actors such as the US Congress and Lithuanian, Latvian, and Estonian diasporas actively pushed for a stronger US stand on Baltic independence. Finally, there was general uncertainty about how to deal with the disintegration of the Soviet Union. The rapidly changing situation in the USSR prevented the US government from having a coherent policy toward Soviet collapse, making it the object of endless hesitations and improvisations. Between 1989 and 1991, Washington and its European allies moved from extreme prudence regarding the Baltic claims to unconditional support for their independence. However, this change was reluctant and driven much more by domestic pressures and last-minute decisions than by realpolitik calculations and long-term strategy.

Moscow's problem with the Baltic countries can be best described in the words of Anatolijs Gorbunovs, a high-ranking Latvian communist who came to fully embrace the independence project between 1988 and 1990: "Gorbachev had no plan: neither how to let us free, nor how to keep us."[2] The Soviet leader indeed had no plan of how to deal with center-republic relations in general and the Baltic situation in particular. At first, around 1987, it seemed that there was no need to worry about Estonia, Latvia, and Lithuania; the three republics were relatively rich and relatively calm, there were no outbreaks of ethnic violence, and their leadership supported Perestroika. Then suddenly, starting from 1990, it was too late. Tallinn, Riga, and Vilnius pushed for independence and engaged in an active foreign policy. Baltic officials traveled to the West and were received at the White House, Élysée Palace, and Downing Street. In reality, of course, the pro-independence shift in the Baltic countries was not at all instantaneous. It had both historical and structural causes, but the Soviet power caught in the tremendous effort of implementing Perestroika reforms had no time, no plan, and no expertise to address grievances in the periphery. Since the early days of the Soviet state, relations between the Soviet center and the republics had been imperial: they were rooted in a system of interaction in which the dominant metropole exerted political control over the internal and external policy—the effective sovereignty—of the subordinate periphery.[3] When, after 1985, both the democratizing rationale of Perestroika and actors in the periphery pushed for reform in center-republic relations that would reduce the power asymmetry at the heart of the Soviet federal system, Moscow was caught unready, hesitant, and overwhelmed by other seemingly more urgent issues.

First and foremost, this book tells the story of how Moscow and Washington tried to deal with independence movements at the Soviet periphery, namely the Baltic countries. This problem at first seemed minor, but as it started to gain more and more international visibility, it risked derailing "the real issues" that actually mattered in the eyes of both Soviet and American leaders—the transformation of the Soviet state and transformation of international order. Second, it is an account of how, at times of profound historical change, marginal actors defy their marginality and find strategies for gaining visibility on the international stage.

In other words, this is a book about superpower struggles with uncertainty and Baltic struggles with invisibility. Through them, it tells a broader story of the Soviet collapse.

As an analytical concept, uncertainty carries multiple implications in international relations. It has been conceptualized either as fear or ignorance due to the lack of information or as confusion and indeterminacy arising from the ambiguity of information.[4] For the Bush administration, the problem was not a lack of information about the situation in the USSR but rather its abundance and ambiguity. The unexpected rise of a reformist leader in the USSR left Americans in uncharted waters, and they struggled to ascribe meaning to Gorbachev's actions and untangle the complexity of the Soviet internal struggles. In 1989 the incoming Bush administration mistrusted the Soviet leader and blamed President Reagan for not seeing the iron fist hidden in the velvet glove.[5] The US initiated pause in Soviet-American relations that lasted from Bush's inauguration day until the autumn of 1989 was directly due to American uncertainty about Soviet intentions. Two key questions preoccupied the American decision makers: was Gorbachev a genuine reformer, and would he be able to survive politically? Both had direct implications for US Baltic policy.

While after the fall of the Berlin Wall it seemed clear that the Soviet Union would not resort to violence to stop the democratization of Eastern Europe, the White House continued to fear a military crackdown in the Baltic republics. Constant American requests not to use force in Estonia, Latvia, or Lithuania were among the few consistent elements in US dealings with the Baltic question. At the same time, American leadership worried that the Baltic drive for independence could destabilize Gorbachev and thus tried different and often contradictory approaches to ease the tensions between Moscow and the Baltic capitals. Yet, Gorbachev's survival was not an end in itself. While cautioning the Estonians, Latvians, and Lithuanians not to put too much pressure on Gorbachev with their claims for independence, the White House did not hesitate to pressure him towards accepting full NATO membership for reunited Germany.[6]

Gorbachev's ambitious reforms pushed the Soviet society into an unknown territory, making uncertainty the everyday experience of all Soviet citizens. The Soviet leader and his advisors had a vision of a new, reformed Soviet Union, but they did not have a clear plan for how to handle the economic and social forces that were unleashed by the reforms. The routines and practices of center-periphery relations in the USSR were established for an authoritarian framework and shaped according to the imperial paradigm in which Moscow had the final say over the republics' affairs. However, the democratizing effect of Perestroika completely changed these dynamics. Starting from 1988, central power had to face something it had not seen before: an increasingly pluralistic and democratic periphery. On the one hand, Gorbachev and his entourage struggled to adapt to the new situation, in which it was not clear whom they could trust and to whom they should talk in the rapidly changing Baltic political landscape. On the other hand, Gorbachev's willingness to dwell upon this problem was limited, as his agenda was already oversaturated with seemingly more urgent issues including failing economic reforms, Armenian–Azerbaijani conflict over the Nagorno-Karabakh region, and international arms negotiations. Gorbachev's liberal advisors were proposing considerable autonomy or even independence for the Baltic republics. At the same time, the conservative forces gradually grew into the idea that force was the only answer to the Estonian, Latvian, and Lithuanian drive for independence. Caught between the two, Gorbachev hesitated and procrastinated, while the three Baltic republics progressed from demands of larger autonomy toward a determined push for independence.

The dynamics surrounding the Baltic question can be better understood by taking a broader perspective on Perestroika and what it meant for both Soviet society and the international community. This book relies on scholarship that conceptualizes Perestroika not just as a project of political and economic reforms but also as an attempt to both forge domestically and project internationally a new Soviet identity.[7] The scope and depth of reforms in both domestic and foreign policy envisioned by the Soviet liberal thinkers required no less than a reconceptualization of key ideas about the nature of the Soviet state and its place in the world. In domestic policies, it meant gradual embrace of such international norms as human rights, free speech, and democracy.[8] As Eduard Shevardnadze put it: "If we want to be a civilized country, we must have the same laws and regulations as the rest of the civilized world."[9] In foreign policy, it demanded the abandonment of what Alexander Yakovlev, one of the key Perestroika thinkers, called the "psychology of the besieged fortress."[10] The encircled revolutionary state was to become a member of a larger Western (and/or European) community, sharing values more important than class interests.[11] A key element in this Soviet paradigm shift was the refusal to use force both internationally and domestically. Although excessive state violence had been one of the pillars of the Soviet system since its inception, Gorbachev initially refused to see it as an option for solving international disputes and internal problems. At the same time the changes that Perestroika brought were never supposed to entail a dismantelemnt of the Soviet empire. While Gorbachev and his allies were willing to recosinder some of the imperial practices and reduce the power assimietry between the center and the republics, they planed to reform not to destroy the Soviet Union. Thus the story of Gorbachev's relations with Lithuania, Latvia, and Estonia is not just a story about the relations between the Soviet centre and the periphery at the time of Perestroika, it is also a story of a deep tension at the heart of the Perestroika project: the incompatibility between the democratisation of Soviet society and the preservation of the Soviet empire.[12]

The United States and its allies were pleased about and responsive to these developments but constantly wary that the window of opportunity opened by Gorbachev's reforms might close. The West's fears of a military coup, civil war, or general collapse of the USSR that could disturb the favorable international situation have often been mentioned in memoirs and scholarly literature.[13] Much less has been written about the fears of Westerners and Soviet liberal forces that Gorbachev himself could halt the reforms and sour East-West relations by starting a crackdown in the Baltics. This book demonstrates how, in the eyes of many, the state of the relations between the rebellious republics and Gorbachev was closely linked to the state of Perestroika. When Gorbachev drifted toward the conservatives and force was used in Vilnius and Riga, Soviet supporters of Perestroika, as well as Western policymakers, became alarmed about the future of Soviet reforms.

These dynamics show the role that norms and normative expectations played during the Perestroika years, both internationally and domestically. Norms, as collective expectations for the proper behavior of actors of a given identity, play both constitutive and regulative roles.[14] In the first case, they define actors' identities, while in the second, they function as standards prescribing behavior. Both Soviet liberal democratic circles and the international community expected the leadership of the newly reformed Soviet Union to find a peaceful solution to the Baltic problem. For the Soviet liberals, rejection of violence as a tool for achieving political goals was part of the larger enterprise of defining a new Soviet identity. Meanwhile, for the West, the Soviet refusal to use force in Eastern Europe was one of the main elements in overcoming the Cold War alienation and recognizing sameness in the former Soviet "other." In other words, while in Soviet internal politics abstention from excessive state violence played a constitutive role, on the international stage it had a regulative function: Soviet compliance with this norm reinforced the image of the new Soviet identity, shaped by the values of liberal democracies.[15]

The struggle for social visibility as a quest for empowerment is a key element in social movements' strategies and small-state foreign policy. Marginalized groups seek recognition from the mainstream to secure their rights: in a Hegelian perspective, freedom requires recognition by the other for its self-realization.[16] In this sense, internal politics are continuously shaped by recognition struggles. While Hegel himself was reluctant to apply his concept of recognition to interstate relations, international relations scholars have claimed that states seek not only recognition in the legal sense but also an international affirmation of their internally forged identity.[17]

The Estonian, Latvian, and Lithuanian independence movements first acted as non-state actors challenging Soviet power. After winning the 1990 elections and proclaiming independence or transition toward independence, they became representatives of three small states with complicated international status. At both stages, they reached out for international support but struggled to be seen and heard. To a certain extent, this was a practical problem that all small states encounter; while larger powers focus on changing the perception that others have of them, small states must first make a considerable effort to be seen.[18] For Estonia, Latvia, and Lithuania, the task was even more complicated. Until August 1991, their independence was not recognized and therefore they were not supposed to have a voice in the Westphalian system of sovereign states. Furthermore, in the eyes of Western policymakers the Baltic question was not perceived as important enough to actually be included in international negotiations at the time of German unification and the first Gulf War.

However, visibility in the international arena was essential for Baltic activists. Since their first calls for independence in 1989, Baltic pro-independence elites had been very skeptical of a scenario in which the USSR would willingly grant independence to Estonia, Latvia, and Lithuania. According to the official rhetoric of the independence movements, Baltic statehood should not depend on the USSR because Soviet power in the Baltic region was illegal. In reality, Baltic leaders simply did not believe that Moscow would ever be willing to let their countries leave the Union. Thus, independence seemed to be achievable only through international negotiations and international recognition. The idea of achieving national independence through the internationalization of the issue was not a new one. For example, the most decisive struggles for the independence of Algeria were carried out in the international arena.[19] Indeed, the situations were similar to the extent that neither Algerian nor Baltic nationalists were able to control their national territory, and thus their claims for sovereignty were abstract and largely dependent on their capacity to delegitimize French or Soviet rule internationally.

At the same time, international visibility had deeper meaning for the Baltic countries, beyond practical considerations. The rise of the Baltic independence movements was, to a considerable extent, an unintentional result of Perestroika. They started off in 1988 as popular fronts created to support Gorbachev's reforms: the three most prosperous Soviet republics[20] were especially eager to reform the Soviet system. Glasnost gave unprecedented freedom of speech to Soviet citizens and revealed deep frustration with Soviet rule in Estonia, Latvia, and Lithuania. Environmental concerns, anxiety over the low birth rates, discontent with the influx of migrants from other Soviet republics, and frustrations generated by long-term contradictions in Soviet nationality policies were amplified by the revelations of the scope of Stalin's repressions in the Baltic republics.

These developments increased ontological insecurity—a collective, socially constructed, and subjective fear about the future of the collective selves, defined as Estonian, Latvian, and Lithuanian nations.[21] By consequence in the late 1980s and early 1990s Baltic activists and governments saw themselves as being engaged in "existential politics" struggling for independence as a precondition of national survival.[22]

In turn, the emerging ontological insecurity accelerated the push toward independence, perceived in large parts of Baltic societies as the only sustainable future for the Estonian, Latvian, and Lithuanian nations. In the context of these existential anxieties, the international community functioned as the significant other that tests and testifies one's existence.[23] What Baltic independence activists sought was not only legal but also existential recognition and affirmation. Political scientist Erik Ringmar has distinguished four types of recognition that individual and collective actors seek: (1) visibility; (2) equal treatment; (3) acknowledgment of actors' individuality; and (4) acceptance by a group in which actors believe they belong.[24] For Estonian, Latvian, and Lithuanian independence activists, all these steps mattered: they wanted to be perceived as European nations, they underlined their specificity in the Soviet context, and they argued that their independence claims were as legitimate as were German calls for unity. This book traces the strategies that Baltic American diaspora, Baltic independence movements, and Baltic governments used for achieving visibility and recognition in both legal and ontological senses.

Much research has been published on the international and internal causes of the Soviet collapse, but very few works have made the connection between the two.

Among the many internal factors that have been viewed as contributing to the fall of the USSR are: the failure of the Soviet ideological project, misguided reforms, economic decline, interethnic tensions, the ethno-federal structure of the Soviet state, malfunctioning of its institutions, and the bid for power by republic elites.[25]

Works that deal with external influences upon the Soviet collapse have mostly focused on the interactions between Moscow as the imperial center and the outside world, especially the United States. Scholars have debated the role that Reagan's foreign policy did or did not play in the destabilization of the USSR and analyzed Bush's attempts to change the international order without destabilizing the USSR.[26] Meanwhile, other scholars have discussed long-term transformations in the Soviet elite's perception of the West and Europe, Western ideas, and universal values.[27] These works largely focus upon decision makers and elites in Moscow, projecting the impression that during the Soviet collapse, the central government still functioned as a gatekeeper between the international community and other Soviet actors. However, notable exceptions include scholarship on the impact that the collapse of Eastern European communism had upon Soviet republics,[28] the role of Ukraine in the Soviet collapse and the US attitude toward Ukrainian independence,[29] and Western (especially West German) attitudes toward Baltic claims for independence.[30] *Politics of Uncertainty* aims at contributing to this emerging scholarship by studying the triangular relations among Moscow, the Baltic capitals, and Washington and highlighting the interconnections between the domestic and external factors in the Soviet collapse.

It has often been argued that, despite their geographical proximity, Estonia, Lithuania, and Latvia are too different to be put under the same "Baltic" label. Indeed, their grouping as the Baltic states is a rather recent phenomenon. In the eighteenth and nineteenth centuries, the world *Balt* was used to refer to the Baltic Germans, who at the time constituted the ruling class in most parts of the current-day Estonia and Latvia.[31] As a result, the Baltic provinces of the Tsarist Empire were Estonia (northern parts of contemporary Estonia), Livonia (Southern Estonia and Northern Latvia), and Kurland (Western Latvia). In the interwar period, the term "Baltic states" appeared for the first time, but it included not three but four countries, linking Finland to its southern neighbors. It was only in the context of the Cold War that the international community started to use the term "Baltic states" to designate Estonia, Latvia, and Lithuania. At the same time, Soviet citizens referred to the three as "Baltic Republics."

The three Baltic nations, often perceived as almost identical, are very different indeed. The Latvian and Lithuanian languages are the last living ones of the Baltic language group, which belongs to the Indo-European family. Estonian is a Finno-Ugric language. Estonians are Protestants, Lithuanians are Catholics, and Latvians are predominantly Protestants, with a Catholic region in the southeast of the country. Furthermore, both Estonia and Latvia have a significant Russian-speaking minority that is mostly Orthodox.

Latvians and Estonians share a similar history, from which Lithuania diverges. The Estonian and Latvian ancestors were Christianized during the thirteenth century by Northern German missionaries with the military support of the Teutonic Order. Lithuanian pagans resisted the Crusaders, and the Duchy of Lithuania was founded in mid-thirteenth century. In 1387 it became the last European country to formally embraced Christianity. In 1569, the Grand Duchy of Lithuania and Poland formed the Polish-Lithuanian Commonwealth. Until 1561 the territory of present-day Latvia and Estonia was part of medieval Livonia, a set of territories governed by local bishops and the Teutonic Order. From 1561 to the early eighteenth century, the former Livonia was divided between Polish-Lithuanian Commonwealth and Kingdom of Sweden. In 1721, the region of present-day Estonia and a large part of Latvia were conquered by Peter the Great. Lithuania and Southern Latvia were included in the Russian Empire after the partition of the Commonwealth by Russia, Habsburg monarchy, and Prussia in the late eighteenth century. In general, the history of Estonia and Latvia was very much influenced by the presence of "Baltic barons", or Baltic Germans who arrived in the region during the Crusades and formed the aristocratic elite of both Latvia and Estonia until the First World War. The history of the Lithuanian people is marked by their relations with Poland. Even after the proclamation of independence in 1918, Lithuania's internal dynamics and its international position were strongly influenced by its conflict with Poland over the city of Vilnius. An authoritarian coup d'état took place in the same year as the one in Poland (1926), while Latvian and Estonian democracies survived from 1918 until 1934.

Despite these differences, all three Baltic countries were occupied by the USSR in 1940, and 43,000 of their inhabitants were deported to Siberia on June 14, 1941.[32] In late June 1941, all of them were occupied by Nazi Germany, and 90 percent of their Jewish citizens were killed by the occupying power and local collaborators. In all three countries, the populations both resisted and collaborated with the USSR and Nazi Germany, but the situation was more complicated in Latvia and Estonia, where Nazi Germany created special Latvian and Estonian Legions in the Waffen SS. Thus, by the end of the war, Latvians and Estonians were fighting in the ranks of the Red Army as well as on the Nazi side. Between 1944 and 1945, about 140,000 Latvians, 75,000 Lithuanians, and 65,000 Estonians left their homelands as war refugees.[33] After the Second World War in all three countries, the so-called forest brothers continued to lead a partisan war against the Soviet Union. In Lithuania, this resistance movement was much stronger than in Latvia and Estonia. On March 25, 1949, 95,000 additional residents of Estonia, Latvia, and Lithuania were deported to Siberia. The most important difference between the three countries during the Soviet period was, that while the ethnic situation did not change much in Lithuania, it was drastically modified in Estonia and Latvia by the arrival of migrants from other Soviet republics, mostly from Russia, Ukraine, and Belarus.[34]

Thus, while the Baltic states' languages, historical experiences, and religious affiliations differ, this book analyzes them collectively for two reasons. First, between 1989 and 1991, the international community, as well as the Soviets, were dealing with the "Baltic question" and did not separate the Lithuanian, Latvian, and Estonian issues. Annexed by the USSR in 1940, the three countries were the only Soviet republics that, in Western perception, legally did not belong to the USSR. They were the only ones with twenty year experience of independent statehood in living memory and the first ones to challenge the integrity of the Soviet Union. Second, in light of their common tragic history and the similar challenges they faced in their quest for independence, all three populations showed a considerable degree of solidarity while their leaders sought to cooperate. In other words, the external actions of Estonians, Latvians, and Lithuanians during these three consequential years can be analyzed together because their situations vis-à-vis the USSR were similar. Likewise, they were similarly perceived by the West, and their leaders opted for coordination and cooperation.

To create a fuller picture of the triangular relations among the Baltic states, the USSR, and the United States, this books relies on research conducted in multiple archives throughout Europe as well as primary sources from the United States and in the Russian Federation.

To convey the Baltic side of the story, it draws on the Estonian national archives, Latvian national and diplomatic archives, and Lithuanian diplomatic archives. To tell the American side of this story, it utilizes, among others, papers from the Bush administration and its key players, congressional records, and the National Security Archive.

The research on the Soviet side of the story has been facilitated by materials from the Gorbachev Foundation, excerpts from Politburo meetings, and documents on Soviet attempts to handle center-republic relations.[35] While these sources provide essential insights into Soviet policies and debates, the selected documents are often only partially published and thus sometimes yield more questions than answers. Beyond these archival sources, the book draws on twenty-seven original interviews carried out with American, Estonian, French, Latvian, and Lithuanian diplomats and officials, as well as with Baltic diaspora activists.

The book traces the raise and resolution of the Baltic questions over a time span of about fifty years. The first chapter covers the period from the occupation of the Baltic states in 1940 until the Perestroika era. Meanwhile, the four other chapters analyze the crucial years between 1989, when the Baltic poplar movements first proclaimed independence as their ultimate goal, and 1991, when three months after the recognition of Estonian, Latvian, and Lithuanian independence, the Soviet Union collapsed.

Chapter 1, "The Origins of the Baltic Question," provides an overview of the three elements that made the Baltic situation a specific case in the Soviet context: the decision in 1940 by the United States not to recognize the annexation of Estonia, Latvia, and Lithuania as legal, the emergence of an active and well-organized Baltic-American diaspora during the Cold War, and the rise of the Baltic independence movements in the late 1980s. In addressing these three topics, the complexity of the Baltic issue is revealed: the legal debate about their international status, the ties between the Baltic diaspora and the US Congress, and the multi-causal roots of Baltic discontent with the Soviet rule.

Chapter 2, "'Have you not noticed our absence?': The Baltic Question during the Annus Mirabilis of 1989," follows the transformation of the Baltic question from a purely internal Soviet nationalities problem to an international issue in 1989. It analyzes the Soviet and American policies toward Estonia, Latvia, and Lithuania in the context of Eastern European revolutions, highlighting the American unwillingness to get involved with the Baltic question, as well as the country's inability to avoid it. The chapter sheds light on Baltic attempts to use the history of the Molotov-Ribbentrop Pact to delegitimize Soviet rule, both at home and abroad. It pays particular attention to the relations between Baltic independence movements and other Soviet actors such as Gorbachev's liberal advisors, Yeltsin's circle, and other republics. The chapter ends with the Malta summit, during which Bush and Gorbachev failed to effectively communicate their respective positions on the Baltic issue.

Chapter 3, "Building a New World Order?" The Lithuanian Crisis of Spring 1990," examines American policy regarding the so-called Lithuanian crisis, a period of increasing tensions between the USSR and the Baltic states, which started with the Lithuanian independence declaration on March 11, 1990, and ended with its suspension on June 29, 1990. The international context and the ongoing talks on German reunification were crucial in shaping not only the American but also the European responses to the Baltic declarations: the Baltic situation had to be appeased before it derailed negotiations on German reunification. It argues that the White House's attempts to defuse the crisis were often hesitant, chaotic, and to a considerable extent driven by congressional pressures and Baltic diaspora grievances.

Chapter 4, "The End of Perestroika?: The Baltic Quest for Visibility and the Soviet Crackdown," looks at the Baltic efforts to engage with the international community during the second half of 1990, which ended with their expulsion from the CSCE Paris summit. The chapter then analyzes Gorbachev's so-called turn to the right, the use of force in the Baltics in January 1991, and the international reactions to these events in the context of the Gulf crisis. It explains the international and Soviet domestic outrage that followed the deaths of twenty civilians in Vilnius and Riga by a general fear that violence in the Baltic countries meant the end of Perestroika. The chapter describes the initial American hesitation to take a strong stand against Gorbachev in the wake of the Gulf War and the subsequent hardening of the White House attitude after the killings in Riga. It argues that international pressures played a crucial role in stopping the Soviet crackdown in the Baltics.

Chapter 5, "The Rise of the Republics, the Fall of the Center: The Baltic Exception and the Collapse of the USSR," underscores US attempts to understand the complexity of the Soviet domestic struggles and predict the possible future of the USSR during the first half of 1991. It describes the increasing power diffusion in the Soviet Union and the growing cooperation between the Baltic states and Boris Yeltsin before turning toward the international recognition of the Baltic states after the August coup. The US and European decisions to restore diplomatic relations with the Baltic states did not mean the abandonment of Gorbachev or acceptance of Soviet disintegration. Rather, it was a final disconnection of the Baltic and Soviet questions.

Thirty years after the Soviet collapse, this book aims to tackle the interplay between international and domestic dynamics in the Soviet disintegration process. Based on extensive archival research, it investigates the triangular relations among the US government, Baltic independence movements, and Moscow during the Perestroika years. Both Washington and Moscow wanted to defuse the Baltic crisis, but neither was certain about how to do it. The United States tried to perform a highly changeable balancing act of supporting Baltic independence without jeopardizing its relations with the Kremlin. Meanwhile, Gorbachev faced an increasingly pressing choice between democratization and preservation of the Soviet empire. In other words, this book studies the relations between those at the top of international and domestic power hierarchies with those situated at their margins. It shows how at the time of deep historical change the disruption of existing power structures causes uncertainty that limits the agency of the powerful and opens windows of opportunity for those seen as marginal.

CHAPTER 1
The Origins of the Baltic Question

We could hardly consider that international peace and stability will really have ceased
to be threatened as long as Europe is faced with the fact that is has been possible for
Moscow to crush these small countries which have been guilty of no real provocations
and which have given evidence of their ability to handle their own affairs.
>   —George Kennan, NSC 20/1, 1948

On April 17, 1990, George H. W. Bush met with a delegation of senators led by Senate Majority Leader Democrat George Mitchell, to discuss the Baltic question. Dissatisfied with the meeting, he later wrote in his diary: "They don't want to make any specific suggestions. They say you are going to do something, but they are not saying what it is, and that's right— Congress has the luxury of doing that."[1]

This encounter summarizes very well the US domestic dynamics surrounding the Baltic problem between 1989 and 1991. The president felt compelled to support the Baltic states but feared jeopardizing US-Soviet relations. Congress found the president's efforts too weak and asked for a stronger US stand in support of Baltic independence. The president complained that Congress was taking the high ground on the Baltic question without considering the disastrous consequences of a possible U-turn in US-Soviet relations.

At the same time, while the various actors involved in US foreign policymaking—the president, the National Security Council, the State Department, the Senate, and the House of Representatives—were divided on the question of *how* to deal with the Baltic problem, everybody involved

Politics of Uncertainty. Una Bergmane, Oxford University Press. © Oxford University Press 2023.
DOI: 10.1093/oso/9780197578346.003.0002

in this debate agreed that the Baltic claims for independence could not be dismissed as a Soviet internal affair.

The two primary factors behind the US interest in these rebellious Soviet republics were the non-recognition policy and the long-established relations between the US Congress and the Baltic diaspora. Both were related to the actors' uses, interpretations, and understandings of the past. In the eyes of the West, the Baltic states had a special legal status because of the events of the Second World War: in the summer of 1940 when Soviet forces entered the territories of independent Estonia, Latvia, and Lithuania, the United States refused to recognize this annexation as legal. The idea that the Baltic states were not legally a part of the USSR was a powerful mental frame through which US decision makers considered at the Baltic situation. At the same time, this legal position would have had limited practical consequences once the Cold War tensions faded had the US Congress not regularly called upon the president to take a more active stand on the Baltic question.

Traumatized by war and displacement, Baltic refugees in the United States built their identity around the idea of the possible re-establishment of Baltic independence. Constant advocacy for a stronger US stand on the Baltic question gave former refugees a sense of purpose and continuity. Over the years, Baltic diaspora had established strong links with several members of the US Congress. During the crucial period of 1989–1991, these senators and representatives actively advocated for the Baltic cause. In other words, the keen interest that the US Congress and the Baltic diaspora took in the fate of the Baltic nations at the end of the Cold War gave the non-recognition policy real substance.

At the same time, the non-recognition policy was hardly a crystal-clear principle from which equally clear ideas about how to deal with the Baltic question would ensue. The non-recognition policy emerged in 1940 as result of the rise of the legalist approach to international relations in the interwar period; from the US national interest, as interpreted in the pre–Operation Barbarossa geopolitical situation; and from personal connections between certain US officials and the Baltic countries. The policy had different functions in different contexts and different meanings for different actors. For most Western countries during the Cold War, it was a legal position and a diplomatic tradition. For Estonians, Latvians, and Lithuanians who left their homelands at the end of the Second World War, it was first an unexpected safeguard against forced return to the USSR, then for many among them an entry ticket to the United States, and finally a reassuring narrative that reinforced the myth of possible return. For the emerging Baltic elites in the late 1980s, the narrative about the illegality of Soviet actions in 1939/1940 became a mobilizing tool domestically and the main argument for independence internationally. Finally, for the Estonian and Latvian right wing, it also became a tool for exclusion: if Soviet action in 1940 was illegal, then the Baltic states were occupied territories, and if the Baltic states were occupied territories, then immigrants from other Soviet republics were merely colonists, not rightful citizens.

This chapter follows these dynamics while laying out crucial context for the 1989–1991 dynamics. First, it explains the origins of the Baltic question by presenting an overview of the 1940 events and the development of the US non-recognition policy. It then describes the Baltic diaspora's lobbying efforts and analyzes the main reasons for the congressional interest in the Baltic problem. Finally, it summarizes the circumstances behind the emergence of the Baltic independence movements in the late 1980s.

THE BALTIC QUESTION FROM THE SECOND WORLD WAR TO THE COLD WAR

The process that led to the Soviet annexation of Lithuania, Latvia, and Estonia can be divided into four stages: the conclusion of the Soviet-Nazi pact on August 23, 1939; the establishment of Soviet military bases on Baltic soil in the fall of 1939; the occupation in June 1940; and the illegal annexation a few weeks later, in August.

This process occurred against the backdrop of broader Soviet attempts to gain control over its western neighbor states, in the anticipation of the upcoming war that Stalin had feared since the late 1920s. After the signing of the Molotov-Ribbentrop Pact and its secret protocol dividing Eastern Europe in Soviet and Nazi zones of influence in August 1939, the USSR attacked Poland and Finland. Just a week after the Baltic occupation, the USSR issued an ultimatum to Romania, demanding the immediate cession of Bessarabia and Northern Bukovina.

In the period between the conclusion of the Molotov-Ribbentrop Pact and the occupation in June 1940, the three authoritarian governments of the Baltic states believed that they might preserve their sovereignty by closely cooperating with the USSR. The military threat that constantly loomed in the background of Baltic-Soviet negotiations left them with little choice. Either they would have to form an agreement with USSR, or they would have to fight and almost certainly lose a war.[2] Thus, in the autumn of

1939, the Baltic states unlike Finland acceded to Soviet demands to establish Red Army bases on their soil. To preserve their legitimacy in the eyes of their populations, the regimes of Lithuania's Antanas Smetona, Latvia's Kārlis Ulmanis, and Estonia's Konstantin Päts insisted both internationally and domestically that their relations with the USSR were friendly and free of any coercion.[3]

On June 14, 1940, the day the Nazi army marched into Paris, the Soviet government presented an ultimatum to Lithuania, demanding for the formation of a new Soviet-friendly government and the free entrance of Soviet forces into its territory.[4] In the early hours of June 15, the Latvian border post at Masļenki was attacked by Soviet troops: three border guards and two civilians were killed; thirty-seven were arrested and brought to the USSR. On June 16, similar ultimatums were made to Latvia and Estonia. Anticipating possible Baltic resistance, Moscow had prepared camps for 50,000–70,000 Baltic prisoners of war.[5] However, the Baltic governments decided not to resist the USSR, and the Red Army occupied their countries in just a few hours. Once again, their authoritarian leaders believed that concessions to Stalin's demands might allow them to preserve some form of independence, or at least avoid large-scale human losses. While the Lithuanian president fled the country, his Latvian and Estonian counterparts remained in place and actually facilitated the Soviet takeover, before they themselves were deported in July. Even in the wake of the Soviet occupation, the general public was still unsure about what precisely the arrival of the Soviet troops meant, and many lived under the illusion that their governments were still able to control the situation.

Meanwhile the Soviet authorities were preparing to legitimize their takeover through rigged elections. On June 7, Stalin's emissaries—the chief of the Leningrad Communist Party Andrei Zhdanov, Stalin's chief prosecutor during the Great Terror Andrei Vyshinsky, and deputy commissar of foreign affairs Vladimir Dekanozov—arrived in Estonia, Latvia, and Lithuania. New governments were immediately formed under their instructions, and in July 1940 Moscow-orchestrated elections were organized in the Baltics. In all three countries a single list of candidates was accepted—that of the "working people." Although before the elections, "working people's lists" advocated friendly relations between the USSR and the independent Baltic states, in late July 1940 the new pro-Soviet parliaments applied for membership to the Soviet Union without holding a referendum on this question. The USSR annexed Lithuania, Latvia, and Estonia on August 3, 5, and 6, 1940, respectively.

US Reactions to the Occupation of the Baltic States

While the official Soviet narrative about the events of 1940 argued that on June 21 1940, "a spontaneous uprising of the working people" had taken place in Estonia, Latvia, and Lithuania, Western diplomats in their personal writings and official reports insisted that the annexation of the Baltic states was carried out under Soviet coercion.[6] For example, three days after the Soviet entry into Latvia, the first secretary of the French Legation in Riga, Jean Jacques de Beausse, wrote in his diary: "We are not here for much longer. The annexation by the USSR is already half done, and the true Latvians are desperate."[7] On July 13 the US minister in Lithuania, after describing the circumstances under which the parliamentary elections were being held in Lithuania, concluded: "Grave doubt and concern arise regarding the possibility of free expression of the true will of the Lithuanian nation through the impending elections."[8]

The United States, which had not yet entered the Second World War, decided to react to the Soviet occupation of the Baltic states in the same way it had to the Nazi occupation of other European countries. In April 1940, following the Nazi invasion of Denmark and Norway, Roosevelt had issued executive order 8389, under which the US Treasury froze all assets of European states occupied by Nazi Germany. On June 15, 1940, this order was amended by the president and applied to the three Baltic states occupied by the Soviet Union.

Furthermore, on July 23, Under Secretary of State Sumner Welles (who was replacing Secretary Cordell Hull) made a public announcement qualifying Soviet actions as predatory. He stated that the United States was opposed to "any form of intervention on the part of one state, however powerful, in the domestic concerns of any other sovereign state, however weak" and to "any activities that were carried out by use of force or by the threat of force."[9] The declaration later turned out to be the beginning and the foundation of the Western non-recognition policy regarding the Soviet annexation of the Baltic states. It lasted over a half century.

The US move can be explained by three different factors: the rise of the legalist approach to international relations in the interwar period; the situation on the international stage in 1940; and the internal dynamics in the US administration.

Welles's declaration on Soviet entry in the Baltic states in 1940 stated that "opposition to all activities carried out by the use of force or the threat of use of force is the founding principle of relations between states."[10] This stand is an example of the gradual change in international relations that occurred after the First World War. During the 1920s, the tragic legacy of the Great War generated transnational attempts to change the basis of international conduct. While secret diplomacy and bilateral alliances were to be replaced by multilateral institutions, the use of force was to be restricted by international law and norms. The most striking example of this was the Kellogg-Briand Pact of 1928. This agreement, signed by more than sixty states, outlawed war and the use of force in international relations. In the light of the Second World War, this document has often been seen as a utopian delusion of the 1920s. However, in a recent study, legal scholars Oona Hathaway and Scott Shapiro have challenged this perception, explaining that August 27, 1928, was a "turning point in world history." Before the signature of the Kellogg-Briand Pact, the legal rights to territory, people, and goods were decided by war, and agreements negotiated at gunpoint were binding.[11] After the signature of the pact, the principle *ex injuria jus non oritur* (law does not arise from injustice) gradually emerged as an international norm. Thus, even if war did not disappear with the signature of the Kellogg-Briand Pact, fighting, or the threat of war, ceased to be a tool with which to create rights over territory.

In 1932, reacting to the Japanese invasion of Manchuria, US Secretary of State Henry Stimson informed the Japanese government that "The U.S. Government does not intend to recognize any situation or agreement which may be brought about by means contrary to the covenants and obligations of the Pact of Paris of August 27th, 1928, to which both Japan and China, as well as the US, are parties."[12] This statement became known as the Stimson Doctrine: the refusal to recognize any international territorial changes that were executed by force. In the summer of 1940, this doctrine was applied to the Baltic case. Baltic assets in the United States reminded frozen despite Soviet demands to transfer them to the "new governments." Latvian and Lithuanian legations in Washington and the Estonian consulate general in New York kept their official status, and Baltic ships were blocked in American ports.

The American press applauded this decision as a selfless application of high moral principles. The United States "had been presented with a choice and had made a decision," a *New York Times* journalist wrote on July 24; "the Russian action had forced the issue of whether the same yardstick should be applied to international morality in all cases or only against governments with which the country had clashed."[13]

Even though, as the journalist pointed out, there had not been serious conflicts between the two United States and USSR, they were initially leaning toward different sides in the next global conflict. While USSR relations with Nazi Germany were more friendly than neutral, the United States observed the rise of Nazi power with great concern.

Whereas European diplomats perceived Soviet actions in northeastern Europe as a continuation of Tsarist imperial traditions,[14] the American diplomats tended to analyze them in the context of the alliance of the two totalitarian powers. For example, a *New York Times* editorial of October 3 stated: "The swift and cold-blooded manner in which sovereign nations are summoned one by one to hear what their future status is to be shows Stalin to be something more than an apt imitator of Hitler. His method of intimidation and conquest is quicker and quieter."[15] US leaders were closely following Soviet relations with the Axis powers and were willing to link their Baltic policy with Soviet attitudes toward Nazi Germany and its allies.

Finally, it has also been argued that there was a link between the fact that many influential American Cold War diplomats had started their careers in the US legation in Latvia and the later American commitment to the non-recognition policy.[16] In late 1930s a group of diplomats within the State Department took an approach dubbed "Riga axiom," which pushed for a more aggressive US policy toward Moscow. Named after the Latvian capital, this perspective was supported by men such as Robert F. Kelley, Loy W. Henderson, Charles E. Bohlen, and George Kennan, who had served there in the late 1920s and early 1930s. Indeed, while Kennan was not especially fond of the Baltic states per se, he saw the annexations as a dangerous breach of international law.[17] In 1941 Kennan, while working in the US embassy in Berlin, warned his colleague Henderson in the State Department against too close US alignment with the USSR, as it would identify the nation "with the Russian destruction of the Baltic States, with the attack against Finnish independence, with the partitioning of Poland . . . and with the domestic policy of a regime which is widely feared and detested throughout this part of the world."[18]

Henderson himself had even stronger links with the Baltic states than Kennan. He had served in the American Red Cross Commission to Western Russia and the Baltic States between 1918 and 1920 and had spent almost six months in the Baltics during the Estonian, Latvian, and Lithuanian wars of independence. Between 1927 and 1930 he was third and then the second secretary to the US legation in Latvia, where he met his Latvian wife, Elise Marie Heinrichson. After having served in the US embassy in Moscow between 1934 and 1938, Henderson became assistant chief of the Division of European Affairs.[19] During these years in Moscow, he became close friends with the Latvian minister to the USSR, Alfrēds Bīlmanis. In 1940 both Bīlmanis and Henderson met again in Washington, DC, when the former was serving as Latvian minister in the United States and the latter worked at the State Department.

On July 15, 1940, Henderson prepared a memorandum on the Baltic situation urging the US government not to recognize Soviet rule in Estonia, Latvia, and Lithuania. "Is the government of the United States," Henderson wrote, "to apply certain standards of judgment and conduct to aggression by Germany and Japan which it will not apply to the aggression of the USSR? In other words is the government of the US to follow one policy with respect to say Czechoslovakia, Denmark, and German-occupied Poland, and another policy with respect to Latvia, Estonia, Lithuania and Finland, which before the end of the year is likely to suffer the same fate as the other three Baltic states?"[20] It was Henderson, too, who prepared the draft of Welles's July 23 announcement that launched the non-recognition policy.[21] While the birth of the non-recognition policy was related to legal considerations, geopolitical calculation, and personal ties, its continuance was mostly due to the rise of the Cold War tensions.

As the tragic events of the Second World War unfolded, the United Sates had to adapt its position regarding the Baltic question according to the changing military and political realities. On June 22, 1941, war between Nazi Germany and the Soviet Union broke out; a few weeks later the Baltic states were occupied by German forces; in late 1941 the USSR and the United States started to fight on the same side; in 1943 the Red Army began to advance toward the West; and in 1944 it reached the borders of the Baltic states. In 1944/1945 it liberated and at the same time reoccupied Estonia, Latvia, and Lithuania.

In principle, the eventual restoration of Soviet power in the Baltic seemed incompatible with the American and British war aims defined in the Atlantic Charter. Issued on August 14, 1941, the charter emphasized that both powers wished to see "no territorial changes that do not accord with the freely expressed wishes of the peoples concerned" and that they looked forward to seeing "sovereign rights and self-government restored to those who have been forcibly deprived of them."[22] State Department officials assured Baltic diplomats in the US that the Atlantic Charter applied also to the Baltic case.[23]

Still, while very promising from the Baltic perspective, the charter played little role in their destiny or in the fate of Eastern Europe more widely. The postwar settlements in Eastern Europe, including the Baltic states, were determined not by principles and ideas, but by the military realities on the ground. By the end of the Second World War, the Red Army was controlling European territories from Berlin to Moscow and from the Baltic Sea to the Black Sea. The United States was not ready to risk a third world war by defying the USSR and, in the light of wartime cooperation, believed in the possibility of substantial dialogue in the future. Thus, the emerging superpower was willing to recognize the whole of Eastern Europe as a Soviet sphere of influence. The situation of the Baltic states, even if closely linked to the fate of the other Eastern European states, was to a certain extent different, as the USSR was not just seeking their inclusion in its zone of influence but a direct re-annexation. From the Soviet point of view, the issue of the Baltic countries was closely linked to the question of Eastern Poland: both "territories" had been part of the USSR between 1939/1940 and 1941, and of Tsarist Russia before the First World War. And both Eastern Poland and the Baltic countries were defined as Soviet zones of influence in the Molotov-Ribbentrop Pact. Avoiding any direct reference to its secret protocols with Nazi Germany, the USSR started to refer to the Curzon line instead of the Molotov-Ribbentrop line. However, when during the Tehran Conference British foreign secretary Anthony Eden maintained that there was no difference between the two, Stalin replied: "Call it what you will, we still consider it right and just."[24] The USSR first sought recognition of its claims in the Baltics and Eastern Poland during the negotiations on the British-Soviet friendship treaty in 1942. In this case the linkage between the Baltic countries and Eastern Poland turned out to be advantageous for the Baltic countries; the UK refused to enter into such a deal, mainly because of its links with Poland, not with the tiny Baltic states.[25]

Both questions were again raised together by President Roosevelt on December 1, 1943, the last day of the Tehran Conference. In his rhetoric, the US president linked both questions to the upcoming US presidential elections of November 1944. He explained to Stalin that, even if he accepted the river Oder as the Soviet-Polish border, he could not voice his support for this plan in public, as there were 6–7 million American voters of Polish descent. Along the same lines, the president emphasized that he fully understood that the Baltic countries "had in history and also recently" been a part of Russia. According to the note taker Bohlen, he even "added jokingly" that he did not intend to go to war with the USSR when its army reoccupied these territories.[26] Still, the president made it clear that the question of the will of the Baltic people and referenda in these territories was important for American public opinion in general, and for Baltic American voters in particular.[27] Indeed, in the 1930s there was already an important Baltic community in the United States, mostly of Lithuanian descent, and it, together with other ethnic minorities, had largely supported the New Deal alliance.[28]

Stalin replied by pointing out that when the Baltic countries "had no autonomy under the last Czar," neither the United States nor Britain had raised the question of public opinion and thus "he didn't quite see why it was raised now."[29] Stalin advised Roosevelt to inform public opinion and "do some propaganda work." He also added that the Baltic nations would have "plenty of opportunities" to express their will under the Soviet constitution but that any international control would be unacceptable.[30] However, when the US president insisted that a public Soviet declaration on such elections in the Baltics would be very helpful to him personally, Stalin avoided making any promises.[31]

As this conversation shows, even if Roosevelt had unofficially agreed to the Soviet annexation of Eastern Poland and the Baltic States, in the case of the Baltic states he tried at least to negotiate a referendum. At the same time, he neither insisted on the issue nor returned to it in his later meetings with Stalin. The Baltic states were thus directly included in the USSR, while the rest of Eastern Europe stayed formally independent. Furthermore, in the Baltic case the USSR made no public promises to hold free elections, while it did make such a commitment as regards Eastern European territories, during the Yalta conference.[32]

However, even if the Baltic question and the Polish eastern border questions were treated together in Tehran, they were not perceived in exactly the same way. While the USSR obtained an official US agreement in Yalta on the Polish-Soviet border, the United States continued not to recognize the legality of the Baltic annexation.

In the wake of the Allied victory, the possibility of recognizing the annexation of the Baltic states was seriously discussed before the Paris Peace Conference of 1946. In a memo to the US delegation, the chief of the European Affairs Division, Llewellyn Thompson, wrote that the USSR might possibly seek *de jure* recognition of the Baltic annexation and thus advised: "It appears that we must sooner or later recognize *de jure* this development which has long since been accomplished *de facto*."[33]

However, this step was not taken, either at the Paris conference or later. First and foremost, the smallness and relative insignificance of the Baltic states played a role. Even if the Soviet Union had included the three foreign ministers of the Baltic Soviet republics in its delegation, it did not aggressively push for recognition in Paris. Meanwhile, the United States did not see how it could use recognition as a serious bargaining chip in its negotiations with the USSR. In 1945, Bohlen wrote that *de jure* recognition would be perceived by Moscow as mere appeasement and nothing more.[34] Second, despite the existence of the wartime alliance, the United States was suspicious of further Soviet intentions. The State Department recommended avoiding serious dispute with the Soviets, but to keep in mind that the USSR might use tactics applied in the Baltics in their dealings with other territories in Eastern Europe, and thus recognition in the Baltic case could have negative consequences in the future.[35]

Finally and most important, the German question, which in the immediate postwar years started to dominate the discussions between the superpowers, had an indirect influence on the Baltic issue. As the disagreement on Germany deepened, the United States, as well as Britain and France, became increasingly more unwilling to make any concessions to the USSR. In other words, the Baltic question might have been solved once and for all in favor of the Soviet Union had there been a general European settlement. Divergences on the German problem prevented such an arrangement and thus also postponed an answer to the Baltic question.

FRAMING OF THE BALTIC QUESTION I: BALTIC AMERICAN DIASPORA

The non-recognition policy was a juridical construct that had no direct impact on the situation in the Baltic states, but it had significant consequences for Estonians, Latvians, and Lithuanians outside the USSR. An important US commitment to the *de jure* continuity of the Baltic states was the support and recognition of the Baltic diplomatic services that continued to function abroad. The US government continued to recognize Baltic diplomats in Washington and New York as the only legitimate representatives of Estonia, Latvia, and Lithuania and annually released limited amounts of frozen Baltic assets so that these legations could sustain themselves.[36]

US, French, and British non-recognition was also of crucial importance for the fate of those thousands of Estonians, Latvians, and Lithuanians who at the end of war ended up in Germany in displaced persons' (DP) camps situated in the occupation zones of one of those three countries. While according to the Yalta agreements Soviet citizens were repatriated during the first years after the war, many against their will, Baltic nationals who were not accused of war crimes were in most of the cases left in the DP camps.[37] On June 28, 1948, Congress adopted the Displaced Persons Act authorizing the "admission into the United States of certain European displaced persons for permanent residence, and for other purposes." The law required that 40 percent of persons allowed to enter should come from areas that had been "de facto annexed by a foreign power," which basically meant that 40 percent of all immigrants could be from the Baltic countries.[38] In all, between 1948 and the early 1950s around 30,000 Lithuanians, 37,500 Latvians, and 12,600 Estonians arrived in the United States.[39]

While the already existing Latvian and Estonian communities combined did not exceed 25,000, an important Lithuanian diaspora already lived in the America. During the second part of the nineteenth century, thousands of Baltic peasants, recently liberated from serfdom, had left their homes in an effort to obtain land and escape the 1867–1868 famine.[40] However, their destinations were not the same; Latvian and Estonian Protestants were welcomed in the Orthodox areas of the empire, but Lithuanian Catholics and Jews were not.[41] Thus around 200,000 Latvians and about the same number of Estonians headed toward St. Petersburg, Central Russia, the Caucasus, and Siberia, but more than 250,000 Lithuanians left for the North America.[42]

According to the US census in 1990 there were 938,958 people in the country with Baltic ancestry: 86.5% of them Lithuanians, 10.5% Latvians, and 3% Estonians.[43] Even if during their first years Latvian Americans worked as manual and farm laborers, "soon they accumulated considerable social and monetary capital, and most of them achieved comfortable middle-class status if not already in the first, then definitely in the second generation," according to sociologist Ieva Zaķe.[44] The same can be said about Estonians and Lithuanians in America. In 1989 the US average family median income was $33,225, while the median income of Latvian American families was $51,209, Estonians $48,922, and Lithuanians $45,361.[45] 51.11 percent of Estonian Americans, 48.47 percent of Latvian Americans, and 39.97 percent of Lithuanian Americans worked in managerial and professional occupations.[46]

Like other diaspora groups the Estonians, Latvians, and Lithuanians formed a community based on (traumatic) dispersion, orientation toward homelands, and boundary maintenance.[47] Baltic Americans spent a considerable amount of time in community-related activities, such as Sunday native-language schools and holiday celebrations. In the early 1950s, they started to invest in the publication of newspapers, books, and journals in their native languages and in the building of Catholic (Lithuanian) or Lutheran (Estonian and Latvian) community churches. In a few years, various diaspora organizations were created. The Lithuanian American Council, having already been founded in 1915, was reorganized in 1940. Its Latvian counterpart, the American Latvian Association, was created in 1951, and the Estonian American Council was established in 1952. These national organizations became members of worldwide umbrella organizations such as the Lithuanian World Community (founded in 1949), the World Federation of Free Latvians (founded in 1955), and the Estonian World Council (founded in 1952). While the center of Latvian and Lithuanian diaspora life was the United States, the center of Estonian activity was concentrated in Sweden, where the largest Estonian community lived. In 1953 the Swedish Estonians established the Estonian government in exile in Oslo, but it was recognized neither by Norway, nor by any other country,[48] and the main diplomatic representative of the *de jure* existing Republic of Estonia remained the Estonian general consul in New York. The Supreme Committee for the Liberation of Lithuania, which was created in 1943 to resist the Nazi occupation, also attempted to assume the functions of a government in exile, but the Lithuanian diaspora was split between factions supporting the committee and those backing Stasys Lozoraitis, the Lithuanian ambassador to the Vatican, who had been designated as the head of Lithuanian diplomacy by the prewar government.

These active and vibrant communities were, however, deeply marked by the traumatic wartime experiences. The grief due to personal loss experienced during the war, and displacement—loss of families, homes, social status and familiar social environments—contributed to the collective longing for the lost Baltic independence. This lost independence became the central narrative of the diaspora communities, shaping their identities and future plans. For decades Baltic Americans believed that Latvia would be liberated in the near future and that they would return home, perceiving themselves as "refugees forced into exile by the communists."[49] Constant affirmation that the republics proclaimed in 1918 still existed and were only temporary and illegally occupied by a foreign power provided a reassuring "sense of continuity and order in events."[50] In other words, the occupation narrative was crucial for Baltic communities abroad because it allowed them to make sense of past traumatic events, sustained the "myth of return," and helped to preserve the images of the individual and collective selves.

An essential part of the daily lives of the Baltic exiles was devoted to gaining more significant US support for their occupied homelands.

Baltic Lobbying Efforts during the Cold War

Baltic American efforts to lobby for a stronger American stand on the Baltic question were accompanied by a constant search for the best possible way to frame the question. Conscious that the fate of their relatively small nations was not a source of significant concern for the international community, Estonian, Latvian, and Lithuanian exiles tried to give it a more universal appeal. The interpretations that were provided by diaspora activists varied depending on the audience, circumstances, and the convictions of the numerous diaspora organizations, but there was always a link made between the Baltic situation and an important international issue. In their lobbying efforts, Balts appealed on the grounds of human rights, anti-communism, and decolonization, but the non-recognition of forcible annexation remained the central element of their campaign.[51]

One of the first successful Baltic attempts to familiarize the broader American public with their cause was the creation and work of the Congressional Select Committee to Investigate Communist Aggression and the Forced Incorporation of the Baltic States into the U.S.S.R., 1953–1955. In the early 1950s, Baltic representatives, as well as diaspora activists, realized that the support of the White House and the State Department had its limits—the emerging US grand Cold War strategy was one of containment, not of liberation of nations under Soviet rule. While the Baltic diplomats representing the no-longer-existing prewar governments avoided any actions that could be perceived as off-limits by the State Department and the White House, individual diaspora activists started to seek contacts with members of the US Congress. In the early 1950s, even in states with high numbers of Lithuanian Americans such as Illinois, California, and New York, it was still very hard for Baltic Americans to influence the congressional election results, but the larger Eastern European diasporic community easily adopted the Baltic cause.[52] The first significant Baltic success in the US Congress was forged by Charles Kersten, Republican from the Fifth Congressional District in Wisconsin, which had a large Polish American constituency. Known for his strong anti-communist stand and links with Senator Joseph McCarthy, also representing Wisconsin, Kersten was approached by a member of the Lithuanian American Congress suggesting the creation of a congressional committee to investigate the annexation of Lithuania, Latvia, and Estonia. In 1953, this committee was created, chaired by Kersten. In 1954 the Select Committee's mandate was expanded to other communist countries, and the committee held fifty hearings in Washington, New York City, and Chicago, as well as in London, West Berlin, and Munich, with 335 witnesses. Their participation in the commission work familiarized Baltic organizations with American politics, strengthened their shared identity based on specific historical narratives, and gave the Balts the opportunity to reinforce the foundations of the American non-recognition policy.[53]

During subsequent years, Baltic Americans grew closer to the Republican Party. This development was part of a larger shift that occurred in the relations between Eastern European ancestry groups and the two major American political parties in the postwar period. Historically the Democrats had been the first to create ethnically oriented structures inside their party and develop a strategy to attract the votes of American ethnic communities. This policy resulted in the ethnic groups' support for Roosevelt's New Deal coalition. However, after the war Eastern European ethnic groups shifted their support to the Republican Party, mostly because of the perceived betrayal during the Yalta Conference. Still, Lithuanian Americans kept strong links with the Democratic Party throughout the Cold War. In 1990, 109,417 Americans of Lithuanian ancestry still lived in traditionally Democratic Illinois, where their predecessors had arrived in the late nineteenth century. During the late 1980s two members of Congress—Representative Dick Durbin and Representative Bill Sarpalius—were of Lithuanian descent, and both of them were Democrats. Even though American Latvian Association was trying to maintain contact with both parties, the majority voted Republican. The American Latvian Republican National Federation was created in 1961 and the Estonian American National Republican Committee in 1973. In the 1960s, Latvian Americans actively participated in the campaigns of Barry Goldwater (1964) and Richard Nixon (1968).[54]

During the early 1960s, the Cold War bipolar system seemed immutable and Baltic independence unattainable in the near future. Under such circumstances, Baltic organizations sought new ways to influence American politics and tested new tactics. In 1961, the Estonian American National Council, the American Latvian Association, and the Lithuanian American Council founded a joint executive bureau—the Joint Baltic American National Committee (hereafter JBANC)—to lobby for the interests of Baltic Americans in the US Congress, White House, and the State Department. At the same time, younger generations of American Lithuanians, Latvians, and Estonians started to become actively involved in diaspora activities. Perceiving the national umbrella organization as too modest and rigid in its approach toward the common cause and inspired by the UN Declaration on the Granting of Independence to Colonial Countries and Peoples, adopted in December 1960, they decided to link the Baltic question with one of the most important issues on the international agenda: decolonization. In 1965 a group of Lithuanian Americans held a rally in Madison Square Park in New York and adopted the *Baltic Appeal to the United Nations*, urging the United Nations "to implement the Declaration on [the] Granting of Independence to Colonial Countries and Peoples in reference to Estonia, Latvia, and Lithuania by restoration of their independence."[55] It was later signed by 128 public figures including Richard Nixon, fifty-four US senators and representatives, seven state governors, six mayors of major cities, and nineteen clergy members.[56] The next year an organization called Baltic Appeal to the United Nations (hereafter BATUN) was registered to advocate on the Baltic question in the United Nations and its member state delegations. In the period between 1965 and 1991, BATUN activists met with 650 UN members and state diplomats to increase their awareness about the Baltic situation.[57]

The 1970s was marked by several events and developments that shattered the Baltic American community. First, while focusing on their traumatic experiences under Soviet occupation, Baltic Americans had failed to seriously discuss the crimes committed during the Nazi occupation and the involvement of their own compatriots in the crimes against humanity and genocide. While Estonian and Latvian Waffen-SS legions, in which around 40,000 Estonians and around 52,000 Latvians[58] were enlisted, did not participate in the Holocaust, members of the Estonian, Latvian, and Lithuanian Auxiliary Police and Security Police did. In late 1944 and early 1945, an unknown number of these war criminals arrived in the West, hiding among the refugees. In the absolute majority of cases the host country authorities failed to detect them among the other displaced persons, so the former members of Nazi security forces settled in Australia, South America, and the United States. In the 1970s and 1980s, thirteen Latvians were tried by US courts for having lied about their collaboration with the Nazis during their entry to the United States or in their citizenship applications. Only two of them, Boļeslavs Maikovskis and Konrāds Kalējs, were ordered to be deported, while others died, were acquitted, reached settlements with the state, or in one case fled the United States.[59] The situation was further complicated by the publication of KGB-prepared brochures in English that deliberately mixed true facts regarding crimes of some individuals with false accusations against others.[60] Until the mid-1980s, frightened by the possible backlash, the ethnic community squashed open discussion of Latvian involvement in the Holocaust.[61]

Second, the emerging normalization of superpower relations during the détente divided the Baltic American community. Younger generation of Estonian, Latvian, and Lithuanian Americans seized the possibility to visit the Baltic countries and establish direct contacts with their compatriots. However, more conservative Baltic Americans were strongly opposed to any contact with Soviet Estonia, Latvia, and Lithuania.

Third, the rise of détente in the 1970s made Baltic Americans wary that the United States might abandon the non-recognition policy for the sake of the normalization of relations between the superpowers. In the context of the West German recognition of the Polish western border in 1970, Estonians, Latvians, and Lithuanians feared that the Western powers might recognize the annexation of the Baltic states while signing the Helsinki agreement. Alerted by this possibility, JBANC and the Baltic World Conference started an important campaign. In March 1974 they met with chief American negotiator in Helsinki, Robert Frowick, and in May with Gerald Ford, then vice president. In February 1975, nine leaders of the Baltic diaspora organizations met with Ford again, in his capacity as

US president.[62] According to the US press, the meeting with the Balts gave rise to a heated debate between the NSC staff led by Brent Scowcroft and the State Department led by Henry Kissinger, the latter being strongly opposed to any steps that might damage relations with the USSR in the wake of the conference.[63]

Baltic Americans were not the only American ethnic minorities who were opposed to the Helsinki Final Act. While Balts were concerned about the possibility of recognition of the annexation, Americans of Eastern European descent feared the Final Act would legitimize Soviet domination in Eastern Europe, and the American Jewish community was worried about the impact of the agreement on emigration from the USSR.[64] The Congress was alerted by its Eastern European constituents, and the House Foreign Affairs Subcommittee held a hearing on August 3, 1974. In July 1975, Baltic Americans sent around 2,000 telegrams to the White House and held a vigil during the nights of July 30 and July 31.

Even if President Ford had no intention of recognizing the annexation of the Baltic states, and despite the Final Act's having no negative consequences for the Baltic situation, Baltic Americans perceived themselves as having lost an important political battle. This perception of American betrayal increased when, for reasons that still remain unclear, members of the Baltic World Conference were detained by the Finnish authorities in Helsinki. Once again, Congress was more receptive to the Baltic grievances than was the president. In December 1975, the US House of Representatives by a vote of 407–0 adopted Resolution 864 reaffirming the continuing non-recognition of the Baltic annexation. In July 1976, a similar resolution was passed in the Senate.

Although the Helsinki Final Act was initially perceived by Balts and other Eastern European ethnic groups as a Soviet victory, in the long term it contributed to the end of Soviet rule in Eastern Europe and the fall of the USSR.[65] Soon after the Final Act was signed, dissidents around the Soviet bloc started to use its human rights provision to illustrate the discrepancy between international commitments by their governments and the everyday reality in the socialist countries. Civil-society activists in the West supported their demands and pushed political elites to discuss Soviet human rights abuses internationally. In the general context of the rise of human rights rhetoric in the 1970s, these questions became an important issue on the East-West diplomatic agenda. Thus, the Baltic American organizations readjusted their discourse on the Baltic question, starting to frame it as a human rights problem.[66] In 1981 a group of young Baltic Americans funded the Baltic American Freedom League, an association with the primary aim of denouncing human rights abuses in the Baltics. From 1981 until 1991, the Baltic American Freedom League organized annual human rights conferences that served as a platform not only for voicing their concern about human rights in the Baltics but also for delegitimizing the Soviet regime and proposing the independence project as an alternative.[67]

Another important success of the Baltic advocacy was achieved in 1982, when Congress passed the Joint Resolution 201 designating June 14—the date of the 1941 deportations—as Baltic Freedom Day. The bill was introduced by a Republican senator from Michigan, Donald Riegle, and co-sponsored by twenty-three Democrats (50 percent of all Democrat senators in the 97th Congress) and nineteen Republicans (35 percent of all Republican senators). It was signed into law by President Reagan on June 18, 1982. Every year in the period between 1983 and 1992, February 16 and June 14 were designated as Lithuania's Independence Day and Baltic Freedom Day. While these actions had no direct impact on the Baltic situation, they showed that the Baltic question had become part of Congress's Cold War rhetoric.

The beginning of Perestroika and the sudden rise of the independence movements not only surprised Baltic Americans but made them question to what extent they could and should cooperate with movements that had members of the Communist Party in their ranks and with institutions created under Soviet law. In this context, the Lithuanian and Latvian legations in Washington and the Estonian general consulate in New York played a crucial role in overcoming the divide between "homelands" and diaspora. These still-existing pre-1940 institutions strategically linked the networks of homeland and diaspora, as their decision to cooperate with the Baltic independence movements legitimized popular fronts in the eyes of Baltic communities abroad.[68] The Baltic diaspora turned out to be a vital asset for the new Baltic governments. Well integrated into their host countries, the members of the diaspora understood Western societies, values, discourses, and languages much better than did the inhabitants of the USSR. Most important, they had over the years developed strong links with the US Congress, which was ready to advocate for the Baltic cause.

At the heart of congressional support was an active group of representatives and senators who either came from constituencies with an energetic Baltic American community or had built their careers around the Cold War and anti-communist rhetoric. While the absolute numbers of Baltic Americans were not significant enough to shift US elections in general, Baltic votes did matter in certain voting districts in several states. According to the US Census of 1990, the largest numbers of Baltic Americans lived in Illinois (117,559), Pennsylvania (108,846), and New York (86,417), while in terms of the percentages of Baltic Americans in their populations, the leading states were Connecticut (1.38%), Massachusetts (1.26%), and Illinois (1.03%). Significant numbers of Baltic Americans also lived in certain voting districts of California and Michigan. Legislators from these states, such as Representatives Bill Broomfield (Republican, MI), Dick Durbin (Democrat, IL), Frank Annunzio (Democrat, IL), Donald Ritter (Republican, PA), Charles Cox (Republican, CA), and Benjamin Gilman (Republican, NY), and Senators Alfonse D'Amato (Republican, NY), Daniel Moynihan (Democrat, NY), Donald Riegle (Democrat, MI), and Paul Simon (Democrat, IL), took an active interest in the Baltic question and sought to obtain more proactive Baltic policy from the White House.

Furthermore, in the years 1989–1991, Republican and Democrat anti-communists such as Jesse Helms (North Carolina), Robert Byrd (West Virginia), and Don Ritter (Pennsylvania) seized the opportunity to criticize Gorbachev while advocating for Baltic independence. As President Bush explained to the Soviet foreign minister Alexander Bessmertnykh in January 1991, many hawks from the US conservative circles "didn't believe in dialogue with the USSR, to begin with."[69] For these Cold War warriors, Gorbachev was nothing more than an iron fist in a velvet glove, and the Baltic situation was the perfect opportunity to point at inconsistencies in his policies. The support voiced by this active group of Baltic allies was echoed by other members of Congress who seized an opportunity to associate themselves with a cause that was generally framed as "just."

To a certain extent, the Cold War warriors were right. In the late 1980s and early 1990s, Baltic claims for independence became the litmus test of Perestroika, highlighting the tensions between democratization and empire. But they were wrong about the very nature of Gorbachev's reforms, which far from being a showcase for the West, represented a genuine attempt to reshape Soviet society. The results of this enormous enterprise even surprised the reformer himself.

GORBACHEV'S UNEXPECTED PROBLEM: THE ROOTS OF BALTIC UNREST

In 1987, Mikhail Gorbachev published the book *Perestroika: The New Thinking for Our Country and the World*, in which he explained the critical questions related to the reforms in the USSR and its relations with the outside world. Very few pages of this work were devoted to the relationships between different Soviet nationalities. While admitting that the process was not "problem-free," the secretary-general claimed that the USSR had resolved the nationality question "in principle" and concluded that "against the background of the national strike that has now spared even the world's most advanced countries, the USSR represents a truly unique example in the history of civilizations. These are fruits of the nationality policy launched by Lenin."[70]

However, by the time the book was published, ethnic unrest had already broken out in the USSR. In December 1986, protests took place in Alma-Ata when the first secretary of the Kazakh Communist Party, Dinmukhamed Qonaev (Kunaev), was replaced by the Russian Gennady Kolbin who had no previous connections with the republic. The upheaval was brutally repressed and the reported number of people killed varied from 2 to 186.[71]

In 1987 the first anti-Soviet protests took place in the Baltics. The first of these was organized in Riga on June 14, 1987, to commemorate the deportations of 1941. In July 1987, Crimean Tatars demonstrated in Moscow, denouncing the 1944 deportations. On August 23 the same year, simultaneous demonstrations occurred in Estonia, Latvia, and Lithuania to mark the fiftieth anniversary of the Molotov-Ribbentrop Pact of 1939. Around the same time, tensions started to rise in Nagorno-Karabakh, an autonomous oblast in Azerbaijan SSR inhabited mostly by Armenians that in the late 1980s sought attachment to the Armenian SSR. Thus, despite Gorbachev's optimism, the "nationalities question" was far from being resolved in the USSR. During the last year of the Soviet Union, it became a metaphor to describe a wide range of problems: ethnic tensions, calls for greater autonomy, and secession attempts. Baltic independence activists played an ambiguous but important role in these dynamics. On the one hand, Estonians, Latvians, and Lithuanians tried to disassociate themselves from other Soviet republics, emphasizing that the Baltic case was unique because of the 1940 illegal annexation; on the other, their drive for independence had a significant impact on the national aspirations of other Soviet republics.

The three Baltic states considered themselves a special case in the Soviet context because their annexation took place only in 1940; their economic performance allowed them to bypass the rest of the USSR by the 1970s; their geographical situation and historical ties exposed them to the revolutionary dynamics in Eastern Europe[72] and made them receptive to Scandinavian and German influences; and the large and well-organized Baltic diaspora lived outside the borders of the Soviet Union. None of these factors alone, and even all of them combined, would have brought independence to Estonia, Latvia, and Lithuania. Being different did not make the Balts independent, but they did enable Baltic societies to seize the historic opportunity offered by Gorbachev's attempts to reform the USSR and push the limits of Perestroika and glasnost further than the Soviet leader and his team had expected. Furthermore, the specificity of the Latvian, Estonian, and Lithuanian situation made their populations especially sensitive to the structural flaws in the Soviet system. The forced Sovietization, ethno-territorial federal system, contractionary nationality policy, traumatic memories of Stalin's repressions and failed economy impacted the lives of all Soviet citizens, but the Balts were the first ones to claim that independence was the only solution to these problems.

Long-Term Causes of the Baltic Unrest

In the late 1980s, the Soviet leader did not expect the Baltic region to become a significant issue in both internal politics and his dealings with the West. After his trip to Estonia and Latvia in 1987, Gorbachev saw no reason for significant concern regarding the Baltic situation and told other members of the Politburo that the mood in the Baltics "was not bad," people's living conditions were "not bad," and their attitudes toward Perestroika "were not indifferent."[73] The calm in the Baltic turned out to be misleading. Two years and four months after Gorbachev's trip, Lithuania proclaimed its independence.

Gorbachev's failure to assess the Baltic situation was part of a larger miscalculation. The Soviet leader genuinely believed in his ability to avoid a major crisis in the Soviet inner and outer empire by supporting reform-minded forces across the USSR and the Eastern bloc.[74] Gorbachev's error was also due to the image that the Baltic republics had in the Soviet collective imagination, which was shaped by enthno-linguistic, racial, economic, and spatial hierarchies.[75] Imperial domination over Central Asian republics was justified through narratives of "backwardness" and "modernisation."[76] Whereas the Baltic countries were perceived as a "civilized" and "advanced" region in which Soviet rule was officially legitimized by the liberation and Soviet victory in the Great Patriotic War. While for foreign journalists Estonia, Latvia, and Lithuania were the Soviet West, for the Soviet people the Baltic republics were not just merely a window to Europe but Europe itself.[77] Consumer goods produced in Estonia, Latvia, and Lithuania became status symbols, and the quality of life in the Baltics attracted not just millions of tourists but also hundreds of thousands of migrants from other Soviet republics. For decades the three countries were used to showcase Soviet success, and in the late 1980s Gorbachev hoped that they would become a testing ground for his economic reforms.

Blinded by the imagined Soviet success story in the region, secretary-general misperceived the mood in the Baltics. The seemingly calm and, in

Soviet context comparatively rich, republics were deeply troubled by the memories of Stalin's repressions, experience with both Soviet repressive modernity (especially its Russifying effects), and contradictory nationality policies.

The rising ethnic tensions that shook the Soviet Union between 1986 and 1991 were not the result of suddenly rediscovered national identities, but consequences of a deep contradiction that a mix of Lenin's and Stalin's approaches to the national question had planted at the heart of the Soviet system.[78] On the one hand, Soviet nationality policy was based on a rigid system of national classification and the promotion of national languages and cultures of titular nations. On the other hand, Soviet official ideology perceived these same national identities as relics of a bourgeois past that were bound to disappear, yielding to the rise of a Russian-speaking "Soviet Man," "a cultural hybrid who would be a synthesis of the cultural richness of all the people of the socialist world."[79] During the Brezhnev era, the official discourse had moved toward the more neutral "rapprochement of nations" (*sblizhenie*), which did not imply complete disappearance of national differences. Yet, since the Second World War the primacy of Russians and the Russian language in the USSR was openly acknowledged, thus reversing Lenin's attempts to weaken Russian nationalism and reinforcing patterns of linguistic, symbolic, and practical dominance. In Soviet Latvia and Estonia, these dynamics were accentuated by the large influx of Russian-speaking migrants from other parts of the USSR.

In the late nineteenth century, Estonia and Latvia, or the so-called Baltic provinces, governed by the Baltic Germans, had been one of the most industrialized and economically developed regions in the Tsarist Empire,[80] and thus after 1945 they provided good bases for further industrialization projects. These development plans needed significant workforces, but in the period from 1939 to 1945 Latvia had lost almost one-third of its citizens and Estonia almost as many: Baltic Germans had left the region in 1939 (14,000 Baltic Germans had departed from Estonia and 52,000 from Latvia);[81] about 66,000 Latvian Jews were exterminated during the Holocaust by the Nazis and their local collaborators; and hundreds of thousands of Latvians and Estonians had perished while fighting in both the Red and Nazi Armies, had left the country as war refugees, or had been deported to Siberia by the Soviets. The hundreds of thousands of workers from other Soviet republics who arrived in Estonia and Latvia changed the demographics of both republics. In 1956, when destalinization in Moscow gave rise to short-lived national communism attempts in Latvia, the local party leadership tried to oppose the influx of migrants and promote Latvian language learning, but by 1959 they were outmaneuvered by their hardline colleagues and removed by Moscow. In 1985, a CIA report asserted that "Latvians now constitute a bare majority of the populations of their own republic and less than 40% of the population of their capital city."[82] Indeed, while in 1945 80 percent of Latvia's population were ethnic Latvians, in 1989 this proportion had shrunk to 52 percent. Meanwhile, in Estonia, there were 94 percent Estonians in 1945 and 62 percent in 1989.[83] Thus in the case of Latvia and Estonia, the Soviet rhetoric about the disappearance of national identities in the communist future seemed to actually materialize. The tensions were exacerbated by the rigid and ethnocentric Soviet approach to nationality. For example, a migrant from Ukraine could not become Latvian, because national identity was defined by birth and fixed in the passport, along with Soviet citizenship.[84] In the context of Russian-language dominance in the USSR, local language learning was neither encouraged nor promoted among the newcomers and thus only 22 percent of Russians living in Latvia and 15 percent of Russians living in Estonia spoke Latvian or Estonian.[85] Meanwhile, 64.4 percent of Latvians and 33.9 percent of Estonians were fluent in Russian.[86]

At the same time, the Soviet system supported the development of national cultures by sponsoring Estonian and Latvian artists' and writers' unions, schools, and cultural activities. As a consequence, Latvian and Estonian national identities had not weakened during the Soviet period; the national intelligentsia was active, and the population was alarmed by the influx of economic migrants. As noted by the CIA in 1985: "These trends, which many Balts think are largely a consequence of deliberate regime policy of Russification, have given rise to fears about their survival as distinct ethnic groups."[87] The impression that the Estonian and Latvian and eventually also Lithuanian nations might disappear was shared by scholars in the West. In 1978, French historian Hélène Carrère d'Encausse wrote: "The eventual extinction of nations having such a strong personality is a historical tragedy that every Balt consciously feels; however, nobody seems to be able to prevent it."[88] Indeed, while in 1945 80% of Latvia's population were ethnic Latvians, by 1989 this number had shrunk to 52%. Estonia experienced a comparatively similar reduction from 94% in 1945 to 62% in 1989.[89]

The demographic situation in Lithuania at the end of the 1980s was very different, as the percentage of ethnic Lithuanians in Lithuania's population had not decreased, but actually slightly increased during the Soviet period, reaching 80 percent in 1989. These differences were due to both long- and short-term structural disparities between the Baltic countries as well as the agency of Lithuanian communists. While a significant number of Lithuanians had perished in the war or were deported by the

Soviets,[90] the loss suffered was smaller than in the case of Estonia and Latvia, mostly because there were no Lithuanian SS legions. The number of Lithuanian refugees who left their country during the last two years of the war was also smaller than in the case of the two other Baltic countries: 140,000 Latvians, 75,000 Estonians, and 65,000 Lithuanians fled to the West during this period.[91] At the same time, Lithuania lost two of its most important national minorities in the period between 1941 and 1946. Ninety percent of Lithuanian Jews were killed during the Holocaust, and 80 percent of Vilnius Poles were "repatriated" to Poland by the Soviet authorities.[92] As noted by historian Violeta Davoliūtė, "By the end of the war, the pre-war urban population (which comprised mostly Poles and Jews) had been cut in half, while the rural population (mostly ethnic Lithuanians) had been reduced only by less than 10%."[93] Having been less industrialized under the Tsarist regime, Lithuania, unlike Estonia and Latvia, was still in 1939 a rural country to a very large extent. During this last year of Baltic independence, 23 percent of the Lithuanian population lived in cities, while for Latvia, Estonia, and the USSR the same number was respectively 35 percent, 34 percent, and 32 percent.[94] Thus, in the Lithuanian case, the Soviet authorities agreed to repopulate the cities with Lithuanians from the countryside, rather than with migrant workers from other Soviet republics, as in Latvia and Estonia. The decisions to avoid large-scale migration to Lithuania were supported and lobbied in Moscow by powerful members of the Lithuania Communist Party, first and foremost its long-serving first secretary Antanas Sniečkus. Unlike the Latvian and Estonian parties, the Lithuanian one was in its large majority composed of ethnic Lithuanians who were willing to take more risks in defense of local interests. In sum, during the Soviet period Lithuania experienced relatively slow industrialization, rapid and traumatic urbanization,[95] and minor immigration from the other Soviet republics.[96] Consequently, at the end of the 1980s, 80 percent of Lithuania's population were ethnic Lithuanians. As in the Latvian and Estonian cases, an approved version of national culture was supported by the Soviet regime, allowing for a Lithuanian cultural renaissance after Stalin's death and the rise of a powerful and influential Soviet-Lithuanian intelligentsia. The Large part of Lithuanian intelligentsia initially embraced Soviet modernization ideology and was inspired by its spirit of internationalism and urbanity.[97] However in the mid-1960s, when the Lithuanian Renaissance was at its peak, Lithuanian cultural elites started to question the meaning of Soviet modernity for the Lithuanian nation and culture and gradually moved toward an idealization of Lithuania's rural past. This shift in Lithuanian relations with Soviet modernity prepared the ground for the intensive debate

about the past that took place during Perestroika and set Lithuanian independence forces in motion.[98]

Perestroika Opens the Gates

The rise of Baltic independence movements was the unexpected result of
Gorbachev's reforms. His push for glasnost and democratization set the
country into uncharted waters: Soviet citizens everywhere, including the
Baltics, saw new possibilities opening before them, but no one (probably
including Gorbachev) knew how far they were allowed to go in exploring
them. In the context of constantly shifting boundaries between the possible and the permissible, Baltic societies found themselves constantly
testing the limits of Perestroika at three levels. Grassroots activists were
pushing the boundaries and carefully watching the reactions of both
local communist leadership and the Kremlin. Local communists were
looking not only at the Kremlin, but also at the rapidly emerging popular
movements trying to figure out how to maneuver between Moscow and
pressures at home.

The first large-scale mobilization in the Baltic countries voiced not political, but rather environmental grievances. From 1986 to 1987, reflecting the
general post-Chernobyl mood in Soviet society, Latvians, Lithuanians, and
Estonians mobilized against Soviet industrial projects such as the construc-
tion of a fourth hydroelectric dam over Latvia's largest river, the Daugava;
the expansion of phosphorite mining in the Virumaa region in Estonia; and
the opening of the third reactor of Lithuania's Ignalina nuclear plant. In all
three cases, the projects were halted, giving Baltic societies their first experience of successful civil-society mobilization. This experience turned out
to have long-lasting consequences, as it inspired the creation of a variety
of grassroots organizations dedicated to environmental protection and the
preservation of cultural heritage.

In Latvia, the Environmental Protection Club (Vides Aizsardzības
Klubs), founded on February 28, 1987, grew into an influential movement
whose members later joined the independence movement. The Estonian
Heritage Society (Eesti Muinsuskaitse Selts) was established in December
1987. In 1988 and 1989, this society spread its activities throughout
Estonia, turning the preservation of monuments and cemeteries into political acts and contesting the Soviet official narratives of the Estonian
past.[99] The Lithuanian Green Movement grew out of a larger ethno-cultural
network movement that had inherited its traditions from the Lithuanian
hippies, hikers, and folk music fan groups active since the mid-1960s.[100]

Unaware of the deep-rooted frustrations in Estonian, Latvian, and Lithuanian societies, Gorbachev believed that the economically well-advanced Baltic region would be particularly receptive to reforms and hoped to use Perestroika there as an example for the rest of the Union. In late 1986, Soviet prime minister Nikolai Ryzhkov visited Tallinn and unofficially suggested that "Estonia could work out something similar to free economic zones in China."[101] The progressive wing of the Estonian Planning Committee seized this opportunity to start a debate about economic management in Estonia, which led to the emergence of the Estonian 1987 self-accounting initiative that aimed at nothing less than placing all economic activity in Estonia under local (and not Moscow's) jurisdiction. The Estonian move was the first Baltic attempt to use the opportunities offered by Perestroika to considerably expand autonomy.

Estonians and their southern neighbors continued to push the limits in spring 1988 when Perestroika came under vicious attack from the Soviet conservative wing. On April 13, 1988, Estonian economist and member of the Communist Party Edgar Savisaar proposed the organization of a Popular Front for Perestroika Support. On June 1–2, a similar initiative was voiced during a congress of the Latvian Writers' Union. Just a day later, the Committee in Charge of Creating the Lithuanian Popular Front was established during a meeting at the Lithuanian Academy of Sciences. On the one hand, Baltic public intellectuals (most of them members of the CPSU) who were behind these initiatives truly supported Gorbachev's reforms as they represented long-awaited changes in the USSR. On the other hand, they used the language of Perestroika to push the limits of these reforms by creating political alternatives to the CPSU.

In the autumn of 1988, the three movements held their founding congress. On October 2, the Popular Front for Perestroika Support (Rahvarinne Perestroika Toetuseks, hereafter Rahvarinne) was created in Tallinn, Estonia; on October 8 the Latvian Popular Front (Latvijas Tautas Fronte, hereafter Tautas Fronte) was established in Riga; and on October 23 the Reform Movement of Lithuania (Lietuvos Persitvarkymo Sąjūdis, hereafter Sąjūdis) was founded in Vilnius. The ethnic composition of the three countries influenced the ideological standing of their respective popular movements. Lithuanian Sąjūdis became a more right-wing nationalist movement, while Rahvarinne and LTF were more center-oriented and had to face opposition from the Latvian and Estonian right.[102] Within six weeks of its founding, Rahvarinne already had 40,000 members in its ranks.[103] In the coming year, the Lithuanian Sąjūdis reached a membership of around 200,000, and the Latvian Tautas Fronte claimed to have 200,500 members.[104]

At this moment, the three movements still benefited from Moscow's support. In the summer of 1988, Gorbachev's advisor and Politburo member Alexander Yakovlev, who was dispatched to Latvia and Lithuania to assess the situation in the region, publicly endorsed the creation of the popular movements, making it impossible for the local communist leadership to harass, censor, or ignore the movements any longer.[105] This signaled that Baltic societies had boldly tested the limits of Perestroika and that Moscow had approved this step.

It has been argued in literature that Baltic nationalists "tricked" Yakovlev into believing their loyalty or that they themselves were manipulated by Gorbachev and the KGB.[106] In reality, Baltic popular fronts at their inception were neither Gorbachev's loyal lieutenants nor his secret enemies conspiring to implement a hidden independence agenda. They were an emerging and not yet fully defined social movement that did indeed look with great sympathy at Gorbachev's reforms first (but not only) because they seemed to promise a brighter future for the Baltic states. How exactly that brighter future would look—as a larger autonomy inside the USSR or as full independence—was not yet clear in 1988.

When it comes to Yakovlev's motivations, they were first rooted in the understanding that Baltic societies were facing objective problems due to the dysfunctional Soviet system and belief, and that if these problems were solved, local leaderships would stay loyal to Moscow. On August 18, 1988, Yakovlev explained his position to the Politburo. He admitted that serious issues existed in the Baltic republics due to Soviet centralism and Soviet industrial and migration policies, and that these problems were causing "pain, resentment, impatience and predominance of emotion over reason" in the republics. According to Yakovlev, the Soviet leadership had to move toward removing the "irritants" that were causing the uproar in the Baltics.[107] While admitting that there were dozens of "screamers" in Latvia and Lithuania who were "taking unacceptable positions," Yakovlev asserted that all in all he had not encountered "nationalist, anti-Soviet, anti-Russian or anti-Perestroika" positions in the two Baltic republics he had visited. This vision was largely shared by Gorbachev. In his memoirs published in the 1990s he remembers that, at the time of the creation of the popular fronts in the autumn of 1988, many of their members were "fervent advocates of reforms and not at all disposed to the secession."[108] In the spring of 1989, Gorbachev was already aware of radical strains in the movements but believed that they could not prevail over what he saw as a moderate majority.[109]

All told, Gorbachev and other reform-minded, liberal communists in Moscow saw the popular movements as a chance both to gain support against the most conservative forces of the Union and to empower the moderate elements in the Baltic societies against the radical nationalists.[110] Indeed in 1989, Sąjūdis, Tautas Fronte, and Rahvarinne had to face opposition from both more radical nationalist forces and conservative Russian-speaking anti-independence and anti-Perestroika groups.

In Estonia, the conservative International Movement of Workers in the Estonian Soviet Socialist Republic (mostly known as the Intermovement) emerged in the summer of 1988. Its Lithuanian counterpart Yedinstvo was founded in November 1988, while the International Front of the Working People of the Latvian SSR or Interfront was established in January 1989. The three organizations, opposed to both Baltic independence and Gorbachev's Perestroika, enjoyed the backing of Soviet conservatives, yet their success in mobilizing significant numbers of supporters among the local Russian-speaking population decreased over time. Their most active period was spring and summer 1989, when in Latvia and especially Estonia they managed to organize large protests against local language and electoral laws. Yet, their nationalist-conservative message lacked novelty and they had little else to offer beyond the defense of the status quo. The status quo, however, became less and less appealing not only to ethnic Latvians and Estonians, but also to Russian-speaking populations in the Baltic countries, especially among the younger generations.[111] Furthermore both Rahvarinne and Tautas Fronte made a considerable effort to encourage fragmentation of what was previously perceived as a Russian-speaking bloc, promoting and supporting distinct Ukrainian, Belarusian, and Jewish identities. Notably in the period between 1987 and 1991, ethnic groups in the Baltics never resorted to physical violence. The three Baltic independence movements explicitly rejected the use of force as a means to achieve political goals.[112] Thus even though the relations between supporters of independence and intermovements remained tense, they were never violent, leaving room for dialogue.

At the same time, in the period between 1988 and 1991, there already existed in all three republics political forces that called for more radical approaches toward the Soviet authorities and Russian-speaking minorities. While the influence of the Lithuanian Freedom League (Lietuvos laisvės lyga) remained limited, the Estonian National Independence Party (Eesti Rahvusliku Sõltumatuse Partei, hereafter ERSP) and the Latvian National Independence Movement (Latvijas Nacionālās Neatkarības Kustiba, hereafter LNNK) grew into important political forces. Both groups rejected any cooperation with Soviet institutions, including participation in Soviet elections. Beginning in summer of 1989, LNNK and ERSP organized the so-called Citizens' Committees—grassroots movements that registered pre-1940 citizens and their descendants. They aimed to organize national elections that would exclude Soviet-era immigrants from the voting body and would elect alternative parliaments that would not be linked with the Soviet institutions. Both movements managed to hold alternative elections in 1990, in which 557,613 Estonians and 707,772 Latvians elected Latvian and Estonian Congresses. While in Latvia, Tautas Fronte managed to remain the main political force, ERSP and the Citizens' Committee movement in Estonia emerged as an important rival of Rahvarinne.

The fourth crucial players in Baltic Perestroika-era politics were the local communist parties upon which Gorbachev and Yakovlev pinned high hopes. Despite Soviet centralism over the years, Moscow had developed a habit of seeing the local communists in the Baltics as being the most apt to deal with the possible surge of Baltic nationalisms.[113] Following the same line of thought, Gorbachev believed that Estonian, Latvian, and Lithuanian communists would be able to not only successfully lead the implementation of Perestroika but also keep the popular movements under control. This proved a miscalculation. A significant number of Baltic communists did indeed embrace Gorbachev's Perestroika, but their willingness and capacity to keep their republics on a pro-Soviet track was limited. Many of them (especially in Lithuania) ended up aligning with the independence project. In the period between 1988 and 1989, while the Baltic countries were still run exclusively by communists, all three republics proclaimed the superiority of their laws over the Union laws and their respective languages as the only official languages. All three restored the use of the interwar-period national flags and authorized the celebration of 1918 Independence Days. In December 1989, the whole Lithuanian Communist Party (CP) declared its support for independence and split from the Soviet CP. In Latvia and Estonia the process was more complex. In Estonia the majority of CP members split from the Soviet CP in spring 1990 and registered an independent Estonian CP. Around the same time in Latvia an independence-supporting minority left the Latvian CP. Even though in crucial years between 1988 and 1991 their influence gradually decreased, they were an important balancing force and mediator in power dynamics between Moscow and governments in the Baltic capitals.[114]

What led to this shift in the trajectories of Baltic communists? It has been argued that Soviet collapse was "national in form, opportunistic in content,"[115] and while opportunism certainly played a role in Soviet collapse it is not the sole explanatory factor, least in the Baltic case. Like everywhere in the USSR, Baltic communist parties and their nomenklaturas had become less ideological and more technocratic during the 1970s, focusing upon the practical problems that their republics were facing. Historically,

Baltic communists, just like other peripheral nomenclatures, were used to the permanent balancing act of proving their loyalty and usefulness to Moscow while limiting Moscow's interference in their affairs, appeasing the local population by accommodating their needs and keeping them under control through coercion.[116] Their margins of maneuver were usually directly linked to power dynamics in Moscow. For example, destalinization gave rise to a short-lived Latvian attempt to national communism. Under Gorbachev, local communists felt that Moscow's grip was once again easing, while the pressure from the local actors was rising. At the same time, the extent of cohesion in the local parties deeply varied. While the Lithuanian party consisted mostly of ethnic Lithuanians, the Latvian and Estonian parties were divided along the ethnic lines.[117] While not all ethnic Latvian or ethnic Estonian communists were sympathetic to the popular fronts, many of them were. At the same time a generational and ideological divide separated older, more conservative communists in the Baltic republics from younger supporters of Perestroika who looked at local activism with understanding and sympathy.[118]

Yakovlev's 1988 trip consolidated the positions of reform-minded communists in the Baltics and reassured them that they and Gorbachev's liberal circles were playing on the same side. These dynamics were especially visible in Latvia, where more conservative party leadership was plotting to distance the reform-oriented party ideological secretary Anatolijs Gorbunovs from local decision-making by ensuring his promotion to the Central Committee in Moscow. Yakovlev's support for Gorbunovs's wish to stay in Riga ended the debate. According to Gorbunovs, during their conversation Yakovlev, who was already facing strong backlash from the Soviet conservatives, made him understand that he saw their positions as similar. Gorbunovs later remembered: "After a moment of silence he told me, 'You are not loved here, Anatoly.' What could I say, if I was not loved, I was not loved. Yakovlev paused and then said: But I am not loved either."[119] This short exchange reveals a broader mindset of Gorbachev and his liberal entourage: in 1988, their perceived line of division in the Soviet society was not an ethnic or center periphery divide, but the standoff between the reformers and the conservatives.

In all three Baltic republics, reform communists not only provided the popular movements with a certain legitimacy in the eyes of Moscow but also limited the divide in the Baltic societies. Although the Communist Party itself become highly unpopular, individual communist leaders (such as Gorbunovs in Latvia, Algirdas Brazauskas in Lithuania, and Arnold Rüütel in Estonia) still had strong appeal to an important part of local populations.[120] However, their capacity to maintain their relevance in the eyes of the local populations was directly linked to their ability to obtain concessions from Moscow. The Kremlin's hesitation to deal with the national question in the USSR pushed local communists toward deeper cooperation with the popular movements.

November 1988: The First Crisis

The first tangible tensions between the Baltic republics and Moscow started in the fall of 1988 due to planned constitutional reforms in the USSR. The conflict highlighted elements that would later play a crucial role in the Baltic shift toward independence.

On October 22, Gorbachev announced his plan to amend the Soviet constitution and to establish a new legislative body: the Congress of People's Deputies. The reform was ambiguous. On the one hand, it did contribute to the democratization of the USSR, but on the other it institutionalized the nomenclature's presence in the legislative body and decreased the influence of the republics' deputies.[121] In the existing system, the Soviet legislative body consisted of two chambers, one of which was elected from national constituencies (thirty-two deputies from each republic and a smaller number from autonomous republics and regions). The new super parliament, however, was planned to consist of 2,250 deputies, of whom 750 would be elected from territorial one-mandate districts, 750 from national constituencies, and 750 from all-Union public organizations such as the CPSU, trade unions, and the Komsomol. Furthermore, the Congress of People's Deputies was planned to have power to create autonomous regions in the territory of republics, approve changes in republics' borders, "ensure unity of legislative regulation on the entire territory of the USSR," and cancel the decisions of republic governments.[122]

Reacting to what they perceived as an assault upon republics' rights, the leaders of Baltic popular movements met for the first time in Riga on November 8, 1988. After discussing other matters such as the plans for Baltic economic autonomy, they agreed to follow the Estonian initiative and collect citizens' signatures against the planned amendments, as well as to push the local Supreme Soviets to declare the supremacy of republic laws over all-Union laws. While all three movements were successful in their first quest—Sąjūdis, Tautas Fronte, and Rahvarinne together obtained around three million signatures[123]—only the Estonians managed to get the local communist-controlled Supreme Soviet to adopt the Declaration on the Sovereignty. This document, voted on November 16, 1988, declared the laws of the Estonian SSR superior to all-Union laws.

While the term "sovereignty" was not new in the Soviet legal system—all Soviet constitutions (1924, 1936, 1977) contained a reference to the sovereignty of its republics—the Estonian declaration was an attempt to give it a true substance. The Estonian Supreme Soviet took a step further by declaring that a Union Treaty should define the future relations between Estonia and the USSR. In the long term, the Estonian declaration had a considerable impact upon the Soviet disintegration process. Between May 1989 and December 1991, all Soviet republics, including Russian SFSR, replicated the Estonian move and, using the formula created by Estonian lawyers, declared the supremacy of the republic laws. In 1988, however, not even Latvia and Lithuania were ready to follow Tallinn's bold example.

Communists in Riga and Vilnius attempted to perform a balancing act between "not provoking Moscow too much" and at least partly satisfying the populations at home. The communist-run Supreme Soviets in Riga and Vilnius expressed the disagreement with the constitutional reform and proposed their own amendments but refused to adopt sovereignty declarations. The demand for a new Union Treaty was supported by popular movements but not voiced by the republic leadership.[124] This turn of events highlighted differences among Estonian and Latvian and Lithuanian internal dynamics, while becoming a test for the relations between Latvian and Lithuanian communists and their respective popular movements. Both Tautas Fronte and Sąjūdis were disappointed, and their supporters protested outside the local Supreme Soviets.[125]

Moscow, however, did nothing to make life easier for Latvian and Lithuanian communists. Gorbachev did not reward their moderation and did not take into account their proposals, despite a rather passionate speech by Gorbunovs at the Supreme Soviet of the USSR.[126] Years later, Gorbunovs admitted to a Latvian journalist that, far from being an independence supporter early on, he initially believed that a new Union Treaty could be an acceptable solution for Latvia. According to Gorbunovs, it was Gorbachev's inflexibility that made him change his mind and first hope for a constitutional reform that would enable a legal withdrawal from the USSR and then to assent with unilateral secession.[127]

The Gorbachev Foundation's selective transcripts of the Politburo meetings show that on November 10, deputy chairman of the Supreme Soviet Anatoly Lukyanov read "an ultimatum from the Balts," which most likely was a letter sent by the three popular movements, and concluded that "they" demand a new Union Treaty.[128] Over the coming weeks the Soviet leadership clashed over how to respond to this challenge. Lukyanov, an early supporter of Gorbachev who over the years had grown critical of what he saw as the excesses and softness of Perestroika, proposed to do the exact opposite of what the Baltic countries wanted. He argued that the constitutional reform should be used to make a transformation of the Union into a confederation impossible and insisted upon the need to adopt a secession law that would block exit from the USSR.[129] Prime Minister Ryzhkov saw Baltic demands as extremist but at the same time admitted that the constitutional reform was limited and spoke in support for Baltic economic autonomy.[130] Gorbachev insisted that the situation should not be dramatized and sent three members of the Politburo—Chairman of CPSU CC ideological commission Vadim Medvedev, former Belarusian party leader Nikolay Slyunkov, and the head of the KGB Viktor Chebrikov—to the Baltic countries. The conservative trio returned from their two-day visit "horrified."[131] They told their colleagues that during their trip they had been besieged by protesters asking for full sovereignty and chanting slogans like "Russians get out of here" or "Do away with the dictatorship from Moscow." In Latvia, Medvedev had seen a "real political inferno" that he had not yet experienced in Moscow: "noisy meetings, pickets, banners, the most heated discussions in university auditoriums, in the streets and squares."[132] The trio was convinced that the Baltic countries and societies were unified in their demands and that that the national intelligentsia was practicing double talk: one narrative for the visitors like them and another for the people in the streets.[133]

After the meeting at the Politburo, Gorbachev's diplomatic aide Anatoly Chernyaev concluded that Gorbachev had to make a choice between Czechoslovakia of 1968 or Finland of 1918, meaning that the secretary-general had to choose between a military intervention and acceptance of Baltic independence. Both options seemed dangerous, yet Chernyaev preferred the second one, as the use of force would mean "the death of Perestroika."[134] Meanwhile Medvedev argued that no major changes should be made to the constitutional amendments; in his view, that would have been too much of a retreat, and deeper reforms of Soviet federalism had to be reconsidered in the future.[135]

At the end, it was agreed in rather vague terms that there had to be a "political settlement" with the republics, but at the same time an "irreconcilable struggle" had to be carried out against nationalists and extremists.[136] In practice, it meant following Medvedev's suggestions: in the short term the Soviet leadership wanted to avoid projecting an impression that it was yielding to the pressures from the Baltic republics. The Declaration on Estonian Sovereignty was annulled by the all-Union Supreme Soviet and the constitutional amendments were adopted disregarding Baltic suggestions. In the longer term, everybody agreed that something had to be done both with the Baltic situation in particular and with center-periphery relations in general.

Although all three Soviet constitutions (adopted successively in 1924, 1936, and 1977) stated the republics' rights to leave the USSR, the procedure to be followed had never been established in Soviet legislation. During the previous decades of Soviet authoritarianism, this was hardly a problem, as secession was unthinkable. However, in the context of Soviet democratization, it was not unlikely that one or more republics might wish one day to exercise this right. This, however, was not part of Gorbachev's plan. During a November 24 meeting Gorbachev told his Politburo colleagues: "About withdrawal from the Soviet Union. We have tried to camouflage this issue, we got caught, they realized that we do not want to allow this."[137]

In the coming months, various actors studied the possibilities of reforming Soviet federalism. A commission consisting of Supreme Soviet deputies, economists, lawyers, and sociologists led by Chairman of the Presidium of the Supreme Soviet of the Byelorussian SSR Georgy Tarazevich was put in place to create proposals "on the delimitation of powers between the Centre and the Union republics."[138] Gorbachev's advisor Georgy Shakhnazarov argued for considerable autonomy for the Baltic republics and proposed a secession law that would make the exit from the Soviet Union a challenging task.[139] Yet none of these initiatives was implemented or followed by tangible measures, either in 1988 or in 1989. In January 1989 the Politburo established a commission chaired by Medvedev to coordinate the actions of the Central Committee departments and ministries in the Baltic states.[140] Other members were Chebrikov and Slyunkov, who had traveled with Medvedev to the Baltic countries in November 1988, as well as Chairman of the Soviet Planning Committee Yuri Maslyukov, Secretary of the CPSU Central Committee Georgy Razumovsky, and Anatoly Lukyanov. None of them was perceived as a friendly figure in the Baltic countries, but the work of the commission had little impact on Baltic-Soviet relations. Soviet policy regarding the so-called national question in general and Baltic issues in particular continued to consist of Moscow reacting to the situation on the ground rather than shaping it.

November 1988 tensions between Moscow and the Baltic capitals sowed the seeds of the future developments in the Soviet relations with Estonia, Latvia, and Lithuania: the emerging cooperation between Baltic popular movements, their expanding societal outreach, the gradual reduction of local communists' margins of maneuver, and Moscow's inflexibility and hesitancy to deal with the national question.

For those who wanted to save the Union of fifteen republics, November 1988 was probably the last moment when it could have been at least attempted by taking the Estonian offer to sign a new Union Treaty seriously. In 1988, the officially formulated demand emerging from the three Baltic states was a large autonomy. During the summer of 1989 the popular mood would shift toward independence. As one member of Tarazevich commission, sociologist Renald Simonyan, later wrote, "1988 it was by no means early but very, very timely, however after June 1989 it was already too late."[141]

Yet these hindsight considerations were not available to the actors at the time. In late 1988, Gorbachev was still optimistic regarding Soviet ability to find a *modus vivendi* with the Baltic progressive forces, but not overly invested in the issue. There were other more urgent problems on his plate such as the Soviet supply crisis, budget deficit, Nagorno-Karabakh, and the arrival of a new American president at the White House. Meanwhile, the leadership of the Baltic movements was far from feeling confident about their future perspectives as the uncertainty about the limits of Perestroika made them envisage all possible future scenarios, including a Soviet crackdown.[142]

CHAPTER 2

"Have you not noticed our absence?"

The Baltic Question during the Annus Mirabilis of 1989

The Hitler-Stalin pact is still shaping the Europe of today, our once-common Europe.
—The call of the Baltic Council to the Nations of the World, August 23, 1989

The main question of the year 1989 was the question of the limits of Perestroika and the limits of the New Thinking. While it has been argued that Eastern Europe revolutions of 1989 were driven by the gradual discovery of the extent of Soviet tolerance for change,[1] US policy during the same year was marked by "nagging suspicion that somewhere out there, there was still a limit to that tolerance," as National Security Advisor Brent Scowcroft wrote to President George Bush.[2] It turned out that the limit was the Soviet border: while Moscow was willing to accept large-scale transformations in the satellite states, the Baltic contestations ran up against the limits of Soviet tolerance during the year of 1989.

Gorbachev's acceptance of Eastern European democratization and the tightening of the grip in the Baltics went hand in hand. Increasingly concerned about the loss of Eastern Europe, the conservative elements in the Communist Party, as well as the Soviet military, amplified their pressure on Mikhail Gorbachev, limiting his scope for maneuver regarding the Baltic situation. At the same time, over the course of 1989, Baltic popular movements declared independence as their goal and Gorbachev started to realize that Sąjūdis, Tautas Fronte, and Rahvarinne, whose creation he had supported, were his challengers rather than his allies.

Politics of Uncertainty. Una Bergmane, Oxford University Press. © Oxford University Press 2023.
DOI: 10.1093/oso/9780197578346.003.0003

The Baltic decisions to seek full independence were influenced by several factors such as the rise of the Estonian Citizens' Committees, Latvian contacts with the diaspora,[3] and, most important, regime change in Eastern Europe. The success of Eastern European revolutions led activists in the Baltic republics to believe that a window of opportunity for historic change had opened. Developments in Hungary and Poland especially influenced Baltic activists. In March 1989, Trivimi Velliste from the Estonian Heritage Society had already urged the Estonian Communist Party to follow the example of linguistically close Hungary and to seek more independence from Moscow.[4] In August 1989, Sąjūdis congratulated the new Polish prime minister, Tadeusz Mazowiecki, with the words "your victory is also our victory."[5]

The Baltic push for independence during the crucial year of 1989 was embedded in the ontological narrative about the illegal annexation of the Baltic states in 1940. This chapter first follows Estonian, Latvian, and Lithuanian attempts to frame both domestically and internationally their quest for independence according to this narrative. It then analyzes the first US reactions to the re-emergence of the Baltic question, contextualizing them within wider US uncertainty about Soviet intentions.

FRAMING OF THE BALTIC QUESTION II: BALTIC INDEPENDENCE MOVEMENTS

In the Soviet Union, questions such as the deportations of Crimean Tatars or the Katyn massacre were part of Soviet "counter-memory" that contradicted the official versions of historical continuity and the governing mythology.[6] In the context of Perestroika and glasnost, different actors—previously marginalized memory communities,[7] reformers, autonomists, separatists—accessed the public space to challenge official versions of Soviet history.

During the crucial years of Perestroika, collective memory became a pillar of mass mobilization in Estonia, Latvia, and Lithuania. The revelations of the scope of Soviet repression in the Baltics—most notably the mass deportations of 1941 and 1949—led to the first mass gatherings in the three countries. From 1987 to 1991 the crucial dates of March 25 (the deportations of 1949), June 14 (the deportations of 1941), and August 23 (the Molotov-Ribbentrop Pact of 1939) were marked by increasingly impressive demonstrations. These gatherings were not only anti-Soviet demonstrations but also formative moments where collective visions of the past were forged and where individual or family memories of Soviet repression found validation through mass protest.[8]

By challenging the hegemony of official history, protesters also questioned the legitimacy of the Union. For decades, discourses on the past had been used to legitimize the relations regarding control, inequality, and hierarchy between the center and the periphery in the Soviet empire.[9] Discussions about Soviet crimes under Stalin reinforced the already existing feeling of ontological insecurity that was generated by the traumatic experience of Soviet modernity. In Lithuania, emerging testimonies about the suffering of the deportees echoed with the troubling memories of urbanization and displacement. In the two other Baltic states, stories about Estonians and Latvians being forcibly removed from their homelands accentuated the feeling that massive immigration from other Soviet republics was a part of a deliberate Russification plan. In this context, independence became to be understood as the only possible escape from the perceived threats.[10]

Beginning from 1987, mass gatherings marked the 1918 Independence Days in the capitals of the three Baltic republics. As the idea of independence as the ultimate goal of the Baltic popular movements started to be articulated, an intense debate emerged between the Estonian popular front Rahvarinne and Estonian right-wing movement ERSP about how the forthcoming independence struggle should be framed. While Rahvarinne argued for the proclamation of the second Estonian Republic, ERSP insisted on the restoration of Estonian state that was proclaimed in 1918. For ERSP, the idea of the restoration of the Estonian state went hand in hand with the restoration of prewar citizenry, thus excluding Soviet-era immigrants from the voting body.

At the same time, restorationism was much more than a tool of exclusion. During the first half of 1989, Rahvarinne embraced the idea of the restored state without seeking to narrow the voting body or rejecting Soviet institutions. In Lithuania, which had not experienced a massive influx of migrants during the Soviet period and where the question of exclusive citizenship was not seriously considered, restorationism became the main argument for independence, just as in Estonia and Latvia.

All told, legal restorationism was articulated as the main frame of the Baltic independence struggle and applied at the critical moments of political decision-making.[11] The following pages will trace Baltic attempts to project this frame outside Estonian, Latvian, and Lithuanian borders. The first step in the pursuit of these efforts was to make the highest Soviet authorities acknowledge the existence of the secret protocol of the 1939 Molotov-Ribbentrop Pact that had divided Eastern Europe into the Nazi and Soviet zones of influence. In the minds of many Estonians, Latvians, and Lithuanians, the secret protocol represented the ultimate argument for independence: if Baltic annexation to the USSR resulted from a secret deal between Nazi Germany and the USSR, then the Soviet rule over the Baltics was illegal, and their independence had to be restored.

While in the West the existence of the Pact's secret protocol was a widely acknowledged fact, in the USSR, it was a strongly guarded secret that was revealed only in the context of Perestroika. As early as August 23, 1987, during a public meeting at Hirvepark in Tallinn, Estonian dissident Tiit Madisson called for the publication of the secret protocol and the annulling of their consequences.[12] A year later, Latvian high-ranking communist Mavriks Vulfsons did the same during a meeting of Latvia's Trade Unions of Creative Professions, which initiated the creation of Tautas Fronte. The debate launched by Madisson and Vulfsons became central in their respective republics. In 1988 the Estonian newspaper *Rahva Hää*, Estonian Russian daily *Sovetskaya Estonia*, Latvian *Padomju Jaunatne*, and the Sąjūdis news bulletin *Sąjūdžio žinios* published the text of the secret protocol. The importance of this debate was critical in the eyes of former chief of the Latvian KGB Boris Pugo. Pugo openly told Vulfsons that by speaking publicly about the secret protocol, he had "destroyed Soviet Latvia."[13]

An open discussion about the Pact was indeed dangerous for the legitimacy of the Soviet rule in the Baltics as it questioned the official version of the Soviet role in the Second World War. The victory against Nazi Germany was one of the founding myths that shaped and redefined Soviet identity.[14] In the Baltic region, this myth legitimated annexation by placing gratitude for the liberation and the supposedly collective guilt for collaboration at the heart of the power relations between Moscow and the Baltic provinces. The revelation of the existence of the secret protocol shattered these dynamics by shedding light on Soviet cooperation with Nazi Germany at the outbreak of the war and called into question the Soviet official narrative about Estonian, Latvian, and Lithuanian voluntary accession to the USSR.

However, while the debate over the Pact shook Estonian, Latvian, and Lithuanian societies, the Kremlin stayed silent on the issue. For many years the Soviet Union had dismissed Western scholarship on the secret protocol, claiming that there was no such document in the Soviet archives and arguing that West Germany copies were fake. Yet, already in 1986, after Eduard Shevardnadze became the foreign minister, the ministry started to look into the issue and reached a conclusion that the USSR had indeed signed the secret protocol, without finding the missing document. Over the following years Shevardnadze and other Foreign Ministry officials discussed their findings with the Central Committee, and by 1988 heads of the CC's key departments such as Yakovlev (Propaganda), Anatoly Dobrynin (International Affairs), and Medvedev (Relations with Socialist Countries) had come to an agreement that the USSR should publicly recognize the existence of the secret protocol.[15] In spring 1988 the Politburo of the USSR had discussed the issue. During the meeting Vadim Medvedev pointed out that Soviet denial, rooted in the argument that the existing copies were fake, was not convincing anymore. "Our silence," he argued, "leaves an impression that we are afraid of something, that we are trying to hide something."[16] Yet, there was nothing to be afraid of, according to Medvedev; the protocol had to be publicly discussed to counter the Baltic narrative (the protocol existed and Baltic annexation was its direct result) with a new Soviet narrative (the protocol existed but the Baltic annexation was still a result of Baltic own free will).[17] Medvedev was backed by former Foreign Minister Andrei Gromyko, while the Deputy Foreign Minister Leonid Ilyichev talked about the paper trail of the "lost" protocol's original in the Foreign Ministry's archives. Yet nothing was done to address the issue publicly throughout the year, repeating Gorbachev's pattern to deal with the Baltic-related issues only when they became pressing. As Anatoly Chernyaev wrote in his diary in late 1989, if the existence of the protocol had been admitted as a "mistake" in 1988, the Soviet power could have avoided the questions over the Pact's becoming, as he put it, a "symbol of separatism."[18] Indeed, over the course of 1989, the issue of secret protocol became the rallying flag of Baltic pro-independence activists. Paradoxically, the first platform used to launch this mobilization was the controversial Congress of People's Deputies, which the Baltic popular movements had opposed in 1988.

The Congress of People's Deputies

The new legislative body established through the Soviet constitutional reform of November 1988 was constituted through two channels. First, the 750 candidates reserved to the all-Union organization candidates were selected over several weeks in March and April 1989. Second, on March 26 the first free elections in the history of the USSR were held, and the Soviet citizens chose 750 deputies from the national territorial constituencies and 750 from territorial districts.

In the Baltic republics, the elections turned into a triumph for the popular movements. Rahvarinne candidates won 29 out of 36 Estonian seats, Tautas Fronte obtained 30 out 40 Latvian seats, and Sąjūdis got 36 out of 42 Lithuanian ones.[19] As Boris Pugo, former first secretary of the Latvian

CP and former head of Latvian KGB, told his colleagues at the Politburo: "In the Baltics the popular fronts have obtained all that they wanted."[20]

On May 12, 1989, the Politburo discussed Baltic election results and Medvedev made an alarming report about the situation in Estonia, Latvia, and Lithuania, criticizing the local communist leadership and emphasizing that nationalist sentiments in the region were on the rise and secession was discussed.[21] According to Chernyaev, the three leaders of the Baltic communist parties who were present in the meeting held their ground, "shooting back" with "irrefutable arguments."[22] Estonian Vaino Väljas and Lithuanian Brazauskas blamed Moscow and the CPSU for their disastrous elections results. Latvian Jānis Vagris asked more sovereignty for the republics and more truthful information about the secret protocol.[23] Gorbachev responded to Medvedev's report and the Baltic politician's rather defiant speeches by reaffirming his full trust and support for local leadership and calling for a nuanced approach to the Baltic popular fronts—a whole movement was not to be confused with its radical wings. His overall attitude was optimistic and rooted in a complete disbelief in possible Baltic secession. "Where would they go?" Gorbachev asked.[24]

The presence of the Baltic popular movements was already felt on the first day of the Congress. On May 25, right after the opening speech by the chairman of the Central Election Commission, a doctor of Russian descent elected from Riga took the floor uninvited and asked the assembly to observe a minute of silence for victims of the April 9 Tibilisi crackdown.[25]

On June 2, Estonian scientist Endel Lippmaa requested the establishment of a commission that would assess the legal and political consequences of the Molotov-Ribbentrop Pact.[26] The request gave voice to heated debates about its long-term implications. As a Russian deputy from Estonia who was opposed to possible Estonian independence pointed out: "Certain ideologues of Rahvarinne push Moscow to recognize that the Molotov-Ribbentrop Pact and its protocol were null and void since the moment of signing. But, no, it is not for the sake of the historical truth, that they seek such recognition; it is to return to the status that this republic had in 1939. In the past things like these were whispered in cafes, said in the silence of artists' studios, but now they are declared loudly so that the whole world can hear it."[27]

The Baltic request was supported by Mikhail Gorbachev, even if his attitude toward the Pact problem was ambiguous. In his speech at the Congress of People's Deputies, Gorbachev repeated the previously established Soviet narrative. He expressed doubts regarding the existence of the secret protocol, "as their originals had not been found." He questioned the authenticity of the existing copies as "Molotov's signature was in German letters."

However, alluding to the Nazi and Soviet invasion of Poland, he admitted that there was something in the fact that "two great forces were moving toward each other and then stopped at a specific line." Still, he underlined that "these were all just assumptions for now" and that "this should be investigated." Along similar lines, Gorbachev emphasized that he didn't believe the claims that Baltic accession to the USSR wasn't "an expression of the popular will." He agreed, however, that this "should be investigated too."[28]

Gorbachev's speech was very telling regarding not only his relations with the Balts but his political strategy on communication in general. The Soviet president very rarely opposed any of the Baltic demands (except that for full independence), but at the same time, he always nuanced his support, without defining its limits clearly.[29] Representing the Soviet president as a master of the art of manipulating people through language, political scientist Matthew Evangelista quotes a member of the Politburo who described Gorbachev's unique ability: "in a stream of words, complicated, intricate phrases, constructed on any kind of basis, with appeals to authorities and to his own experience, to make his interlocutors into his allies. And in the end, all that verbiage so confused the issue that each of the opposing sides began to think that the general secretary actually supported its position."[30] Such a strategy can also be seen in the Molotov-Ribbentrop Pact debate: the secretary-general's speech at the Congress could have been interpreted as an invitation to find out the unknown truth or equally as a support for a commission that would put an end to the unfounded rumors about the existence of the secret protocol.

The Baltic demands for investigation were hard to reject, as they were formulated according to Gorbachev's own principles of glasnost and supported by one of his closest advisors, Alexander Yakovlev. Yakovlev, who in June 1989 became the chairman of the commission, later admitted in his memoirs that Gorbachev never put any obstacles in the way of the commission's work. However, both he and Boris Yeltsin have accused Gorbachev of actually having kept the Soviet originals of the secret protocol in the archives of the Kremlin and thus having openly lied to the Congress.[31] Indeed, as it later became known, the Russian original of the secret protocol had been kept for years in the archive of the Politburo in a sealed envelope. In 1987 the new head of the Central Committee General Department, Valery Boldin, opened the envelope and according to his memoirs informed Gorbachev about its contents.[32] Even if Boldin's active role in the August putsch against Gorbachev might cast doubts about the sincerity of his testimony, the fact that the envelope was opened in 1987 has been confirmed by historians.[33] According to Andrei Grachev (deputy head of the CPSU Central Committee's International section in 1989), Gorbachev knew about the secret protocol but was unwilling to add a "fatal argument" to the already heated debate over Baltic independence, and thus wanted to delay the discovery of the secret protocol as long as possible.[34]

The work of the commission ended with partial Baltic victory. Six months later, on Christmas Eve 1989, the Congress recognized the existence of the protocol and condemned it by a vote of 1,435 to 251. It did not, however, pronounce on the events of the summer of 1940 or the question of the legality or illegality of the Baltic annexation. The work of the commission that led to this outcome can be seen as a microcosm of larger Soviet political battles. During the final years of the USSR, collective representations about the past became a contested territory in which various groups promoted conflicting views to gain control over the political center or to legitimize separatist orientations.[35] The work of the commission provides an example of these battles but also reveals long-term trends in Estonian, Latvian, and Lithuanian relations with other groups involved in Soviet power struggles.

Baltic Independence Movements, the Molotov-Ribbentrop Pact Commission, and Soviet Political Circles

The chair of the commission, Alexander Yakovlev, was one of the leading architects of Gorbachev's reforms. Often accused of treason for his endorsement of the Baltic popular movements,[36] Yakovlev, like other members of Gorbachev's liberal circles, looked at Baltic countries with sympathy, which to a large extent was due to the socio-cultural appeal that the Baltic region had in the Soviet collective imaginary.[37] The perceived "Europeanness" and "Westernness" of the Baltic republics had a special meaning in the context of Perestroika. The liberal advisors who shaped Gorbachev's reforms belonged to the long-standing Westernizer current of Russian intellectual thought.[38] Annihilated by Stalin, the pro-European tradition (in its socio-cultural, not Cold War political sense) re-emerged in the 1960s among young Russian intellectuals, survived Brezhnev era, and became the driving force of the New Thinking. The affinity for Europe, understood as a civilization, as an intellectual tradition, as a political project, and most importantly as a model from which the USSR should learn, led to a special sympathy for the three countries that were perceived as the most Western of Soviet republics.[39]

Even when in 1989 it became clear that the Balts started to turn away from the collective Perestroika project and seek full independence, important figures in the Baltic leadership managed to maintain good relations with some of Gorbachev's key collaborators. Advisors such as Georgy Shakhnazarov and Anatoly Chernyaev argued for considerable autonomy for the Baltic countries.[40] At the moments of greatest tension between Moscow and the Baltic capitals, Latvian members of the Congress of People Deputies reached out to Shakhnazarov and Chernyaev seeking their help and mediation.[41] The Balts would similarly value their relationships with interior minister Vadim Bakatin.[42] When it came to Yakovlev, the leader of Tautas Fronte, Dainis Īvāns, called him the "most intelligent man in Gorbachev's circles."[43] Yet the aims of the Baltic deputies and Yakovlev differed. While the Balts wanted to shape their key argument for independence, Yakovlev wished to push forward the Perestroika project. In 1988, Yakovlev became the head of the Politburo commission in charge of studying Stalin's repressions and was actively involved in Soviet-Polish discussions about the Katyn massacre. The debate over the Pact, in his view, was another problematic conversation that Soviet society had to face in order to deal with the Stalinist legacy.

Initially, during the commission's meetings, the Baltic deputies constantly clashed with two other men from Gorbachev's closest circles: the head of the International Department of the CPSU and former Soviet Ambassador to Germany, Valentin Falin, and the director of the Institute of the USA and Canada of the Soviet Academy of Sciences, Georgy Arbatov. Both Falin and Arbatov were initially very skeptical about the Baltic interpretation of Soviet history, even though Falin knew about the discovery of Soviet originals in the CC archives.

While the relations between the Balts and Gorbachev's liberal advisors were often complicated, the leadership of the Baltic popular movements developed an increasingly close relationship with the circles around Boris Yeltsin. Just like Gorbachev's liberal advisors, Yeltsin's circles were attracted by Baltic "Europeanness." While they were not part of the 1960s generation intellectual cohort, they definitely were on the side of those embracing the European destiny of Russia and the USSR in the late 1980s Soviet standoff between the liberalizing Westernizers and nationalist neo-Stalinists. Many Russian liberals shared Baltic views on the market economy and copied their political strategy to enhance the agency of the Russian SFSR.[44]

On the commission, Yeltsin's supporters were represented by a professor from Omsk University, Alexey Kazannik; director of the Moscow State History and Archive Institute Yury Afanasyev; editor in chief of *Ogonyok* magazine Vitaly Korotich, and writer Vasil Bykaŭ, secretary of the Soviet Writers' Union. Not all of them initially had the same opinion regarding the Soviet-Nazi pact, and not all were equally active in the commission work. The main Baltic ally was Afanasyev, deputy chairman of the commission, historian, and an influential leader of the Congress Interregional Deputies Group that united Russian Democratic forces. During the months of the commission's work, Afanasyev supported the Baltic perception of the Soviet past.

Finally, the commission included two deputies from Moldova and Ukraine and one each from Belarus, Armenia, and Kyrgyzstan. Relations between the Baltic movements and other Soviet republics were ambiguous. At first, adopting the Polish slogan "For our freedom and yours," Baltic activists perceived their struggle as inseparable from the emancipation of other Soviet nationalities. Influenced by the example of the Crimean Tatars, the Balts inspired autonomist activities in Georgia, Armenia, Azerbaijan, Moldova, Ukraine, and even the Federal Republic of Russia.[45] But Baltic interests and those of other Soviet republics did not always converge. Despite the initial enthusiasm for the idea of solidarity among Soviet nationalities, the leaders of the Baltic movements soon started to question the usefulness of their close association with other Soviet republics, and gradually adopted a discourse highlighting their uniqueness in the Soviet context.[46] As far as the work of the commission was concerned, the opinions of the representatives of the different republics varied according to the implications that the condemnation of the secret protocol might have had for their own people. Estonia, Latvia, and Lithuania were not the only Soviet republics whose destiny was shaped by the Nazi-Soviet deal. In 1939 the Pact had also allocated Eastern Poland and the Romanian region of Bessarabia to the Soviet zone of influence. In 1940, Bessarabia had become the Moldavian SSR, while the territories of former eastern Poland were divided between the Ukrainian SSR and the Belarusian SSR. Fearing for the territorial integrity of his republic, Ukrainian minister of foreign affairs Volodymyr Kravets repeated the Soviet official narrative claiming that the secret protocol was a Western forgery.[47] Supported by Falin and Arbatov, he argued, that since Ukrainians and Byelorussians populated the Polish territories that were ceded to the Soviet zone, the USSR had contributed to the re-establishment of the "territorial integrity" of Ukraine and Byelorussia. Meanwhile, Moldovan deputies, such as the writer Ion Druță and the chairman of the trade union council of Moldova Grigore Ereme, supported the Baltic arguments about the illegality of the secret protocol. Another member of the commission, the very popular Kyrgyz writer Chingiz Aitmatov, also backed the Baltic cause.

Despite the initial controversies, documentary proof from Finnish, US, and West German archives provided by Baltic members of the commission played a crucial role in convincing the skeptics such as Fallin, Arbatov, and

Kulin to publicly admit the existence of the protocol. As Kazannik explained to the Congress on December 23, 1989: "I took these documents and tried to analyze them as a jurist. To what conclusion did I come? That the secret protocol[s] have indeed existed!"[48]

While the commission was debating the existence of the secret protocol, the leaders of the popular movements began to take bolder steps in their attempts to shape the framework of the move to Baltic independence.

The Baltic Way and the Limits of Perestroika

In the context of sweeping change in Eastern Europe, the leaders of Rahvarinne, Tautas Fronte, and Sąjūdis were reflecting on their future strategy. Since November 1988, Edgar Savisaar, Dainis Īvāns, and Vytautas Landsbergis had been cooperating closely, meeting almost every week to co-ordinate their activities.[49] Avoiding holding meetings in the Baltic capitals, the chairmen used smaller cities such as Pärnu (Estonia), Cēsis (Latvia), and Šiauliai (Lithuania). During the meeting of July 14, 1989, Estonian leader Edgar Savisaar proposed the organization of a human chain from Tallinn to Vilnius via Riga on August 23, 1989, to commemorate the fifty years since the signing of the Molotov-Ribbentrop Pact. His Latvian and Lithuanian counterparts embraced the idea, and a formal agreement was signed on August 15 in the outskirts of the city of Cēsis.

On August 23, the largest mass gathering in the history of the Baltic countries took place when around two million Estonians, Latvians, and Lithuanians joined hands, forming a 430 mile long chain, "the Baltic Way," from Tallinn in the North to Vilnius in the South.[50]

This event was not only a milestone in the Baltic pro-independence mobilization and a powerful message from the Baltic states to Moscow, but it also increased Baltic visibility on the international stage. On August 23 and 24, for the first time in their history, Estonia, Latvia, and Lithuania came under the spotlight of the global media. The Baltic Way and the anniversary of the Pact made front-page news in the United States, the UK, France, Italy, West Germany, Denmark, Sweden, and Finland.[51] Western media coverage obviously did not mean automatic Western support for the Baltic cause. For example, the wording chosen by the British press was more prudent and skeptical than that of the French media.[52] However, all the reports contributed to the spreading of the Baltic message about the illegality of Soviet rule.

On the eve of the Baltic Way, Sąjūdis, Tautas Fronte, and Rahvarinne issued an appeal to the "nations of the world." Drafted by Estonians and ratified by all three popular movements, it was then sent by Sąjūdis to the United States and relayed to the leading Western media. The document reflected all the main arguments that Estonians, Latvians, and Lithuanians were deploying at the international level. In the first part of the text, the Balts argued that the illegality of Soviet actions in 1939 made Soviet rule illegal in 1990. At the same time, they framed the Baltic cause not only as an issue of international law, but also as a chapter in the anticolonial struggle, calling for "abolishing the last colonial possessions in Europe." The text also went to great lengths in affirming the Estonian, Latvian, and Lithuanian commitment to human rights, civil rights, freedom, equality, and Europe. The wording shows the Balts' efforts to shape their independence project according to internationally accepted values. On the one hand, this language was meant to make the Baltic cause more attractive to the West. On the other hand, it reflected genuine Baltic willingness to claim European identity by conforming to European normative expectations.

Newspapers quoted the Baltic appeal in Norway, West Germany, France, and the United States.[53] In the US Congress, Senator Jesse Helms drew his colleagues' attention to the question posed at the end of the appeal: "Have you not noticed our absence?"[54]

In the United States both the *New York Times* and the *Washington Post* published the full text of the secret protocol, but the stand of their editorial boards on the Baltic question differed. The August 27 the *Washington Post* editorial "The Captive Nations" drew a very positive image of the Baltic independence movements and called for US support for Baltic self-determination.[55] Meanwhile, in the columns of the *New York Times*, Anthony Lewis took a more cautious approach and called for some sort of compromise between the Baltic republics and Gorbachev.[56]

The Soviet leadership, however, was no longer willing to compromise. The Baltic situation was not the only problem on their plate. The day after the Balts joined hands in protest, Solidarity's Tadeusz Mazowiecki had become prime minister in Poland, while East German refugees were flooding into Hungary. Gorbachev's acceptance of Polish and Hungarian reforms was met with great concern by Soviet conservatives. Determined to stop what they saw as the erosion of Soviet power, the conservative members of the Politburo pushed for a harshly worded condemnation of the Baltic actions. On August 27 the Soviet Communist Party issued a statement condemning the "nationalist hysteria" in the Baltic states and warned: "Things have gone too far. The fate of the Baltic peoples is in serious danger. People should know into what abyss they are being pushed by the nationalist leaders. The consequences could be disastrous for these peoples if the nationalists managed to achieve their goals. The very viability of the Baltic nations could be called in question."[57]

To the great surprise of certain Western journalists, the harshly worded Central Committee statement was signed by all members of the Politburo including Mikhail Gorbachev. In France, *Libération* qualified the Soviet statement as a threat,[58] *Quotidien de Paris* found in it "the old, insulting doublespeak from the quiet days of Brezhnev era nostalgia."[59] On August 30, David Remnick in the *Washington Post* wrote that, "Like many Westerners, some activists in the Baltic republics refuse to believe that a reformer like Gorbachev could have anything to do with something as scathing and reminiscent of the pre-glasnost days of Soviet politics as last Saturday's Central Committee statement denouncing the independent political movements."[60] Indeed rumors circulated that the document was published without consulting Gorbachev or that he was somehow pressured into signing it.[61] Sąjūdis leader Vytautas Landsbergis tried to make excuses for Gorbachev and told the foreign press that Gorbachev had had no choice but to sign the document: "If they called him up and told him that all the rest had signed, he couldn't but sign."[62]

Soviet liberals such as Anatoly Chernyaev were not proud of the statement and were skeptical about its possible impact on the Baltic drive for independence. "But what is it to the Balts?" he wrote in his diary. "In their civilized manner they could be sailing away from the USSR for years."[63]

After the Baltic Way, the Soviet leader attempted to warn the Balts about the limits of what was acceptable, while at the same time trying not to spoil relations with the supporters of Perestroika in the Baltic communist parties. On September 13, during a meeting with the Baltic leadership, Gorbachev told the Estonians, Latvians, and Lithuanians not to pay too much attention to the statement and "to go forward," keeping in mind that the Soviet Union should be preserved, unity of the Communist Party maintained, and all nationalities considered as equal.[64] In other words, despite Gorbachev's liberal foreign policy and his universalistic rhetoric, he was not willing to make concessions to the Baltic countries—the Union had to be kept intact.[65] While Western media and Baltic pro-independence activists expected Gorbachev to show in the Baltic case the same tolerance for change that he showed in the Polish and Hungarian cases, the Soviet leader saw a strict difference between the satellite states and the Soviet republics. The former were free to choose their own path, while the latter had to realize their self-determination without leaving the USSR.[66]

The meeting with the Baltic communist leadership did not go well. Without directly challenging Gorbachev's red line—unity of the Communist Party, unity of the state, and ethnic equality—they did not hide their discontent. None of them had been warned about the Central Committee's harsh statements in advance, and all of them were fighting to maintain their political relevance in the context of increasing pro-independence mobilization at home, yet due to Moscow's procrastination over the federal reforms they had no alternatives to offer.[67]

Between September 19 and 21, 1989, the long-awaited CPSU Central Committee Plenum on Nationalities Policy took place. Addressing thousands of delegates from all over the Soviet Union, Gorbachev rejected Baltic arguments about the illegality of Soviet actions in 1940, stating that "there is no basis for questioning the decision by the Baltic republics [in 1940] to join the USSR and the choice made by the people there to be part of the Soviet Union."[68]

Speaking about the nationality problem in the USSR in general, the first secretary refused to accept secession (which actually was authorized by the USSR constitution) as being part of peoples' rights to self-determination: "Claims that national self-determination in the USSR has not been achieved in reality, and attempts to equate self-determination with secession (and thereby impair this universal principle of resolving the problem of nationalities) are futile and should be vigorously condemned."[69] While the impossibility of secession was pointed out, the plans for reforming the Soviet state remained vague. The plenum ended without offering any substantialy new answers to the question about the future of the multi-ethnic Soviet state.[70] Two weeks after the plenum, Estonian Rahvarinne and Latvian Tautas Fronte declared independence as their primary goal. In early November it became clear that the Communist Party of Lithuania was planning to secede from the Communist Party of the USSR. On November 16, 1989, the secretary-general of the Lithuanian Communist Party faced an angry Politburo and openly stated that the leadership of the party was no longer able to cope with the pro-independence pressures not only from Sąjūdis but also from inside the party itself.[71]

The existing partial publications of Politburo meetings clearly show that its members were fully aware that the Baltic states were moving toward independence.[72] Yet the central government's actions to counter it were very limited. In November the Politburo finally backed the Baltic economic autonomy project that had been discussed at various levels since 1987. Yet this was too little, too late. While the economic autonomy was an exciting project in 1988, it was not something that could dissuade independence supporters from pursuing their goals. On December 2, a long letter from Gorbachev was sent to the Communists of Lithuania pleading to maintain the unity of the Communist Party of the Soviet Union. The Lithuania CP ignored his demands and broke from the CPSU on December 24, 1989.

BUSH'S SPECIAL CASE: INTERNATIONALIZATION OF THE BALTIC QUESTION

According to Secretary of State James Baker's memoirs, the question of whether "Gorbachev would be able to survive" dominated his life in the period from 1989 to 1991.[73] This, however, is not a fully correct assessment of the situation, as during the first year of the Bush presidency his administration was as much if not more preoccupied with the question of to what extent Gorbachev could be trusted.

Since the arrival of Gorbachev at the leadership, the USSR had accumulated important symbolic capital by successfully projecting a new Soviet identity that corresponded to the ideological preferences of Western liberal democracies. On the one hand, the shaping of the new collective Soviet self-understanding was a part of the Perestroika project. As one Soviet official wrote in 1988: "By Europe, we should understand not only the political phenomenon but also a definite model as to how we live, think, communicate with other people. The processes that are going on today in our country . . . have the dimension of a movement towards a return to Europe in the civilizational meaning of the term."[74]

On the other hand, the image of the new Soviet Union was an instrument that the Soviet leadership deployed to achieve political goals on the international stage. Both Gorbachev and his closest advisors, such as Yakovlev, were determined to deconstruct the hostile image that the Soviet Union had in the West.[75] And their quest was successful. Already in 1987, Ronald Reagan admitted that the Soviet Union was no longer the "evil empire" that it had been in 1983.[76]

However, the incoming Bush administration was much more skeptical than Reagan's team. Gorbachev, who was very aware of Bush's skepticism, believed that the changes in the attitude originated in the new National Security Council.[77] Indeed, the national security advisor, Brent Scowcroft, suspected Gorbachev of using East-West summits to gain popularity, without producing any substantial change at home.[78] In early February 1989 the senior director of Soviet and East European affairs, Condoleezza Rice, drafted a memo entitled "Getting Ahead of Gorbachev," in which she argued that weakening NATO remained the main objective of the Soviet leadership.[79] In her eyes, Gorbachev's military retreat from Eastern Europe was a tactical move to gain the upper hand in the US-Soviet standoff by charming the international community. All in all, Rice advised that the best way to deal with Gorbachev's moves was to slow down the pace of US-Soviet interactions, while consolidating domestic support and strengthening relationships with US allies. Robert Blackwell, who served as the special assistant to the president for European and Soviet Affairs, found Rice's analysis "an outstanding paper."[80] In early March, Scowcroft sent the memo to the president, who read the document and found it "interesting."[81]

In May both Secretary Baker and President Bush publicly stressed that the United States wished Perestroika to succeed. However, the new administration opted for a "pause" in Soviet-American relations. At the same time, the cooling in this relationship did not imply more significant support from Washington for forces in the USSR or in Eastern Europe who were challenging the existing status quo.

The pause initiated by Washington coincided with the acceleration of "negotiated revolutions" in Poland and Hungary. Over the spring and summer of 1989 an intensive dialogue between governments and opposition in Warsaw and Budapest became the driving force of Polish and Hungarian democratization. Policymakers and historians are divided over their assessment of the role the United States played in these events. Even if actors such as Bush, Baker, and Robert Hutchings have claimed that the United States encouraged and supported Eastern European revolutions,[82] historians have mostly agreed that the US policy was reactive rather than proactive and focused on gradual rather than revolutionary change.[83]

All the elements that shaped the US attitude toward Eastern Europe during the first half of 1989—prudence, skepticism, preference for controlled change, fear of a Soviet backlash—played a role in the White House's initial reactions to the unrest in the Baltics. The possibility of large-scale destabilization and the probability of a Soviet backlash was higher in the Baltic case than in Eastern Europe, for the simple reason that Estonia, Latvia, and Lithuania were *de facto* part of the Soviet Union. Yet two factors pushed the Bush administration to raise the Baltic question with the Soviet Union after the Baltic Way: congressional support and the non-recognition policy.

For policymakers in the Bush administration, non-recognition policy was a legal position and a diplomatic tradition. It would have been impossible for the Bush administration to break with this tradition without causing significant damage to its reputation and credibility.[84] At the same time, it was also one of many historical narratives that decision makers used to make sense of the rapidly changing situation in Eastern Europe and the USSR.

During the crucial years of 1989 to 1991, history in general, and the Second World War in particular, became a frequently evoked topic during the meetings of European, Soviet, and US politicians. When French president François Mitterrand met Margaret Thatcher to discuss the German rush to unification, the British prime minister showed him a map of interwar

Europe, arguing that a united Germany would claim its former territories in Eastern Europe.[85] When Gorbachev and Shevardnadze confronted West German foreign minister Hans-Dietrich Genscher over Helmut Kohl's Ten-Point Plan, they did not hesitate to compare the West German chancellor with Hitler.[86] When Western powers started to contemplate the eventual disintegration of the USSR, their attitudes were shaped by lessons from the past about the disastrous consequences of imperial collapses.[87] And when it came to Baltic independence particularly, George Bush said that his main fear was the repetition of the 1956 Hungarian events—a situation in which the United States would raise the hopes of local populations without being able and willing to provide concrete support in the case of a Soviet crackdown.[88] Meanwhile, Mitterrand argued that the USSR was capable of violent reaction to Baltic independence claims because according to him, "historically, these areas were part of Russia."[89]

These references to the past were undoubtedly used as a rhetorical device to convince the other, and oneself, to justify a decision and to explain a complicated situation. At the same time, perception of the past was also a source of personal beliefs about international relations and other countries. As political scientist Robert Jervis has noted, private memories and interpretations of history, especially the last major war, do play a role in the shaping of the perception of decision makers as well as of ordinary citizens.[90] Facing the sweeping changes of the late 1980s and early 1990s, actors used narratives about the past to make sense of the rapidly changing situation and to reduce the uncertainty they had to face. In other words, at the Cold War endgame lessons from the past were both internalized and instrumentalized by the policymakers.

The 1940 non-recognition was one of those perception shaping narratives. There was precious little that Bush or any other Western politician knew about Estonia, Latvia, and Lithuania, but they were all aware of the fact that their respective countries had not recognized the 1940 annexation as legal. In the period 1989–1991, this narrative became central in the US understanding of the Baltic question: in the eyes of US policymakers, the Baltic states were not Soviet republics like the others. This perception of the Baltic and Soviet situation did not mean immediate support for independence, but it made it impossible to dismiss the Baltic problem as a Soviet internal affair, and it made it possible to discuss it with the Soviet officials.

One month after the Baltic Way, Eduard Shevardnadze visited Washington, DC. While George Bush did not raise the Baltic question with the Soviet foreign minister, James Baker did discuss it with his counterpart. In his memoirs, Baker explains: "I wanted him to understand that our

Baltic policy was rooted in historical and domestic political realities, and the president could not shift away from this position even if he wanted." When Baker insisted that "it would be hard to sustain positive relations if you find it necessary to use force," Shevardnadze assured him that nobody intended to use force against Estonians, Latvians, and Lithuanians, as "the use of force would mean the end of Perestroika."[91] This first discussion on the Baltic question between a key official of the Bush administration and the Soviet foreign minister became a pattern for later United States and Soviet communication on the topic. In the following two years, the White House and State Department repeatedly insisted that for historical reasons (meaning the non-recognition) the United States was interested in the Baltic situation and that use of force in the Baltics would harm US-Soviet relations. US officials also implicitly or even explicitly made their interlocutors understand that they were facing domestic pressures to take an even stronger stand regarding the Baltic problem.

This domestic pressure came first and foremost from Congress. As noted by foreign policy analyst James Lindsay, congressional influence over US foreign policy cannot be measured merely by its capacity to legislate its own political preferences.[92] The legislative branch can use other, more indirect means to shape the external actions of the United States. One of these indirect methods consists of putting pressure on the president, so that, to protect his image and credibility, he anticipates Congress's moods on specific foreign policy issues and shapes policy accordingly. One of the pressure-building tools that Congress often used was passage of resolutions that clearly expressed the stand of one or both chambers on US Baltic policy even though they did not create laws and were not enforceable.

After the Baltic Way, Republican Senator Bob Kasten and Democrat Senator Robert Byrd proposed a resolution related to the Baltic situation.[93] The text urged President Bush and Secretary Baker to raise the Baltic question in their conversations with the Soviet leadership and to call upon the USSR to respect human rights, norms, peoples' right to self-determination, and the Helsinki Final Act. A similar text was adopted by 98–0 in September 1989.[94]

Another pressure-building tool was that of direct letters to the president. In October 1989 the chairs of the Ad-Hoc Committee on the Baltic States and Ukraine, Democrat Dennis Hertel (Michigan) and Republican Don Ritter (Pennsylvania), prepared a letter for George Bush calling for "a more active and visible Baltic policy."[95] Framing the Baltic question as a "regional issue," the members of the US Congress contested the Soviet claims that the Baltic problem was an internal affair and had to be resolved according to the Soviet constitution.

On October 31, ten days before the fall of the Berlin Wall, the White House and the Kremlin announced that the Soviet and American presidents were going to meet in Malta in early December. Rumors surrounding this meeting reinforced the anxiety of Baltic allies in Washington.

A Secret Deal at the Malta Summit?

The summit, secretly planned since July, quickly became the subject of speculation on both sides of the Atlantic.[96] In the United States and Europe, it was thought that the meeting might have been scheduled to seek a superpower agreement on Germany. Once again, historical narratives were revived to speak to about the current events. As James Baker noted in his memoirs: "The question in everybody's mind was: would Malta become Yalta II? Would the superpowers form a condominium and decide the German question by themselves?"[97]

Rumors about a secret Soviet-American agreement were bolstered by the recollection of suggestion that former secretary of state Henry Kissinger had made to President Bush one year earlier. On December 18, 1988, Kissinger had met with the president-elect and recommended that he negotiate a deal with the Soviet president that would consist of two promises: on the Soviet side not to use force in Eastern Europe, on the American one, "not to exploit any economic or political changes that occurred there at the expense of 'legitimate' Soviet interests."[98] Historian Michael Beschloss and Strobe Talbott, who in 1989 worked as a reporter, have claimed that the president was initially interested in Kissinger's suggestion, and the former secretary of state mentioned his idea also to Mikhail Gorbachev during his trip to the USSR in January 1989.[99] The idea was sharply criticized and denounced as "Yalta II" by Assistant Secretary of State Rozanne Ridgway and her deputy for Soviet affairs, Thomas Simons.[100] In an interview for this book in 2012, Thomas Simons explained that Kissinger's plan had never been implemented because of its unpopularity in the State Department.[101]

Similarly, Robert Hutchings in his memoirs wrote that, despite Secretary Baker's "flirting" with the idea of engaging directly with the Soviets on Eastern Europe, a possible secret deal was neither on the agenda nor ever given serious consideration by any senior administration official.[102] Baker himself told the *New York Times* on March 28 that "the West should not rush into such a plan because the counter-argument also had appeal: Why strike a deal that would grant the Soviets any type of formalized status in Eastern Europe when countries in the region, like Poland and Hungary, are already moving toward a more Western orientation in their economies and political systems?"[103] Kissinger's diminished influence in the Bush administration, due to his conflict with Baker, seems to have contributed to the rejection of his plan.[104] At the same time, the US administration held back from Eastern European affairs during the eventful first part of 1989, giving credence to doubts as to whether Kissinger's plan had left traces on US policy.

In this context, the Estonians, Latvians, and Lithuanians in the USSR and in the United States feared that a similar deal could be made regarding them. Rumors circulated that Gorbachev would propose not to intervene in Eastern Europe if the United States overlooked repressions inside the USSR. In the Baltics, talks about a possible US-Soviet deal resonated not only with the Gaullist myth of Yalta but also the Molotov-Ribbentrop Pact debate, feeding into a more general historical narrative about Western betrayal. In early November, the American ambassador in Moscow, Jack Matlock, received a delegation of deeply concerned Baltic independence movement leaders, eager to know if the United States and the USSR were about to make a deal on their independence. Even though Ambassador Matlock insisted that the Balts "had plenty of things to worry about, this was not one of them," the anxiety persisted.[105]

As the summit approached, the White House continued to receive letters from supporters of the Baltic states in the Congress and from Baltic diaspora organizations. On November 1, a message was sent by the Joint Baltic American Committee (JBANC) requesting a meeting with the president and other Baltic American leaders.[106] By the end of November, seventeen senators had written to the president asking him to raise "the question of the occupied Baltic States" during the meeting with Mikhail Gorbachev in Malta.[107] Another message was sent by thirty-two representatives, expressing their concern about possible American concessions regarding the Baltic states.[108] However, in a memorandum to the president, Baker advised him to flag the US commitment to the non-recognition policy but also to explain that Washington was not seeking to destabilize the USSR and did not have a "preconceived notion about the agreement that the Baltic states might arrive at through a democratic process of self-determination."[109] In other words, the secretary of state suggested that Bush should signal that Baltic independence was not a US goal and should reassure his Soviet counterpart that the United States was not going to exploit the Baltic situation.

While the summit preparation documents and recent scholarship[110] clearly show that the United States was not predisposed to or interested in making any deal with the USSR regarding Eastern Europe, Philip Zelikow (director of European security affairs at the National Security Council from

1989 to 1991) and Rice in their memoirs, as well as Talbott and Beschloss in their book, have claimed that a "Kissinger style" agreement was actually explicitly reached on the Baltics. According to these accounts, which seem to be influenced by each other, Bush during the meeting promised not to interfere in the Baltics if Gorbachev abstained from the use of force in the region.[111] As explained by historian Timothy Naftali, "he had told Gorbachev in Malta that despite the official position he would treat Lithuania as an internal matter of the USSR as long as Gorbachev promised not to use force in the Republic and agreed that eventually the principle of self-determination should be extended there."[112]

However, the memoirs of George Bush, the summit preparation documents, and the transcript of the Gorbachev-Bush meeting in Malta do not confirm this version of events. The declassified Soviet transcript shows that George Bush first mentioned the Baltic question on the first day of the meeting, suggesting that this "extremely complicated issue" should be discussed "confidentially."[113] The US transcripts reveal that Bush returned to the Baltic issue during a restricted bilateral session on the second day of the summit. Interestingly the transcript does not provide Bush's wording verbatim but indicates that "the president described a question that he had been asked about the Baltic states." Responding to this, Mikhail Gorbachev talked about the Russian minorities in Estonia and Latvia, framed Baltic separatism as a "danger for Perestroika," and concluded that "if the US has no understanding, it will spoil relations with the US more than anything else."[114]

According to the Bush memoirs, he replied by pointing out that the United States would have to respond to any use of force by the Soviets there. However, according to the transcript, the wording chosen by the president was more neutral: "if you use force—you don't want to—that would create a firestorm."[115] Both the transcript and the Bush memoirs show that Gorbachev, unlike Shevardnadze in September, did not explicitly reject the possible use of force.

The discussion about the Baltic countries reveals broader dynamics of the summit. Historians and actors have long debated how to assess the Malta meeting in the context of the Cold War endgame. Some have argued that it was a lost opportunity; others have insisted that it was crucial in terms of trust-building between the two leaders or in terms of the Soviet-American bargaining over the German reunification.[116] However, historian Sergey Radchenko has pointed out that when it came to fundamental questions, such as the interpretation of the end of the Cold War, the two leaders talked past each other.[117] In the eyes of the president, the United States had won the Cold War but was willing to do the Soviets a favor by not publicly claiming the triumph. For Gorbachev, the Cold War ended because of the New Thinking and Perestroika, and it was America's duty to help him with these projects.

It seems that a similar misunderstanding had occurred regarding the Baltic question. There is a certain discrepancy between the contents of this short discussion that appears in the transcripts and the far-reaching conclusions that its participants drew from it. Scowcroft has written that he himself came away from this exchange convinced that "Gorbachev understood clearly what a neuralgic issue the Baltics were . . . and that he would restrict himself to non-coercive measures."[118] At the same time, in a letter written by Mikhail Gorbachev to George Bush in spring 1990, during the so-called Lithuanian crisis, the Soviet president refers to "a fundamental mutual understanding regarding the conduct vis-à-vis Lithuania" reached in Malta.[119] The Bush administration had left the summit feeling that Gorbachev had understood that the use of force in the Baltics would provoke a strong US reaction and thus would not do it. Meanwhile, Gorbachev was under the impression that Bush had realized the dangers the Baltic issue represented for Perestroika (and in consequence the common good) and thus would not intervene in the affair.

While the precise details of the Malta meeting remain unclear, it can be seen as the beginning of the US involvement in the Baltic question at the highest level. December 1989 was the first time since the end of the Second World War that a US president invoked the Baltic issue with a Soviet leader. At this stage, the Bush administration did not ask for Baltic independence; it merely hinted at "a firestorm" that the Soviet use of force would provoke in the United States. At the same time no such remarks were made regarding other Soviet republics, and no other Soviet republics were discussed at the summit.

International relations scholar Joshua Shifrinson has argued that the Malta summit was crucial in reducing American anxiety about possible hostile Soviet reaction to German reunification.[120] Political scientist Jacques Lévesque has pointed that it was after the fall of the Berlin Wall that the United States started to believe that the USSR was not going to use force to maintain its influence in Eastern Europe, including East Germany.[121] By early December 1989, the US president had lost his previous caution and preference for slow, controlled change and agreed to support the German Unification—thus challenging "the most basic ingredient of the European balance of power."[122] It was not just the realization that the Soviet Union did not indeed plan to use force to prevent change in Europe, but also the shift of the object of this change: a possible German reunification was more important for the Bush administration than changes in Eastern Europe for several reasons. First, because of its geopolitical and economic importance, the German Question had always been at the heart of the Cold War conflict. The Cold War began first and foremost over Germany, not Eastern Europe. Second, reunification directly touched upon US interests as it involved a vital member of the North Atlantic alliance—West Germany. Bush's embrace of German reunification plans did not mean equally active support for revolutionary changes in Eastern Europe and even less in the Soviet breakaway republics. During 1990, all changes in the European and Soviet status quo would be measured against their possible impact on German reunification.

CHAPTER 3

Building a New World Order?

The Lithuanian Crisis of Spring 1990

You think Lithuania is an internal matter, but it has a real impact on my political situation.
—George Bush to Mikhail Gorbachev, June 1, 1990

On March 11, 1990, the Republic of Lithuania proclaimed the restoration of its independence. The Lithuanian decision inspired its Baltic neighbors, angered Moscow, and put the international community in a difficult position. Already in early 1989 during Spain's presidency of the European Economic Community, Spanish diplomats had described the dilemma that Western states were facing when dealing with the Baltic question: "The Western world is faced with an obvious contradiction: either lose this opportunity to support the Baltic states, with the consequent breakdown of the principles held until today (non-recognition of the absorption), or rather support openly the Baltic claims for independence, reducing Gorbachev's maneuverability and creating new difficulties for Perestroika."[1] On the one hand, for fifty years, most Western countries had argued that the annexation of the Baltic states by the USSR in 1940 was illegal and that thus, *de jure*, Estonia, Latvia, and Lithuania were not part of the USSR. On the other hand, since 1944/1945 these three Baltic states had been controlled by the Soviet Union, which by 1990 was led by a cooperative and reform-oriented statesman.

The function of the international recognition of states has long been a topic of debate. The declaratory school of legal scholars argues that such recognition is simply an acknowledgment that a political entity has

Politics of Uncertainty. Una Bergmane, Oxford University Press. © Oxford University Press 2023.
DOI: 10.1093/oso/9780197578346.003.0004

satisfied the criteria of statehood laid down in the Montevideo Convention (1933): a permanent population, defined territory, effective government, and a capacity to enter relations with other states. The constitutive school, on the other hand, claims that the act of recognition, rather than just acknowledging the existence of a country, actually participates in its creation, and when the new state's existence is contested, it consolidates it.[2]

These two legal interpretations of recognition reflected the differences between Lithuanian, and later also Estonian and Latvian, expectations of the international community and the attitude of Western capitals toward the Baltic question in spring 1990. Lithuanians hoped that the international recognition would consolidate their independence and make the USSR accept their freedom as a *fait accompli*, or at least improve their position vis-à-vis Moscow. The international community, however, argued that Baltic independence could not be recognized until governments in Tallinn, Riga, and Vilnius had established effective control over their territories and populations. As Estonia, Latvia, and Lithuania could hardly establish this control by force, Soviet consent to Baltic independence became a crucial precondition of international recognition.

The recognition question was not just a legal matter. It was first and foremost a political problem. In Europe as well as in Washington, it was clear that the answer to the Lithuanian proclamation was actually an answer to the Baltic question and a decision regarding the integrity of the Soviet Union. As a CIA report on February 28 noted, future Baltic independence would most certainly fuel separatist aspirations in other Soviet republics such as Moldova, the Caucasus, and eventually Ukraine.[3] Furthermore, the international context was particularly tense: talks on German reunification in 2 + 4 format (two German states and four occupying powers) started on March 14, with the sensitive question of German NATO membership on the table.[4]

The measures taken by actors in Washington, as well as in European capitals, were shaped by the feeling that they were living through a period of crucial historical change, but that they had minimal time to shape these changes to their own advantage. The Lithuanian crisis risked complicating, if not halting, the transition to the post–Cold War order and thus had to be defused. Yet the rapidly changing situation in the USSR and the confusing signals from Moscow made it very hard for the United States to determine the best way to proceed.

Between March 11, when Lithuania proclaimed its independence, and late June 1990, when Vilnius agreed to suspend its declaration, the United States tried various approaches, and more than once made last-minute changes in their policies. Congress actively participated in this process, pushing the White House toward a harder stance on the Baltic question. This chapter will follow these chaotic dynamics leading up to the last-minute reversal of Bush's Baltic policy at the Washington summit.

THE UNWELCOME INDEPENDENCE

On January 12, 1990, two months before the Lithuanian proclamation of independence, Mikhail Gorbachev arrived in Vilnius. For the secretary-general, the visit was crucial as he feared that Lithuania's independence would establish a dangerous precedent, weakening not only the unity of the USSR but also his position in the Soviet power structures. The trip turned into a failure as Gorbachev once again seemed to be "late" in his response to the developments in the Baltic republics. The time when elites in the Baltic countries would have been able and willing to accept significant autonomy instead of full sovereignty was over. Public opinion was demanding independence; Lithuania was preparing for Supreme Soviet elections in February 1990, and candidates endorsed by Sąjūdis were running on a pro-independence program. The secretary-general also failed to propose a meaningful alternative plan to his Lithuanian interlocutors. In late 1989, Gorbachev's advisors such as Chernyaev and Shakhnazarov had strongly encouraged him to undertake direct negotiations with Sąjūdis and to propose that the Baltic republics sign a new Union Treaty giving them special status within the USSR, but the Soviet leader had not followed this advice. Instead he came to Vilnius empty-handed.[5]

While claiming full respect for Lithuanian rights to self-determination, Gorbachev insisted that Soviet laws and constitution had to be respected. During a speech in Vilnius, he pledged to prepare the missing secession legislation soon, without specifying when. At the same time, he clearly stated that he himself was against an eventual Lithuanian independence.[6] According to Andrei Grachev, the Soviet leader came back to Moscow shaken and surprised by the impossibility of challenging the Lithuanian drive toward independence.[7]

In February and March 1990, Supreme Soviet elections were held in the Baltic countries, and the pro-independence movements won the majority in their respective Supreme Soviets. During the February 24 elections in Lithuania, candidates endorsed by Sąjūdis obtained 91 out of 141 seats in the Supreme Soviet of Lithuania. During its first session on March 11, 1990, 124 members of the newly elected parliament voted in favor of restoring the independence of Lithuania. Vytautas Landsbergis, the leader of Sąjūdis, was elected chairman of the Lithuanian parliament and economist Kazimira Prunskienė became the first female prime minister of Lithuania.

This of course was not a complete surprise for the Soviet leadership, since at least October 1989 it had become absolutely clear that the Baltic countries were aiming for independence. Yet only on March 2 had the Politburo started to seriously discuss the need to take the initiative and prepare a new Union Treaty. Gorbachev admitted that there was no clear plan of how "to defend the federation" and ordered his Politburo colleagues to work on it.[8] On March 12, government and Politburo members clashed over the question of how to react to Lithuania's declaration. While Shevardnadze was inclined to take a conciliatory tone with Vilnius and opt for dialogue, others disagreed, and the conversation became "rude" and "aggressive."[9]

On March 15, the Soviet Congress of People's Deputies declared the Lithuanian proclamation null and void. Meanwhile, events quickly were unfolding in the two other Baltic countries. During the March 18 elections in Latvia and Estonia, candidates supported by Latvian Tautas Fronte won 131 seats out of 201, while in pro-independence forces obtained 73 out of 105 in Estonia.[10]

On April 3, in an attempt to block Baltic independence, the Soviet Congress of People's Deputies adopted the promised secession law. The new legislation required the republics to follow a rather complicated procedure. First the Supreme Soviet of the republic in question, or one-tenth of the Soviet citizens living in the republic's territory, had to request a referendum on secession; second, two-thirds of the republic's inhabitants had to vote for it; third, the question had to be considered by the Congress of People's Deputies, which had to establish a transition period during which military, economic, and other matters were to be settled between the republic and the USSR; and fourth, at the end of the transition period the Congress had to adopt a decision confirming that the process had been completed and that its results were satisfactory for all involved parties.[11] Thus, the final decision would be in the hands of the Congress of People's Deputies.[12]

The White House followed the standoff between Moscow and Vilnius with deep concern, fearing a breakout of a major crisis that would jeopardize the ambitious international agenda of spring 1990.

In the Shadow of German Unification

The unexpected fall of the Berlin Wall had shattered the international status quo, giving decision makers in both Europe and the United States the chance to define the future of the European order. The spring of 1990 was what international relations scholars call a "window of opportunity"— a moment in history when decision makers believe that by acting quickly they can exploit a change in domestic/international circumstances to enact essential policy changes.[13] As noted by Mary Sarotte, after the fall of the Berlin Wall various groups of actors competed and struggled vigorously to recreate order in a way most advantageous to themselves.[14] Crucially for US policy toward the Baltic question, the US plans for the post–Cold War European order mainly concerned Western, not Eastern, Europe.

During the spring of 1990, the most urgent Western objective was to successfully handle the "grand bargain" between the West and the Soviet Union on the reunification of Germany, and this necessarily involved maintaining good relations with the USSR.[15] While the USSR had consented in principle to German reunification, American and West German perceptions on how the reunification should be handled differed from Soviet ones.[16] The USSR was looking for an agreement that would restrict the military possibilities of a united Germany, determine its Eastern border, and, most important, redefine the European security system, undermining NATO. Meanwhile, West German and US ambitions basically consisted of integrating East Germany into West European/West German structures. The main issue in the negotiations was German NATO membership. For the United States, it was the key objective, while the USSR did not want to see a united Germany as a NATO member.[17]

Scholars of the late Cold War period have long debated the eventual Western promise not to expand NATO toward the east as a trade-off for German reunification. While all of them agree that no written agreement on this question was ever concluded, some argue that the general spirit of the negotiations might have led the Soviets to believe that a future NATO enlargement toward the east was unimaginable.[18] It has to be noted that 1990 the Bush administration was indeed not planning the expansion of the North Atlantic Alliance beyond Germany. The question was discussed only in October 1990, when despite the Defense Department's enthusiasm about such a possibility, the White House and the State Department argued that such plans should not be included in the US foreign policy agenda.[19]

At the same time, the United States was not willing to seriously consider the possibility of replacing NATO with a new pan-European structure that would also include Eastern Europe. To reassure the Soviets during the German reunification negotiations, the White House used rhetoric that seemed to show support for the Conference on Security and Cooperation in Europe (CSCE) as a fundamental institution in the new international post–Cold War order. Functioning as a follow-up mechanism to the conference that had adopted the Helsinki Final Act in 1975, CSCE was the only international framework that assembled all European states (except Albania), the USSR, Canada, and the United States and thus seemed the perfect framework for a more inclusive European order. The American statements made in 1990 seemed to be in line with Soviet plans for a "common European home" in which the CSCE would play the leading role, while NATO and the Warsaw Pact would either be dissolved or be turned into political rather than military alliances. In reality, the Bush administration saw the strengthening of the role of the CSCE as a threat to American influence in Europe and had no intention of making a real contribution to it.[20]

The United States was ready neither to drastically reshape European order by abandoning NATO, nor to aggressively expand it eastwards; in 1990 American decision makers liked the idea of strengthening their presence in Eastern Europe, but there was no clear strategy for doing this or a desire to promote this at the expense of US-Soviet relations. The American focus was on the integration of united Germany into US-dominated transatlantic structures, while its interest in Eastern Europe was limited. In other words, US politicians saw German reunification as an opportunity to secure and strengthen the US presence in Western Europe, but not as the platform for aggressively expanding American influence into Eastern Europe. This overall attitude toward Eastern Europe had a direct impact on the White House's reactions to Lithuanian independence; instead of trying to use the Lithuanian independence declaration to amplify its influence in the region, it was mainly concerned about how it might complicate the German reunification negotiations.

This concern was shared by West Germany, as Bonn was anxious to avoid any linkage between unification and other European problems.[21] When the Poles, with the support of the French and the Soviets, insisted that the German-Polish border question should be discussed at the same time as the unification, West Germany made an effort to push the eastern border question out of unification talks to a separate treaty.[22] And when Lithuania proclaimed its independence, Helmut Kohl openly told the Soviet ambassador in Bonn that he would not be involved in developments in Lithuania and wanted to maintain good and friendly relations with the USSR.[23] In May, he went so far as to ask the Lithuanian prime minister Prunskienė to put Lithuanian national aspirations on hold so that they would not jeopardize the achievement of German ones.[24]

Bush and his Western European counterparts were conscious that the window of opportunity that had opened was to a considerable extent due to Gorbachev's willingness to accept changes in the international status quo. A deterioration in East-West relations or, even more, a regime change in Moscow would certainly mean a closing of that window. Thus, the Baltic question was weighed against the matter of Gorbachev's political survival. During a meeting in Key Largo, Florida, in April 1990, George Bush told François Mitterrand that, when it came to Lithuanian independence, the Soviet military might be "more concerned than previously."[25] His counterpart agreed, indicating that "if we go too far, we will get a military dictatorship."[26]

At the same time, the non-recognition policy and the interest that the US Congress had taken in the Baltic question made it impossible for the Bush administration to dismiss the Lithuanian declaration as a Soviet internal problem. On March 11, the White House affirmed the continuous non-recognition of Baltic annexation and called upon the Soviet government to start negotiations with Lithuania.[27] From the White House's perspective, the Baltic states could become independent only with Moscow's full consent, and talks with Gorbachev were the only way this consent could be obtained.

This stand deeply dissatisfied the Lithuanian leadership as well as the Baltic diaspora in the United States and their allies in Congress. The leaders of the great powers were not the only ones who saw the spring of 1990 as a lifetime opportunity to introduce long-awaited changes. The Baltic governments and diaspora activists realized that the international system was changing, and they wanted to secure the place of Estonia, Latvia, and Lithuania in the new European order, whatever that order might be. By choosing the 2 + 4 format for dealing with the German question, the West basically opened a Pandora's box of persisting Second World War issues. The Japanese Northern Territories re-emerged on the international agenda, and until mid-July Poland insisted on the necessity of signing a peace treaty for the Second World War, which among other issues would address its western borders.[28] In this context, Estonians, Latvians, and Lithuanians saw an unprecedented opportunity for them too—after all, their loss of independence also resulted from dynamics arising from the Second World War. As the foreign ministers of the three Baltic states pointed out in the fall of 1990: "Reunification by no means spells the definitive end of the Second World War; we Estonians, Latvians and Lithuanians are still the victims of that war."[29] The Baltic attitude regarding the general calls to slow down their push for independence was best summarized by Jonas Mekas, a Lithuanian American filmmaker who has often been praised as the godfather of the American avant-garde cinema. On March 29, the *New York Times* published his op-ed with a telling title: "No, My Friends, We Won't Go Slow."[30]

In contrast to Western heads of state, Lithuanians and the Baltic leaders generally did not trust Gorbachev. The constitutional secession process established by the Soviets would mean submitting Baltic independence to long proceedings that could take years and to a vote at the Congress of People's Deputies. Such an option was unacceptable. Nobody could guarantee that the Congress's vote would be favorable, and time was of the essence.[31] Like the West, the Balts feared the hardening of the regime in the Soviet Union and wanted to leave the Union before that happened.[32] Thus, for the supporters of Baltic independence, the question of international recognition was imminent and urgent: the historical opportunity had to be seized before it was too late. As Estonian foreign minister Lennart Meri put it in May 1991: "If we cannot solve the Baltic question now, we will not have another chance within the next hundred years."[33]

In the days and weeks following the Lithuanian independence proclamation, the US president had to face growing pressure from both Congress and the Baltic diaspora, as well as members of the American press, to take a stronger stand in support of Lithuanian independence.

American Domestic Pressures

The Lithuanian independence declaration gave the Baltic question unprecedented visibility in US domestic debates. During the crisis, the *New York Times* was the newspaper that most actively reported on the Lithuanian issue. In the period between March 11, when Lithuanian independence was proclaimed, and the end of June, when the crisis seemed to be partially resolved, the *New York Times* mentioned Lithuania in 623 articles. The *Washington Post* followed with 358 pieces.[34]

Yet the visibility that the American press coverage gave to the Baltic question did not immediately mean support for Lithuanian independence. The US press was far from unanimous on the issue, but there were supporters of the Lithuanian cause among the columnists of leading US newspapers, such as William Safire and A. M. Rosenthal from the *New York Times*.[35] Sympathetic editorials were also published by the *Washington Post* and the *Wall Street Journal*.[36] Meanwhile, the *New York Times* columnist Leslie H. Gelb blamed Lithuania for provoking Gorbachev and putting him in a problematic situation vis-à-vis the Soviet conservatives.[37] At the same paper an op-ed by John B. Oakes expressed concern that "the Lithuanian leadership is inviting not only the economic crackdown that has already begun but the possibility of full-scale military repression."[38] Both the *St. Louis Post-Dispatch* and the *St. Petersburg Times* (Florida) supported the administration's approach, explaining that Washington officials had to maintain a delicate balance between support for Lithuanian independence and support for Gorbachev.[39]

The Baltic question, or the issue of Lithuanian independence, was not a significant concern for the American public opinion as such. A *Time* magazine and CNN poll, conducted in April 1990, showed that only one-quarter of people surveyed agreed that the United States should pressure the USSR on the Lithuanian question, while two thirds did not see this issue as a significant concern for their own country.[40]

At the same time, actors supporting the Baltic cause were using platforms important enough to obtain the attention of the White House. When discussing the Lithuanian crisis of spring 1990 in the memoirs co-written by George Bush and Brent Scowcroft, the National Security Advisor remembers "the very heavy pressures" that the White House had to face from Congress, Baltic Americans, and the press, while the president complained about Congress not fully understanding how complicated his position was.[41]

An active number of US senators and representatives were indeed critical of the cautious American approach to Baltic independence and managed to mobilize both chambers to express their support through the means of congressional resolutions. The Baltic diaspora, despite being only one million strong, flooded the president with angry letters until the White House Public Liaison Office pointed out that "there was a problem with Lithuanian groups" and that the president should meet them.[42]

The US non-recognition policy, as well as its Cold War anti-communist rhetoric, had given the Baltic diaspora the impression that, even if Baltic independence was not the United States' top priority, the American superpower was supportive of the Baltic cause. Thus, when Lithuania proclaimed its independence on March 11, 1990, most Baltic Americans hoped for immediate recognition and were deeply disappointed by the administration's cautious approach. In their view, recognition was the only genuine form of support; anything less than that was reinforcing Soviet rule in the Baltics. For example, by late March 1990, a Vietnam War veteran of Lithuanian descent, Walter V. Kazlauskas, wrote to President Bush: "But, can we as leader of the democratic world afford to withhold the act of recognition, while continuing to voice on human rights and democratic principles? I think not. Every moment of delay strengthens our bond with the Soviet Union and makes us a partner in the acts of suppression."[43]

Baltic Americans who had been involved in the activities of the Republican Party were the most active and the most disappointed. On March 31, the chairman of the Lithuanian-Republican National Federation,

Jonas Urbonas, informed the president that "it has become very hard" for him to convince Lithuanian Americans that the US government was truly supporting Lithuania.[44] The same day a Lithuanian American member of the Republican Party from Illinois wrote to the president's chief of staff, John Sununu, describing a rally that had been held in Chicago and had gathered around two thousand participants:

> The signs promoting Lithuania were equalled by signs critical of the president. Speakers include Congressman Durbin and Senator Simon, both of whom spent time eliciting crowd response by critiquing the president. Republicans, including myself though I am Lithuanian, were best off not to speak. . . . Failure to act will have adverse effects upon Republican prospects here in Illinois this fall.[45]

As the Soviet pressure on Lithuania increased, the letters sent to the White House became harsher in tone, and both Latvian and Lithuanian Republicans used their loyalty toward the party as leverage. For example, on May 4, Lucija Mazeika, from the Californian Republican Heritage Groups Council, emphasized that Lithuanian American support for the Republican Party and the president himself was eroding.[46]

While the Baltic American Republicans felt deceived by their party, other Baltic Americans were disappointed by the attitudes of their country. In the context of Lithuania's isolation on the international stage, attitudes of the United States toward the ancestral lands—Lithuania and the other the Baltic states—were identified with attitudes toward the diaspora. In other words, in the perception of Baltic Americans, Washington had to support the Baltic countries because the United States "owed" it to them as loyal American citizens. On April 7 the North American support groups of Tautas Fronte movement sent the White House a letter, signed by more than 243 individuals, that stated: "We have served in all branches of the United States military services here and abroad, and many of us have given our lives for democracy and freedom. We . . . have taught, invented, saved lives and done everything possible to make this country the best in the world. It is, therefore, that we are saddened that your response to the oppression to Lithuania, Latvia and Estonia had not been strong enough."[47]

Letters expressing similar sentiments were received from the Lithuanian American Community, the Latvian American Association, the Supreme Committee for Liberation of Lithuania, the Federation of Lithuanian Women's Club, and the Knights of Lithuania.[48] Balts living outside the United States addressed the White House because of its key position in the international system.[49] Demands for stronger US support for Lithuanian independence were backed by other American ethnic communities that could relate to the Baltic situation because of their own historical experiences, such as the Polish American Congress, the Ukrainian Congress Committee of America, the New York Republican Heritage Groups Council, and the Center for Taiwan International Relations.[50]

One of the most influential supporters of the Baltic cause was Robert T. Davis, a career diplomat who had served as US ambassador in Poland from 1971 until 1978. Like the Baltic Americans, he insisted that hesitation in recognizing the independence of Lithuania was a "tacit encouragement to the Soviet government."[51] On April 8, Davis's letter was published in the *Washington Post*.[52]

Although the Baltic diaspora was active in voicing its discontent, it was not necessarily representative of US public opinion. While the majority of the public simply did not have a strong opinion on the Baltic question, some concerned citizens also wrote to express their support for George Bush and/or Mikhail Gorbachev. For example, on May 9, Peter Sørensen from Santa Monica, a personal acquaintance of the Bush family, wrote to the president that, even if he was supportive of Baltic independence, the survival of Gorbachev was vital for US interests.[53]

Yet the Bush administration saw Baltic activism as a source of concern, and by early April a decision was made to invite a group of influential Baltic Americans to meet the president at the White House. On April 11, 1990, George Bush, James Baker, and Brent Scowcroft met with the leaders of the leading Baltic American organizations: the Supreme Committee for the Liberation of Lithuania, the Lithuanian American Republican National Federation, the Baltic American Freedom League, the Lithuanian American Community, the Lithuanian American Council, the American Latvian Association, the Joint Baltic American National Committee, and the Estonian American National Council. Before the meeting, Lithuanians, as well as Latvians and Estonians, had been in touch with the governments and activists in the Baltics. Valdis Pavlovskis, president of the Latvian American Association, had just returned from Riga; Mari-Ann Rikken, from Estonian American National Committee, had spoken with Estonian dissident Tunne Kelam; and Kazys Bobelis, president of the Supreme Committee for the Liberation of Lithuania, had talked with Lithuanian president Landsbergis on the phone. Thus, the Baltic diaspora served as a link between Vilnius, Tallinn, and Riga and the White House. Pavlovskis informed the president that Latvia was preparing an independence declaration on May 3, Rikken spoke about the activities of the Congress of Estonia, while the Lithuanian Americans asked for immediate recognition of Lithuania. The debate revealed a profound contradiction between the way the US president perceived the situation and how it was seen by Baltic Americans. For the diaspora activists, the Baltic question was the most important issue, while for Bush it clearly was just one of the problems on the international agenda.[54] The president argued that, if a military takeover in Moscow was averted in the short run, Lithuania and the other Baltic states would eventually find their way to self-determination, but Baltic Americans were not willing to wait. For them independence had to come immediately. "The time is now, Mr. President," Angela Nelsas, president of BAFL, told Bush at the end of the meeting, "and the person is you."[55]

The April 11 meeting did not convince Bush that he should proceed to immediate recognition, nor did it reassure Baltic Americans about the administration's good intentions regarding the Baltic countries. As during the Cold War, it was in Congress that they found the strongest support for their cause.

As in the autumn of 1989, the supporters of the Baltic cause in Congress attempted to alter US policies by using direct and indirect means of pressure. In March and April, they mobilized their colleagues to adopt resolutions signaling congressional preferences for a stronger US stand on the Baltic question. In May and June, they proceeded to more direct pressures, blocking the ratification of the US-Soviet trade treaty.

On March 21, ten days after the Lithuanian declaration of independence, Senator Helms (NC) and his Republican colleagues Senators D'Amato (NY), Armstrong (CO), Kasten (WV), Humphrey (NH), Pressler (SD), and Murkowski (AK) proposed a resolution calling for the president to recognize the independence of Lithuania. As the debates on the decisions dragged on, Republican leader Robert Dole called the White House and the State Department to get the opinion of the administration. The National Security Advisor Brent Scowcroft as well as Under Secretary of State Lawrence Eagleburger saw the resolution as potentially harmful for the Lithuanian cause since, according to them, it might upset Soviet-Lithuanian negotiations.[56]

This exchange revealed essential differences in the basic perception of how the Baltic problem could be solved. While the administration thought that Lithuania could become independent only through negotiations with the USSR, the Baltic supporters in the Congress hoped that an international recognition could impose Lithuanian independence upon the USSR. Once again, the framing of the Baltic situation was shaped by a narrative of waiting and opportunity. While Bush wished the Lithuanians would be slower and "more reasonable" in their drive for independence,[57] senators supporting the Baltic cause stated that the time to act had come.[58]

The Senate was divided regarding the resolution, as many senators shared the administration's concerns about the impact that an immediate recognition would have on the Baltic situation.[59] At the same time, the moralizing language that was used to frame the Baltic question made it hard for senators to oppose it without harming their public image. During the March 21 debates, as well as later, members of Congress framed the Baltic/Lithuanian question as a question of "right" and "wrong," as a question of continuity of US foreign policy, and as a question of principle and morals.[60] They appealed to the fact that the non-recognition policy had been established by President Franklin Roosevelt and maintained by every American president since.[61] Several senators and representatives drew parallels between the events of 1776, the values of the Founding Fathers, and the Baltic drive for independence.[62] Support for the Baltic cause was identified with what was perceived as essential "American values" and as support for human rights.[63]

Even after Helms's resolution was rejected by a vote of 56–36 on March 21, the next day a new text was proposed, this time by the Senate majority leader George Mitchell and minority leader Robert Dole. The latest version of the Lithuanian resolution was very similar to the first, and to some extent even stronger, as it clearly stated that Soviet use of force in the Baltics "would have serious consequences on US-Soviet relations."[64] The resemblance between the two texts allowed Senator Helms to claim that the senators had not approved his resolution under pressure from the White House, and then changed their minds overnight because of the demands from the Baltic diaspora.[65] This interpretation was misleading, as there was one crucial difference between the two texts. Mitchell's resolution, prepared in coordination with the White House, expressed unequivocal support for Baltic independence but remained flexible in its expectations about the US president. While Helms's resolution "urged the president to recognize the Lithuanian Independence," the one proposed by Mitchell "urged the President to consider the call of the elected Lithuanian Government for recognition."[66] The document was approved unanimously.

On April 4, Democrat Lee Hamilton from Indiana proposed a similar document in the House of Representatives. The resolution was prepared by Hamilton himself and the representatives of two states with significant American Lithuanian populations, Representative Richard Durbin of Illinois and Representative William Broomfield of Michigan. The House adopted the resolution as HConRes289, with a 416–3 vote.

The White House regarded this congressional activism with concern, and it was one of the factors that pushed the Bush administration to take a stronger stand on the Lithuanian issue.

During the second half of March, the Bush administration started to move toward a stronger stand on the Baltic situation. On the one hand, it was anticipating the congressional mood and acting accordingly.[67] On the other hand, the administration itself became increasingly concerned that the Soviet Union might use force in Lithuania.[68]

During these weeks, tensions were rapidly rising between the USSR and its western republic. While Gorbachev insisted that no discussion between Vilnius and Moscow would be possible before the annulment of the Lithuanian declaration, Lithuania claimed that it was fully open to starting a dialogue, but categorically refused to annul its decree. In the eyes of the Soviets, the proclamation was unlawful and unconstitutional; in the eyes of Lithuanians, they were not legally part of the USSR and thus did not have to comply with the Soviet constitution. Lithuania hoped that the Baltic question could be solved through international negotiations just like the German one, while the Soviet president found this idea "ridiculous."[69]

Moscow responded by launching an intimidation campaign in Lithuania. Men who deserted the Red Army or refused the draft were persecuted, and several public buildings were taken by force. On March 18, the United States received information that the Soviets had started significant military preparations in the region.[70] Meanwhile, alluding to the breakdown of the Prague Spring in 1968, the diplomatic aide to the Soviet president noted in his journal on March 22: "Today at the Politburo might have been the 'Charnyna Tizsa' for Lithuania. Things are moving towards Czechoslovakia-'90. I am horrified. Everyone was chiming in with the most vulgar and conceited great-power sentiments. Yakovlev and Medvedev kept their silence. What should I do? . . . If he [Gorbachev] makes a massacre in Lithuania, I am not only going to leave. . . . I will probably do something else besides."[71]

The use of force was, to a certain extent, a red line for the Bush administration, an issue more important than the independence of the Baltic states. It mattered not so much for the sake of the Baltic nations but because the images of Soviet tanks in the Baltic capitals would complicate US-Soviet relations at a time of crucial negotiations by reducing Bush's maneuverability vis-à-vis domestic pressure groups. Over the next three months, the US government and its European allies attempted to ease the tensions between Vilnius and Moscow. It was a task made more complicated by general uncertainty regarding the probable effects of international interference. Although there was a consensus in the Western capitals that too much pressure on the Soviet Union should be avoided, the rapid escalation of tensions between Vilnius and Moscow, as well as the confusing signals coming from the Soviet leadership, made Western policymakers unsure about the appropriate levels of pressure to exercise. The White House (as well as Bonn and Paris to a certain extent) was torn between fear of not doing "enough" to de-escalate the crisis and concern about aggravating the situation by doing "too much." This led the US government to envisage and try out various policy options, instead of developing one consistent approach to the Soviet-Lithuanian problem. The possible courses of action discussed at the different levels of the US administration were: the signaling of US concerns through private and public communication; soliciting the allies to plead for a peaceful solution in the Baltic; suggesting a referendum in the Baltic states; calling and/or writing to Lithuanian president Landsbergis; suggesting the suspension of the Lithuanian declaration; providing economic assistance to Lithuania; introducing the issue to the United Nations or at the International Court of Justice; providing American or Czech mediation in the conflict; and refusing to sign the Soviet-American trade treaty.[72]

At first, the Bush administration tried to persuade the Soviets to show restraint by signaling its concerns through private communication. In these conversations, the US side also attempted to propose eventual solutions for the Lithuanian crisis, namely a referendum and/or a suspension of the Lithuanian independence declaration. When these attempts did not prove fruitful, the White House started to consider not signing the new Soviet-American trade treaty.

Quiet Diplomacy

The American approach to the Lithuanian crisis was based on the idea that US concerns should be communicated to the Soviets privately. While Lithuanians were deploying considerable efforts to gain international visibility for their cause, the White House was trying to deal with the Lithuanian issue outside the public sphere. The private communication was chosen as a trust-building measure and as a safe option that would limit the destabilizing effects of the Lithuanian crisis.

In March and April, Bush sent two unpublicized letters to the Soviet president about the Baltic situation. Secretary Baker talked about the Lithuanian question in all four meetings that he had with his Soviet counterpart between March and May. In addition to talking about the issue one-on-one, Baker also wrote Shevardnadze a letter and called him at least twice. This communication at the ministerial level was prioritized to underline America's active interest in the issue, but without turning it into a significant presidential-level problem in US-Soviet relations. The Soviet side, nevertheless, was annoyed by the American activity, and by the end of May Gorbachev asked Baker if events in Nagorno-Karabakh or Vilnius really should be taking up more time in US-Soviet relations then Perestroika.[73] Ironically, the US aim was precisely to avoid having the Baltic question take over the superpowers' relations and to defuse the crisis before it became violent.

The first Soviet-American ministerial discussion after the Lithuanian proclamation of independence was reassuring. During a meeting in Namibia on March 20, Secretary of State Baker again asked Minister of Foreign Affairs Shevardnadze not to use force in Lithuania. Shevardnadze assured his counterpart that the Soviet Union had no intention of doing so.[74] However, over the following days, Soviet paratroopers seized the headquarters of the Lithuanian Communist Party, which since December 1989 had taken a pro-independence stand. Moscow also announced restrictions on foreign travel in Lithuania, requested that US diplomats visiting Vilnius be removed from the republic and ordered Lithuanians to surrender their arms.[75]

Alarmed, the United States increased the pressure on Moscow. Baker wrote to Shevardnadze, Under Secretary of State Eagleburger summoned the Soviet ambassador, and the US ambassador to Moscow contacted the Soviet Ministry of Foreign Affairs. The three men repeated the same message: "the use of force or intimidation in Lithuania would have negative consequences on the relations between the United States and the Soviet Union."[76] To coordinate a multilateral approach, the White House expressed its concerns to the Allied governments and invited them to plead with Moscow in favor of a peaceful solution in Lithuania.[77]

The news that the White House received from Europe was not reassuring. The Baltic countries' closest neighbors in Scandinavia feared large-scale repressions in the Baltic countries. The international press reported that the Swedish island of Gotland was prepared to accommodate a possible wave of Baltic refugees.[78] Meanwhile the French embassy in Copenhagen informed that a Danish warship was sent to the eastern parts of the Baltic Sea, and that Danish military radars were put on alert.[79] On the diplomatic front, the Swedes, the Norwegians, and the Danes were multiplying their calls for Soviet restraint in Lithuania.[80] After a phone conversation with the Soviet president, British prime minister Margaret Thatcher warned George Bush that she found Gorbachev depressed and evasive on the issue of the non-use of force.[81] Massachusetts Senator Ted Kennedy and Chairman of the Joint Chiefs of Staff Admiral William James Crowe, who both traveled to Moscow in March, reported that the Soviet president was non-committal regarding abstention from the use of force in the Baltics, while the Soviet military was ready to crush Lithuania.[82]

Facing this unexpected escalation, the White House felt compelled to propose a more concrete solution to the Lithuanian crisis. On March 29, Bush sent a private letter to Gorbachev suggesting the possibility of organizing a referendum in Lithuania. The letter was carefully worded and stressed the pressures that the American president was facing at home, while at the same time asking Gorbachev to move away from "confrontation, ultimatums and demands" and proceed to "reasoned discussions" with Lithuanians.[83]

On March 29, the US ambassador to the USSR, Jack Matlock, who was on his way to Washington, was awakened at his hotel in Frankfurt and instructed to return to the USSR. The president's letter and very detailed instructions on how to deliver it awaited him in Moscow. On March 30, Matlock met with Yakovlev and read him the document before handing it over.[84] The answer from Gorbachev's advisor was firm: "no discussion is possible on a referendum without the cancellation of the declaration of independence of Lithuania."[85]

The letter once again revealed that the main US concern in the Baltics was not the question of Lithuanian independence, but a possible Soviet use of force in the rebellious republic. As Baker explained to Shevardnadze a couple of days later, "It is clear that all that is needed right now is one incident where you feel the need to go in and restore order. And we are going to be put in a position where we are simply not able to defend what is going on and what you are doing."[86]

The discussion between the Soviet foreign minister and US secretary of state about the Baltic question that took place in Washington on April 4 was one of the most extensive and most detailed Soviet-American exchanges on the issue. It lasted for three and a half hours and continued the next day over dinner. Nevertheless, it did not lead to a better understanding between the two superpowers on the Baltic question and only increased American perplexity. The root of the problem was their different perception of the Estonian, Latvian, and Lithuanian situation. For Baker, the Baltic states were not Soviet republics like the others; for Shevardnadze, they were an integral part of the USSR. During most of the conversation, the two men talked past each other. When Baker stressed the heavy pressure that he and the president were facing domestically, Shevardnadze pointed out that Gorbachev too had faced pressure from internal forces when the United States invaded Panama in late December 1989. When Baker explained that for the United States the Baltics "were different" from the other Soviet republics, Shevardnadze claimed that just like all the other republics they were bound by the 1977 constitution.[87] When Baker suggested that Lithuania might have a special referendum on its independence, Shevardnadze argued that the secession law that Lithuania refused to respect already envisaged a referendum.

Even if, as Shevardnadze argued all through the conversation, the Soviet Union did not plan to use force in Lithuania, Baker was not reassured. The next day during a discussion over dinner, he explicitly asked Shevardnadze not to impose direct presidential rule in Lithuania and "to discourage the Russian minority in Lithuania from organizing demonstrations which could potentially lead to clashes."[88]

During the discussions on both days, the Soviet foreign minister went to great lengths to frame the Lithuanian independence claims as potentially dangerous for the general progress of Perestroika. He accused Lithuanians of having acted irresponsibly and having deceived the Soviet leadership. He called the Lithuanian acting president Landsbergis "inexperienced, naïve and dangerous."[89] He invoked Polish and Russian minorities and alleged Belorussian claims to Lithuanian territory, to suggest that Lithuania's situation was not much different from Armenian-Azeri conflicts in the Caucasus. He reminded his counterpart about the risk of widespread destabilization in the USSR and Eastern Europe and of the rise of a military dictatorship.

As Baker pointed out, such widespread destabilization was precisely what the United States wanted to avoid. The Americans believed that the task could be achieved by defusing the crisis through a direct dialogue with the rebellious republic and through a referendum. By the end of the conversation, however, the director of Bush's Policy Planning Staff, Dennis B. Ross, who was serving as note taker and interpreter during the meeting, asked Shevardnadze directly what should be done for a Soviet-Lithuanian dialogue to begin. The Soviet minister responded that Lithuania should revoke their independence declaration.[90]

The American side had heard from both Gorbachev's main advisor and his foreign minister that the Soviets were not interested in any negotiations with Lithuania unless Vilnius returned to the status quo ante. Trying to break the deadlock, Baker suggested a compromise: maybe the Lithuanians could suspend and not entirely revoke their independence declaration.[91] The suggestion was first been made during the April 5 dinner, and while Shevardnadze avoided a direct answer, the secretary of state started to envisage the suspension of the declaration as the ideal face-saving solution for both the Soviet and the Lithuanian sides. During April the White House pursued this possible solution for the Lithuanian crisis, leaving the referendum option aside. However, instead of publicly suggesting the suspension of the Lithuanian declaration, it encouraged Paris and Bonn to promote the option.

A Franco-German Initiative?

Although the proposal to suspend the Lithuanian independence declaration has become known mostly as the "Franco-German initiative," in reality, it was as much Washington's initiative. It was conceived by the United States and then embraced by France and West Germany as a way to get the Lithuanian question off the international agenda, at least until the German reunification negotiations were over. The French response to the Lithuanian crisis was primarily influenced by the German position on the Baltic question. The spring of 1990 was a crucial moment in French-German relations: by the end of March, Mitterrand adopted a more supportive public discourse on German reunification, and by mid-April France and West Germany launched the transformation of the European Community (EC) into a political union.[92] A mutually beneficial deal was made between Kohl and Mitterrand: the first would get a rapid unification, and the second a quick European monetary union.[93] In this context France perceived the Lithuanian crisis as an unnecessary obstacle toward smooth German reunification or even a risk for European stability.[94] The news from the Soviet Union was not reassuring, either for Paris and Bonn or for Washington, as Vilnius and Moscow seemed to escalate into a spiral of fierce conflict over sovereignty in Lithuania.

On April 1, the two leading Soviet newspapers published an "Appeal from the president of the USSR to the people of Lithuania" in which Gorbachev warned Lithuanians that "just indignation" was mounting against them and threatened to transfer a part of Lithuania's territory to Belorussia and Kaliningrad.[95] On April 3, Lithuania answered by claiming that it was fully open to starting a dialogue, but at the same time continued to adopt legislation that reduced effective Soviet control over Lithuania.[96] On April 13, Moscow threatened Lithuania with an embargo if it did not repeal laws that abolished Lithuanian conscription in the Soviet army and established new national identity cards for citizens of Lithuania.[97] The Lithuanian government did not rush to respond to this threat, indicating that the whole country was preoccupied with celebrating Catholic Easter.[98] On April 17, the USSR announced its economic blockade against Lithuania, further escalating the crisis. Eight days later, Chancellor Kohl and François Mitterrand sent an official letter to Vytautas Landsbergis, asking him to temporally suspend Lithuania's independence declaration.[99]

The White House was very reluctant to show open and official support for the Franco-German letter,[100] but behind the scenes, the US secretary of state had been a strong supporter of the initiative. Indeed, on April 18 Baker had once again called Shevardnadze to warn him that coercion in Lithuania might affect US-Soviet trade relations and also discussed the possibility of suspending instead of annulling the Lithuanian declaration.[101] Following this call, the White House reached out to a Republican senator from Indiana, Richard Lugar, asking him to discuss the possible suspension of Lithuania's declaration with Vytautas Landsbergis.[102] Using the heavyweight senator with good connections to the Lithuanian diaspora as intermediary allowed the Bush administration to engage with the Lithuanian side while avoiding the publicity that intergovernmental contacts would attract. While far from enthusiastic, both Shevardnadze and Landsbergis agreed to consider the solution proposed by the Americans.

On April 21 James Baker met French foreign minister Roland Dumas, who like the American secretary of state would later in his memoirs claim to be at the origin of the suspension idea.[103] While their presidents discussed world politics and shared their somewhat similar views on the Lithuanian crisis, Baker and Dumas agreed that France would officially propose this option to the Lithuanian government.[104] However, once the Franco-German letter was made public, views on the initiative started to differ also inside the Bush administration. While the suspension of the Lithuanian declaration had seemed like a good idea to the secretary of state, Deputy National Security Advisor Robert Gates and Senior Director for European and Soviet affairs Robert Blackwell believed that the United States should not openly support a document that could be seen as an attempt to dissuade the Baltic states from accessing their independence.[105] Indeed, when on April 24 Chancellor Kohl and President Mitterrand publicly suggested the suspension of the Lithuanian declaration, the French opposition blasted the initiative as "open support of oppression" that inspired "discomfort" and "shame."[106] Fearing a similar backlash at home, the White House officially abstained from showing public support for the letter.[107]

The Bush administration's hesitations regarding the possible suspension of Lithuanian independence showed yet again the double challenge that it had to face in crafting a policy that would defuse the crisis without upsetting either the USSR or Congress. During March and April, discretion and quiet diplomacy had seemed the best way to deal with the situation. However, after the Soviet embargo against Lithuania was put in place, the White House started to consider escalating public pressure on the USSR.

Economic Pressures

By the end of April, the White House became increasingly concerned about the impact that the Lithuanian crisis was having on its image and credibility, in terms of both its relations with the USSR and US domestic politics. The Soviet leadership seemed to ignore American warnings and violate the assurances that they gave during every ministerial meeting.[108] The White House was anticipating strong congressional reactions to the Soviet embargo and wanted to "capture the agenda" instead of giving the impression that it was acting only under congressional pressure.[109] In this context, the Bush administration, and above all the National Security Council, started to consider moving from quiet diplomacy toward public pressure, and from general warnings toward concrete economic action against the Soviet Union.

By the end of the month, the Soviet Union and the United States were supposed to conclude negotiations on the new trade treaty. If ratified, the agreement would grant reciprocal Most Favored Nation (MFN) tariff treatment to the products of each country. The treaty had both practical and symbolic importance. Granting MFN status to the Soviet Union would require repealing the 1974 Jackson-Vanik amendment that restricted US trade relations with countries with non-market economies that did not respect freedom of emigration and other human rights. Thus symbolically, the trade treaty would be an acknowledgment of the change that Perestroika had brought to the Soviet Union and an affirmation of the new quality of Soviet-American relations. Practically, this treaty was the only contribution that the United States was willing to make to rescue the failing Soviet economy. The Soviet Union was actively seeking economic aid, but unlike West Germany, which had expressed its readiness to furnish vital credit, Washington was unwilling to provide substantial financial assistance.

One of the first to publicly suggest that Soviet actions in Lithuania could jeopardize the ratification of the trade treaty was Senate Majority Leader Mitchell.[110] Behind the scenes, the idea to link the Lithuanian question with the trade treaty was vigorously defended by the team of National Security Advisor Brent Scowcroft. In their view, the best response to the Soviet embargo was the suspension of negotiations on the trade and tax agreements, and withdrawal of US support for the Soviet application for observer status in the General Agreement on Tariffs and Trade (GATT) organization.[111] At first it seemed that this option would prevail in the Bush administration. On the morning of April 23, Brent Scowcroft wrote to the president, informing him that he and James Baker had both agreed on the suspension, and that Condoleezza Rice was already preparing the elements of the explanations that the president should provide to the press when announcing the decision.[112] However, later that day Baker and Scowcroft clashed over the Lithuanian question during an NSC meeting. While Scowcroft argued for immediate sanctions, the secretary of state supported sanctions only in the case of use of force against Vilnius.[113]

On April 25, the Scowcroft team was still preparing the press releases, letters to the Allies, and the president's speech announcing the US refusal to sign the treaty, but no public announcement was made.[114] Despite the NSC's willingness to proceed to public pressure and active measures, the president once again had opted for private communication with the Soviet leader.

On April 29, Bush wrote again to Gorbachev informing him that the United States would not be able to conclude the trade treaty if the USSR did not manage to start a dialogue with Lithuania. "Here is the basic reality," Bush explained, "there is no way Congress will approve the MFN under the current circumstances. Further, under existing circumstances, I will not be able to recommend approval."[115] Bush reminded Gorbachev of his administration's restraint and understanding during the previous months but insisted that the Baltic states were a particular case for the United States because of the non-recognition policy. At the same time, George Bush stressed his desire to preserve good relations with the USSR. "You have done too much, and we have gone too far to see matters between us revert to tension and anxiety. . . . Please, know that this was not an easy letter to write."[116]

On May 2, the president received a rather angry answer from Gorbachev, in which the Soviet leader lamented the administration's departure from its "previous reasonable position" and urged it not to interfere in Soviet internal affairs.[117]

Before sending the letter to the Soviet president, Bush had met with the congressional leadership on April 24 and got the impression that the legislators understood and supported his approach to the Lithuanian crisis.[118] Yet, on April 25, one day after President Bush told the press that he was not going to proceed to sanctions against the USSR, he was harshly criticized in the Senate.[119]

On May 1, Senator D'Amato, together with his colleagues DeConcini, Mikulski, Helms, Murkowski, and others, proposed Amendment 1569, urging the president not to submit any US trade agreement or send legislation for Senate approval until the USSR lifted its embargo and entered into negotiations with Lithuania. Commenting on the proposed text, D'Amato explained that it had to be seen not only as an attempt to support the Lithuanian struggle but also as a clear message to the president. "I would not like to see a situation," he stated, "where the president would submit the treaty package, the most favored nation status, to this body and put us in a situation where we should decide whether or not we are going to turn our back on our leader."[120] The amendment was adopted by a vote of 73–24.

While the Senate was proceeding toward direct pressure upon the Kremlin as well as the White House, the Lithuanian leadership increased its efforts to gain visibility on the international stage.

THE ROAD TO WASHINGTON SUMMIT

After the victory of the independence movements in the February/March 1990 elections, all three Baltic republics were ruled by governments that actively worked toward the restoration of Estonian, Latvian, and Lithuanian sovereignty. The ultimate goal of the Baltic external action was the international recognition of Baltic independence. The strategy to achieve this goal was the internationalization of the Baltic question. While the Western powers tried to avoid linkage between the German and Baltic questions, Lithuanian policymakers and activists were actively seeking foreign involvement in their standoff with the USSR. In contrast to the White House's quiet approach, the Lithuanian leadership was working hard to gain visibility on the international stage.

Paradoxically, in Vilnius, the French-German letter was seen as a positive development. In Lithuania's view, the fact that two heads of state directly communicated with the Lithuanian president was seen as an acknowledgment of their autonomy from Moscow and a step toward recognition. The demand for Lithuania to temporarily suspend the effects of its independence declaration, but not to annul the statement itself, was also perceived as an approbation of Lithuanian desire for independence.[121]

Determined to seize the opportunity, the Lithuanians started an active foreign policy. On May 2, 1990, Landsbergis wrote to Mitterrand that Lithuania was prepared to "freeze some laws that interfered with Soviet interests." At the same time, he publicly asked for the mediation of France and Germany.[122] Prime Minister Prunskienė left the country for a tour of Western capitals in search of support. On May 3 during a conversation with American congressional representatives, she insisted: "By this act [the Franco-German letter], the French and German heads of state effectively become mediators and participants in the research of the solution for Lithuania, although they have not expressed such an intention. Suggesting a course of action simultaneously means accepting a certain amount of responsibility."[123]

On May 3 Prunskienė was received by George Bush, on May 9 by Margaret Thatcher, on May 10 by François Mitterrand, and on May 11 by Helmut Kohl. Before arriving in the United States, she had also seen the prime ministers of Norway and Sweden and the foreign ministers of Demark and Canada. The fact that these meetings took place shows the ambiguous attitude of the Western powers toward the Baltic question and toward the Soviet disintegration process itself. On the one hand, the Western powers genuinely feared destabilizing the power of Mikhail Gorbachev, but on the other they were meeting with a leader of what Gorbachev perceived to be a separatist republic. After the meeting with Prunskienė, the White House announced that the president personally, and the US government more generally, were committed to the self-determination of the people of Lithuania,[124] yet it still refused to recognize its independence.

The Bush administration was aware of the symbolic weight of the meeting and hoped that it would ease the Baltic American disappointment about US policy. Before the meeting, Scowcroft sent the president carefully drafted talking points that were supposed to support the suspension of the independence declaration, without giving the impression that the United States was asking Lithuanians to yield in the face of Soviet intimidation.[125]

Three different accounts exist of the Bush-Prunskienė meeting: one by the US president; one by Joseph Kazickas, an influential member of the Lithuanian American diaspora; and one by Beschloss and Talbott. According to the last source, Prunskienė proposed postponing the implementation of Lithuanian independence until 1992.[126] According to Kazickas, she stated that the United States had the obligation to recognize independence. Like Kazickas, Bush recalls telling the Lithuanian prime minister about his fears of a repetition of the 1956 Hungarian scenario, about his commitment to helping Lithuania through quiet diplomacy, and about other crucial issues on the international agenda.[127]

One of the main reasons behind the Western willingness to meet with Prunskienė was their hope of "reasoning" with the Lithuanian leadership to persuade them to dialogue with the USSR. The French president, for example, advised Prunskienė to avoid offending Gorbachev,[128] while Thatcher suggested that the Lithuanians should not expect international recognition any sooner than five years.[129] Kohl, in his turn, told Prunskienė that, if Lithuania suspended the effects of its declaration, all Western countries would support it.[130] In contradiction to this, he later reported to the British foreign minister that he had told Prunskienė not to harbor illusions about any practical support from the West.[131] When Prunskienė mentioned the high hopes that Lithuania had about Mitterrand's visit to Moscow, scheduled for late May, the French president replied that he would not go to Moscow as a negotiator, but if he could help, he would.[132]

The Soviet leadership, however, was not pleased with the idea of a Western mediation in the Lithuanian affair. Before seeing Prunskienė, Kohl met Shevardnadze in Bonn for 2 + 4 negotiations. During a conversation with the chancellor, the Soviet foreign minister let him understand that the Lithuanian question was a Soviet affair, and no external intervention would be tolerated.[133] Consequently, Bonn informed Paris that the German side wished to take no further steps regarding the Lithuanian situation.[134] Unpleasantly surprised by this turn of events, Mitterrand asked Prunskienė twice if Gorbachev was disappointed by the French-German letter.[135]

The main difference between the attitudes of Kohl, Bush, Thatcher, and Mitterrand were that Mitterrand, Thatcher, and Bush did not pressure Lithuania to suspend its declaration. By contrast, Kohl, eager to avoid all obstacles to reunification, explicitly asked the Lithuanians to freeze it.[136]

At the end of May, a French diplomat noted: "Mrs. Prunskienė's international tour showed Vilnius the limitations of Western support at this stage."[137] Paradoxically, at the same time it became clear that the support Lithuania would obtain from inside the Soviet Union was stronger than might have been expected.

Strengthening the Baltic Alliance

The first and perhaps the most critical process for Lithuania was the consolidation of the "Baltic Alliance." Even though the three independence movements of 1988–1990 had cooperated very closely, their governments in 1990 chose different paths toward independence, with Estonia and Latvia opting for a more gradual approach.

Latvian and Estonian elections were held on March 18, the same day as those in East Germany. While the East Germans largely supported the pro-unification alliance for Germany,[138] the elections in the Baltic republics ended with the victory of the Estonian and Latvian independence movements. Thus, declarations of full independence by Supreme Soviets became possible. However, in Estonia and Latvia, political elites decided not to take the step immediately. The chances of obtaining full control over Estonian and Latvian territories without confrontation with the USSR were meager. The Latvian and Estonian leadership worried that, if their actions were too radical, Moscow could quickly destabilize the two republics by instrumentalizing the Russian-speaking part of the populations,

48 percent of the former republic, 38 percent in the latter. In the Estonian case, the Estonian National Independence Party was strongly opposed to the idea that independence could be declared by a Soviet institution.

Thus, instead of declaring independence during its first session on March 30, the Estonian Supreme Soviet declared the state authority of the USSR illegal in Estonia and announced a transition period toward independence. The same day a new government was formed, and the leader of Rahvarinne, Edgar Savisaar, became prime minister. High-ranking communist Arnold Rüütel, who had served as the chairman of the Supreme Soviet of the Estonian SSR since 1983, was reappointed for this position, and thus would internationally assume the functions of acting president of Estonia.

Even though the Estonian approach was much less radical than the Lithuanian one, Gorbachev threatened Estonia with an embargo. In an attempt to ease the impending storm a joint delegation of Latvian communist leadership and Tautas Fronte met with Gorbachev on April 22, 1990, and informed the Soviet president about the forthcoming independence vote at the Latvian supreme Soviet. Gorbachev, in turn, emphasized that no negotiations could follow a unilateral move and proposed to the Latvian side to either follow the recently adopted secession law or accept a large autonomy inside the USSR.[139]

On May 4, in the presence of Vytautas Landsbergis, the Latvian Supreme Soviet declared the annexation of Latvia by the USSR illegal and voted to start a transition period toward full independence. The constitution of 1922 was partly reinstated, but the majority of Soviet laws were kept for the transition period. Similarly, as in Estonia, the top leadership positions were shared between the unraveling communist establishment and the popular movement. One of the leading figures of the Tautas Fronte, Ivars Godmanis, became prime minister and Gorbunovs was reappointed as chairman of the Supreme Soviet.

In an attempt to obtain Gorbachev's support, Gorbunovs sent him a letter arguing that Baltic independence was a logical result of Gorbachev's reforms: "5 years ago you were brave enough to take the historic step that began a new era. . . . We believed in you, we followed you. . . . The statement of May 4 opens the door for a transitional period, a period of honest dialogue. We believe that our neighboring states are facing a new phase of close economic, political and personal cooperation."[140]

However, Gorbachev was not impressed. On May 6, the leader of the Latvian Communist Party (opposed to independence), Alfrēds Rubiks, appeared on national television to explain that neither he nor Gorbachev saw any difference between the Latvian approach and the Lithuanian one.[141]

Alarmed, Latvian members of the Congress of People's Deputies asked Georgy Shakhnazarov and Anatoly Chernyaev to make sure that Gorbachev read Gorbunov's letter carefully. Still unimpressed by the message, the Soviet president responded with two presidential decrees that declared the Estonian and Latvian declarations invalid.[142]

The Baltic cooperation, which during the crucial years of 1990 and 1991 became one of the main axes of Estonian, Latvian, and Lithuanian foreign policy, was not without its problems. First of all, the Lithuanian leadership found the Latvian and Estonian hesitations in proclaiming full independence dangerous for the common cause.[143] Meanwhile, Estonians and Latvians considered the Lithuanian move misguided and reckless.[144] As noted by political analyst Anatol Lieven: "The Lithuanian declaration of independence placed the Latvians and Estonians in a difficult position. Honor suggested similar declarations of full independence: it will be many years before Lithuanians forgive their Baltic neighbors for their failure to issue these."[145]

In the period of affirmation of national identity, the representatives of the three countries were often upset by the Western incapacity to see any differences between them and thus ended up competing against each other in their attempts to distinguish their state from its neighbors. However, these controversies remained minor, as the Baltic cooperation was crucial for all three states. Their geographical situation, legal status, and past experiences were so similar that it seemed obvious that either all or none of the Baltic countries would achieve independence.[146] According to the chairman of the Tautas Fronte, Dainis Īvāns, the cooperation was also driven by what were perceived as lessons from the past, namely willingness to avoid the errors of 1940 when Estonia, Latvia, and Lithuania had failed to coordinate their policies against the USSR.[147]

On May 12 in Tallinn, the three Baltic Supreme Council chairmen renewed the Treaty of Mutual Understanding and Cooperation signed by the Baltic States in Geneva on September 12, 1934. At the same time, the Baltic Council was established to coordinate actions taken for the achievement of full independence.[148] The three leaders also sent a joint letter to George Bush calling for his support in the name of international law and historical justice.[149]

Unexpected but important support also came from other Soviet republics. Boris Yeltsin, who at the end of May became the chairman of the Supreme Soviet of Russian SFSR, stated on several occasions that the embargo against Lithuania should be lifted. On May 29, the Leningrad City Soviet voted a resolution urging the president of the Soviet Union to lift the blockade and start the negotiations. On May

31, the Soviet Socialist Republic of Moldova recognized Lithuania as an independent state.

Even if Lithuania's position seemed to be strengthened, the situation remained blocked. Lithuania did not want to freeze its declaration without any guarantees from the West and without any sign from the Kremlin that this action would be considered sufficient to lift the embargo and begin talks on independence. Moscow, at the same time, showed no willingness to compromise. On May 17, Prime Minister Prunskienė went to Moscow and had a brief meeting with Gorbachev. A member of the French ministry of foreign affairs noted that afterward Lithuania could no longer have any illusion about the firm commitment of Gorbachev.[150] On May 22, Gorbachev received the Latvian acting president, Anatolijs Gorbunovs, and the Estonian acting president, Arnold Rüütel. According to Rüütel, the meeting "was frustrating for everybody present."[151] Estonian prime minister Savisaar, who was also present at the encounter, later wrote that Gorbachev and Soviet prime minister Ryzhkov threatened their guests with direct presidential rule and made menacing allusions to the Soviet repressions of the 1940s.[152]

Meanwhile, the situation on the ground in all three Baltic countries was deteriorating. On May 13, Anatoly Chernyaev recorded in his journal his concerns not only about the situation in the Baltic republics but also about the effect that eventual violence in this part of the USSR might have on the international position of the Soviet State: "I am very afraid. . . . If slaughter breaks out, it will be the end, truly the end because it is clear whose side Gorbachev will take. It will be game over for the trip to the US and to everything in general, after all, we are on the eve of a Russian Congress and the Russian Party Conference."[153]

On May 15, pro-Soviet crowds tried to storm the Latvian and Estonian Supreme Soviets. In both Tallinn and Riga, hundreds of independence activists came to protect the buildings, and for several hours a physical clash seemed inevitable. The standoff ended without escalation to violence, but the situation remained tense. By early June the CIA reported that Lithuania had started to feel the effects of the Soviet blockade. While the hardships that the population was facing were not extreme, living standards were quickly deteriorating: hot water and gas were often unavailable; gasoline sales had been banned for private cars, while the bus services were cut by a third; about 5 percent of the labor force was laid off; and large parts of the population were underemployed.[154]

In this context, the White House had to make a decision regarding the Soviet-American trade treaty that was supposed to be signed during a Bush-Gorbachev meeting in Washington.

The Baltic Question at the Washington Summit

The Washington summit, scheduled to start on May 30, coincided with a complicated geopolitical environment. On the one hand, the United States was seeking Soviet consent for German NATO membership, which the USSR was not willing to grant. On the other hand, the USSR was looking for Western economic aid, which the United States was not ready to provide.

The ongoing Lithuanian crisis made the situation even less comfortable, as it became increasingly harder for US decision makers to track what exactly was going on in Soviet-Baltic relations. Between May 16 and 18, James Baker met Gorbachev, Shevardnadze, and Prunskienė in Moscow, and each side told him a different story regarding the state of their negotiations. While Gorbachev informed Baker that Prunskienė was willing to suspend the independence declaration,[155] Prunskienė herself explained that Lithuania would suspend any laws that the USSR found "offending" but not the declaration itself.[156] While assuring the Lithuanian prime minister that the United States "was on their side," Baker once again encouraged her to consider the suspension of the declaration.[157]

At the same time, there was a growing sense both in the US executive and legislative branches that Lithuania and the Baltic states had done their share of compromising. On May 15 Republican minority leader Dole stated that Latvia and Estonia "have gone the extra mile to meet any legitimate Soviet interests," while the actions of the Soviet Union toward the Baltics "appeared provocative."[158] Likewise, at the end of May 1990, the US government informed its European allies that Lithuania, Latvia, and Estonia had gone far enough in the direction of compromise and that the Soviet Union was responding inadequately.[159]

During May, the Bush administration became more and more assertive about its intention not to sign the Soviet-American trade treaty. Already on May 4 during a meeting in Bonn, Baker had warned Shevardnadze that it might be difficult to sign the agreement during the upcoming summit because of the Congressional opposition. The Soviet foreign minister responded that it would be an unfortunate indication of what was happening to the Soviet-American relationship, but it would not be a tragedy.[160]

At the same time, the Bush administration also started to use the Lithuanian situation, along with ongoing Soviet assistance for Cuba, as two main excuses for not providing large-scale financial assistance to the USSR. On May 17, Bush met with Helmut Kohl, who urged the United States to financially support the USSR. Bush explained that "his hands were tied" because of the domestic reaction regarding Soviet actions against Lithuania. Kohl insisted that East-West relations could not be determined by the

Baltic question, but Bush "remained firm."[161] When the Soviet president asked for US credit during the Gorbachev-Baker meeting that took place the next day in Moscow, Baker launched into to a long monologue in which the Baltic situation and Cuba were highlighted as fundamental issues that reduced the White House possibilities to provide financial assistance.[162] As late as one day before the summit, Baker, Bush, and Scowcroft agreed that the Baltic situation, Cuba, and the lack of far-reaching economic reforms should be cited as the principal barriers against financial aid.[163] Even when Kohl called Bush on May 30, the day of Gorbachev's arrival in Washington, DC, and insisted that Gorbachev needed help "very much," Bush remained non-committal and said that when it came to the "economic side," the United States "had problems related to Lithuania."[164]

In sum, it seemed that the Americans were entering the summit negotiations with no plans to sign the trade treaty. Yet on June 1 it was signed, along with other US-Soviet agreements on topics including chemical weapons, student exchanges, and civil aviation. This last-minute change of plans was first and foremost due to Gorbachev's emotional appeals to Bush. Facing harsh criticism at home for the "loss of Eastern Europe," the Soviet leadership needed something tangible to bring back from the summit before the 28th Congress of the Soviet Communist Party, scheduled to begin on July 2.

In his memoirs published in 1996, Bush recalls how during the first evening in Washington, Gorbachev told him personally that failure to make the trade agreement would be a disaster for him.[165] It seemed that, once again, the two superpowers had misunderstood each other. Gorbachev had come to Washington convinced that the trade treaty was going to be signed.[166] Bush was surprised by this and during a one-to-one session on June 1 read out loud to Gorbachev the letter that he had sent him in late April. When Bush insisted that Congress would never approve the trade treaty, Gorbachev replied that Bush had chosen the Baltics over him. When Bush suggested discussing the issue the next day at Camp David, Gorbachev answered that it was no longer his problem and that the decision was in American hands.[167]

The one-to-one session ended at 11:48 A.M.; the signature of various US-Soviet accords was scheduled for 6 P.M. In the six hours in between, Bush decided to again change the US approach to the Lithuanian crisis and to sign the treaty. The White House wanted neither to destabilize Gorbachev's power nor to jeopardize US-Soviet relations. The first day of the summit had shown some progress toward Soviet acceptance of German NATO membership, but it was not the breakthrough that the American side had hoped for. As the United States did not plan to provide the Soviets with large-scale economic assistance, the trade treaty was the only practical "carrot" that the Bush administration was able to offer to soften the Soviet stance. According to Bush's memoirs, he and Baker agreed that the treaty would be signed with two conditions: one public—the passing of the emigration law—and the other secret—the lifting of the embargo and beginning of negotiations with Lithuania.[168]

The Congressional response was immediate and as harsh as Bush had predicted. On June 6, Democrat Representative Richard Durbin, whose mother had arrived in the United States as a refugee from Lithuania during the Second World War, proposed an amendment to the Omnibus Export Amendments Act of 1990 that would bar the easing of restrictions on exports to the Soviet Union until the president had certified that Moscow had entered serious negotiations with Lithuania "for the purpose of allowing Lithuanian self-determination."[169] The House of Representatives voted 390–24 in favor of the amendment and consequently clearly positioned itself in opposition to the president.[170] While Bush publicly made clear that he was willing to facilitate commercial exchanges with the USSR despite the problems in the Baltics, the House made an equally clear linkage between trade and Lithuanian independence.

Four days after the congressional vote on exports, the Soviet president let the three Baltic leaders know that, if they attended the Union Council on June 12, he would receive them to discuss the eventual solution for the crisis. The proposal was not innocent, because the three Baltic countries claimed that, after their declarations, Soviet affairs did not concern them anymore and they had no reason to be at the Union Council. Still, the three leaders arrived in Moscow on June 12. The meeting was tense. Gorbachev strongly insisted that the Baltic declarations should be suspended. When Rüütel stated that Estonia's aim was full independence, Gorbachev threated him with direct presidential rule in Estonia.[171] When Gorbachev asked Landsbergis about his views on the future of the Soviet federation, Landsbergis responded that he could not comment on the internal affairs of the Soviet state.[172] Gorbunovs emphasized that compromises that Moscow was asking from them would be perceived as capitulation at home. Yet he was willing to compromise: if Latvia's May 4 declaration was recognized as valid by the Soviet authorities, Latvia would be willing to suspend it for the time of negotiations.[173]

On June 13, Lithuanian prime minister Prunskienė had a much more productive bilateral meeting with Soviet prime minister Ryzhkov.[174] After the meeting, Prunskienė told the press that Lithuania could temporarily suspend its independence declaration. "It will be possible to suspend the act only for the duration of the talks, and they will not go on forever," Prunskienė explained. "They will last for a specific period of time."[175]

The dialogue that began that day led to a moratorium on the Lithuanian proclamation and the lifting of the Soviet blockade in late June 1990. In addition, negotiations over the independence of the three Baltic countries were scheduled to begin immediately.

The immediate crisis seemed to be resolved. At the same time, the situation remained very unfavorable for the three Baltic countries: their attempts to obtain permanent Western involvement in the Baltic question had failed, and thus Lithuanians, Estonians, and Latvians had to negotiate their independence with the USSR by themselves. They were not the only ones to find the situation troubling. A few days before the announcement of the moratorium, the Lithuanians sought to consult with the US government on the subject. Instructions to back the moratorium option were sent to the US embassy in Moscow. The same day, the special advisor to the president for national security affairs, Peter Rodman, wrote in a note to his colleagues: "I think we should be ashamed of ourselves."[176]

CHAPTER 4

The End of Perestroika?

The Baltic Quest for Visibility and the Soviet Crackdown

If force is not used against us, we will certainly achieve our goals. But if force is used, then
we are going to be thrown back so far into totalitarianism that we will not be able to find
our way out again.

—Deputy Chairman of the Supreme Soviet of Latvia Andrejs Krastiņš to
the US diplomat George Krol, December 1990.

After the suspension of the Lithuanian independence declaration
in June 1990, the White House started to lose interest in the Baltic
problem. The situation on the ground seemed to have calmed. Lithuania,
the most rebellious of the three republics, had backtracked, and the embargo that the USSR had used to coerce Vilnius into obedience was lifted.
Its Nordic neighbors Latvia and Estonia had shown proof of cautiousness
by declaring a transition toward independence but not the independence
itself. All sides, including the Soviet Union, had declared themselves willing
to negotiate, thus raising US hopes for the compromise-driven solution for
the Baltic independence claims.

At the same time, beginning in July 1990, critical developments on the
international stage distracted the world, not just from the Baltic issue but
even from Soviet internal events in general. While the German reunification process and the 2 + 4 negotiations approached their end, Saddam
Hussein's Iraq invaded Kuwait on August 2. The Baltic governments felt

Politics of Uncertainty. Una Bergmane, Oxford University Press. © Oxford University Press 2023.
DOI: 10.1093/oso/9780197578346.003.0005

that they were losing their international momentum and redoubled their efforts at raising their visibility on the global stage.

The relaxation of tensions in Soviet-Baltic relations was short-lived. Starting from November, Mikhail Gorbachev once again hardened his policies in the Baltic states, and in January an attempt was made to crush the Lithuanian and Latvian drive for independence by force. Suddenly the Baltic countries found themselves in the spotlight of the international news, while Gorbachev faced unexpected outrage, both domestically and internationally. Western reactions, however, were driven not so much by their concern about the fate of the Baltic nations as by their fear that the use of force in Vilnius and Riga might mean the end of Perestroika.

This chapter traces the Baltic attempts to increase their international visibility, which ended with their expulsion from the CSCE summit in Paris in November 1991. It then turns to the events leading up to the Soviet use of force in Lithuania and Latvia and the international response to the attempted crackdown.

BALTIC FOREIGN POLICY IN THE FALL OF 1990

As Estonian prime minister Edgar Savisaar later wrote in his memoirs, 1990 was neither an easy nor a happy year for Baltic foreign policy.[1] That autumn, as German reunification approached and the Gulf War crisis deepened, Estonians, Latvians, and Lithuanians became anxious that the West might put the Baltic question aside or even resolve it to Soviet advantage. While the United States strongly preferred an internally negotiated Soviet-Baltic solution to the Baltic problem, decision makers in Tallinn, Riga, and Vilnius continued to hope for the active involvement of the global community.

On September 5, the three acting presidents and three prime ministers of the Baltic countries met in Tallinn and explicitly asked for the opening of international negotiations on their independence, claiming that the Baltic issue had to be resolved in a "3 + 4" setting. Always fearful of a possible great power agreement that would seal their fate, the they insisted that the Soviet Union was not, and had never been, authorized to represent the interests of the three republics.[2] The only substantive reaction to this statement came from the US Senate, which adopted a unanimous Senate resolution reaffirming the US continued refusal to recognize the 1940 annexation of the Baltic states as legal.[3]

Facing their incapacity to gain active Western involvement in their dealings with the USSR, Baltic diplomats focused on increasing their visibility and presence on the international stage. In the context of their ongoing struggle with Moscow over the legitimate power in the Baltics, communication with foreign countries carried particular significance for the Baltic governments: it was an affirmation of sovereignty. As Lennart Meri, Estonian minister of foreign affairs at the time, declared: "We restore contacts around the world. We don't do this for you, but for us. By restoring contacts, we are restoring Estonia."[4] By requesting meetings with Western leaders, sending them letters, and asking for observer status at the CSCE, the Balts not only tried to capture the world's attention but also to obtain acts of recognition that usually were reserved for sovereign states. During Prunskienė's trip to the West in May 1990, her advisors were particularly sensitive to both the content of the meetings and their form, seeing the venue, the length, and the setting of the encounter as symbolical gestures and political messages.[5]

After the suspension of the Lithuanian independence declaration, it was Latvia's and Estonia's turns to seek contacts with high-ranking foreign officials. Their first attempts to meet the American president turned out to be challenging. When in June the Latvian legation in Washington contacted the White House about the possibility of arranging a meeting between George Bush and Latvian prime minister Ivars Godmanis, the administration was initially reluctant. The tensions between Moscow and the Baltic capitals seemed to have eased, and the administration was somewhat unwilling to undermine Gorbachev by having direct contacts with representatives of the Soviet republics. According to the information that Baltic diaspora activists possessed, the White House had recently refused to receive the leader of Kazakhstan for the same reasons.[6] Once again members of Congress played a crucial role in influencing the president's stand on the Baltic question. After receiving a negative answer to their request, the Latvian legation and the diaspora organization activated their network in Washington and sought help among member of Congress with a record of support for the Baltic cause, namely Minority Leader Bob Dole and Republican Bob Kasten from Wisconsin. According to diaspora activist Ojārs Kalniņš, a call from influential Democratic Senator Robert Byrd, who had served in the Senate for over forty years, played an essential role in the decision of the White House to finally meet with the Latvian prime minister.[7] For the Latvian as well as the Estonian government, this decision was crucial. As the Latvian foreign minister pointed out to George Bush, the trip to the United States put them on "a new political level."[8] It created a precedent of direct communication with the US president and contributed to the symbolic capital of the Latvian and Estonian governments.[9]

For the White House, the decision to meet with the Latvian delegation established a routine procedure in their dealings with the Soviet republics: the president would receive the leaders of the Baltic states, while senior White House officials would meet with high-ranking visitors from other Soviet republics.

George Bush welcomed the Latvian prime minister Ivars Godmanis and his foreign minister, Jānis Jurkāns, on June 30, and received Estonian prime minister Edgar Savisaar and his foreign minister, Lennart Meri, on October 12.[10] During the meeting with the Latvians, the president remained very careful and spoke only to ask questions, while his interlocutors focused on conveying a positive image of Latvia, rather than requesting solid support. Coached by Latvian diaspora organizations, Godmanis tried to deconstruct the perception that Latvian and Baltic independence had something to do with political radicalism and could destabilize Gorbachev or the USSR. Godmanis spoke at length about Latvian economic reforms and the transition to a market economy. He emphasized that Latvia had good working relations with the Soviet prime minister and that his aim was to press "ahead peacefully and normally."[11] Similar tactics were used by the Estonian prime minister, who later wrote in his memoirs that he wanted to take the conversation a step further than Prunskienė and Godmanis but was not sure how far he could go while staying within the limits of what was acceptable for the United States.[12] Just like his Latvian counterpart, he insisted on Estonia's good intentions toward the USSR, but unlike Godmanis he talked about the issue that at the era of Strategic Arms Reduction Treaty (START) negotiations was close to Bush's heart—Estonian opposition to the placement of Soviet missiles on the Estonian territory. Significantly, the only concrete demands that the Latvian delegation made were what Foreign Minister Jurkāns called "tangible proof of our sovereignty": observation status at the CSCE and an opening of a US information center in Riga.

These two questions—the participation in the Helsinki process and an institutionalized foreign presence in the Baltic capitals—were key elements of Baltic diplomacy in 1990 and 1991. The so-called information bureau was the formula created by the Balts and the Scandinavian countries that allowed to intensify the exchanges without proceeding to recognition and opening of embassies. The quest for CSCE membership, or at least observer status, was of crucial importance for Estonians, Latvians, and Lithuanians, as it was seen as providing both visibility and a move toward recognition. First, the participation in international organizations was one of the critical elements of statehood. And second, in 1990 it seemed that the CSCE might become the cornerstone of the new European order. It was the only organization that assembled all European states, and since 1975 had proven its efficiency as a framework for dialogue, as well as a follow-up mechanism for the Helsinki process. For the Balts to be part of CSCE meant being part of the new post–Cold War European order. Furthermore, they perceived the CSCE Paris summit, scheduled for November 1990, as the final settlement of the Second World War legacies and thus wanted the opportunity to remind the world by their presence that their situation was still unresolved.[13]

In early June 1990, the three countries applied for membership of the CSCE, and a few months later the three foreign ministers, Estonian Lennart Meri, Latvian Jānis Jurkāns, and Lithuanian Algirdas Saudargas, made a joint statement asking for observer status at the Paris summit. They tried to connect their situation with larger issues on the international agenda such as German reunification and the invasion of Kuwait.[14] The question of Kuwait was particularly interesting for the Balts, as it seemed that principles that were being invoked by the US president to consolidate an international coalition against Iraq could one day be applied to their case. On September 11, when explaining the US position regarding the situation in the Gulf, George Bush had laid out a vision of post–Cold War world "where the strong respect the rights of the weak."[15] Attempting to take the US president at his word, Meri, Jurkāns, and Saudargas insisted that the Soviet rule in the Baltics was a foreign occupation just as much as Iraq's invasion of Kuwait. "While Kuwait has been forced to endure two months of brutal foreign occupation, the occupation of our countries has lasted for fifty years," they argued.[16] The three foreign ministers then turned to a pan-European discourse, pointing out that, "bound to the continent" by their culture and heritage, they wished to take their "rightful place in a united Europe."[17] This emotional appeal was designed not only to ask for access to the CSCE but also to shape Western perceptions of the Baltic states. By affirming their "Europeanness" the Balts were insisting that they were not "the others," intent on destabilizing the European system, but legitimate members of it.

The initial support for Baltic participation at the Helsinki process came from the countries for whom the Baltic question was not a remote problem of the Soviet periphery, but a regional issue. During the second part of 1990, all Nordic countries, with the exception of Finland, whose foreign policy was still anchored in its Cold War traditions, started to voice their support for the Baltic cause.[18] Geographic proximity, historical ties, and in the Swedish case a large Estonian diaspora increased the visibility of the Baltic question in Sweden, Denmark, and Norway. They were joined and often led by Iceland, which historically had not had strong ties with the three Baltic countries, but whose government saw the Baltic question as an opportunity to increase its own visibility on the international stage, while defending a cause that its foreign minister Jón Baldvin Hannibalsson personally saw as just. In the Danish case, Baltic independence was seen as beneficial to Danish security interests as Copenhagen preferred to have three small democracies rather than the autocratic Soviet power as their neighbors in the Baltic Sea region.[19] In Sweden, which unlike most of other European countries had recognized Baltic annexation as legal, and thus had diplomatic representations in Riga and Tallinn, two different policy perspectives coexisted. On the one hand, the Swedish government balanced between supporting the Baltic countries and staying prudent vis-à-vis Moscow. On the other hand, Swedish diplomats on the ground found these efforts insufficient and pushed for even more active Swedish involvement.[20] Norway always joined its Nordic neighbors in expressing support for Baltic sovereignty, but its stand was stronger in 1990 under the Conservative government of Jan Peder Syse and then under the Labor government of Gro Harlem Brundtland that came to power in November 1990.[21] During the second half of 1990, the Scandinavian countries were more and more often joined by Poland, which had embraced the idea of the independence of its neighboring Soviet republics.[22]

During the summer, Denmark and Iceland had spoken in favor of Baltic aspirations to join NATO, the United Nations, and the Nordic Council, and had lobbied for Baltic participation at the Paris summit.[23] During the ministerial meeting in New York on October 1, the Swedish foreign minister, Sten Andersson, insisted that arrangements should be made to provide the Baltic states with the opportunity to follow the CSCE process.[24] Similarly, the Polish foreign minister Krzysztof Skubiszewski stated that Poland would support any arrangements that would allow "these old European people" to be associated with the CSCE process.[25] Both Norwegian and Danish foreign ministers claimed that the Baltic states fulfilled conditions for full membership.[26] Icelandic foreign minister Jón Baldvin Hannibalsson not only pledged his government's unreserved support for the Baltic group but also called for the restoration of Baltic independence.[27]

Meanwhile, Germany, France, and the United States were much more prudent. The Treaty on the Final Settlement with Respect to Germany was signed on September 12, and the official reunification was set to take place on October 3. During this sensitive period the German leadership wanted no complications in its relations with the USSR. Kohl was deeply grateful to Gorbachev for allowing the unification to take place, but the concluded agreement still had to be ratified.[28] At the same time, the American side was becoming more cautious in its relations with the USSR, as it hoped to sign the Conventional Armed Forces in Europe Treaty during the Paris summit as well as conclude START negotiations shortly; furthermore, it also needed Soviet support to obtain a UN mandate for the war against Iraq. The talks related to the Iraq situation that Bush and Gorbachev had conducted in Helsinki in early September 1990 had not been successful: Bush was opting for military intervention, while Gorbachev was advocating negotiations.[29] The next meeting of the two heads of state was scheduled to take place during the Paris summit, and the administration was trying to avoid any tensions beforehand.

As in spring 1990, strong support for the Baltic cause came from the US Congress. Twenty-two members of the Congress, evenly divided between Democrats and Republicans, sent a letter to President Bush asking him to do everything possible to enable Estonia, Latvia, and Lithuania to participate in the Paris summit, either as full members or as observers. The letter emphasized that, as the annexation of the Baltic countries had not been recognized, they were *de jure* independent European states and thus eligible for CSCE membership.[30]

The non-recognition policy argument was also used in France, the host of the Paris summit, which had to decide whether to invite Estonia, Latvia, and Lithuania to the conference. Initially, the French delegation to the CSCE was opposed to the Baltic presence. French diplomats indicated that, according to the statutes of the conference, only European states existing in 1973 could apply for admission. But on July 14, 1990, the legal affairs department of the French Foreign Ministry rejected this argument, explaining that as France had not recognized the annexation of the Baltic republics, the three countries had not ceased to exist as states for France in 1973.[31]

The final decision regarding the Baltic presence was left to Pierre Morel, a high-ranking French diplomat who was leading the French delegation at the pre-conference negotiations in Vienna. Marked by his encounters with the Baltic diaspora representative in Paris at the beginning of his career, and committed to the French non-recognition policy, Morel was willing to find a solution that would allow the Balts to take part in the conference.[32] In a series of meetings with both Latvian foreign minister Jānis Jurkāns (who was also representing the two other Baltic states) and the head of the Soviet delegation, he negotiated a compromise: Baltic delegates would attend the summit, but instead of having observer status they would be invited as guests of the executive secretary of the conference. Both sides accepted the proposed solution, even if the Soviet side was disposed to rather "close their eyes" on the Baltic presence than to welcome it.[33]

On November 18, Estonian foreign minister Lennart Meri, Latvian Jānis Jurkāns, and Lithuanian Algirdas Saudargas met with James Baker in Paris. The US secretary of state reassured Baltic officials that his country stood by the non-recognition policy, but as usual made no more concrete promises regarding the support for Baltic independence.[34] In the evening the trio had an appointment with the head of the European Affairs Department at the French Foreign Ministry, Jacques Blot, who asked the three ministers to remain discreet during the conference. Even though the Baltic representatives agreed to these terms, they had no intention of going unnoticed. By the next morning, they had told Reuters News that they were going to attend the summit as distinguished guests of the French Republic.[35] At the same time, the *Toronto Star* reported that the foreign ministers of all three Baltic republics had been invited to the summit as guests, but that they intended to unofficially act as equal participants.[36]

On the morning of November 19, the Baltic ministers took their places in the conference hall next to the representatives from the Red Cross and Order of Malta. According to the memoirs of Latvian representative in Paris Aina Nagobads-Ābols, just after the arrival of the Baltic delegations, Soviet defense minister Dmitry Yazov entered the room, fixed his eyes on the Baltic delegations, and then left. A few minutes later, a member of the French organizing team approached the Baltic ministers and asked them to leave the conference room.[37]

According to French diplomats such as René Roudaut, Philippe de Suremain, and Pierre Morel, as well as Foreign Minister Roland Dumas, on the morning of November 19, Mikhail Gorbachev had found out about the Baltic presence and threatened to leave Paris if the Baltic ministers were not removed from the conference. Facing the probable failure of the summit as well as the Conventional Armed Forces in Europe Treaty, Dumas yielded to the Soviet request.

In the short term, the exclusion from the summit played in the Balts' favor as it gave them more visibility than they would have had sitting in the audience next to the Order of Malta. Denmark organized a press conference for them, and the international press reported on their situation.[38] Furthermore, their physical absence from the conference did not mean that the Baltic cause was not invoked. Norwegian prime minister Gro Harlem Brundtland, Polish prime minister Tadeusz Mazowiecki, and Danish prime minister Poul Schlüter called for Baltic inclusion in the Helsinki process.[39] The press especially took note of the speech by Václav Havel, who described the participation of the Baltic countries in the Helsinki process as an important element of future European integration. Havel, the president of the Czech and Slovak Federation, also emphasized that observer status should be accorded to the Baltic states "for the time being," implying that in the future the Baltic countries should have full membership. The *Independent* later reported that Gorbachev canceled his meeting with Havel the next day.[40] The most supportive statement was that by the Swedish prime minister, Ingvar Carlsson, who insisted that for him it was difficult to envisage "a future Europe in peace and cooperation without the full participation of Baltic people." Ignoring the exclusion of the Baltic ministers, he greeted Baltic representatives as distinguished visitors at the conference.[41] Meanwhile Gorbachev, without mentioning the Balts explicitly, warned the CSCE members that "Militant nationalism and mindless separatism can easily bring conflict and enmity, Balkanization, and what is worse, Lebanization of different regions."[42] In a private conversation with Mauno Koivisto, he went even further, telling his Finnish counterpart that fascism was on the rise in the Baltics.[43] Bush, whose main aim for the Paris summit was to obtain an agreement with the Soviets regarding intervention in Iraq, did not mention the Baltic question at all.

While the removal of the Baltic dignitaries from the Paris summit actually increased their visibility, the symbolic violence of the act caused Estonian, Latvian, and Lithuanian officials to perceive the incident as a major failure of their foreign policy. Saudargas was outraged, and Jurkāns concluded: "We were treated as if we were nothing."[44] Meri tried to stay optimistic, seeing the exclusion from the summit as a possibility to attract sympathy and attention from the world. But even for him, November 19 was a symbolic low point for Baltic diplomacy.[45]

That evening, the Latvian representative in Paris, Aina Nagobads-Ābols, with the financial support of the World Union of Free Latvians, organized a reception to celebrate the seventy-second anniversary of Latvian independence, proclaimed on November 18, 1918. The idea behind the celebration was to point out the continuity of the Baltic countries and to give supporters of Baltic independence an occasion to manifest their solidarity. The event was initially arranged for 100 guests, but in the end more than 200 attended. Among the guests were the prime minister of Iceland Steingrímur Hermannsson, with all the members of his delegation, as well as Danish, Polish, Austrian, and Hungarian foreign ministers. Sweden sent its deputy foreign minister and Finland its ambassador to UNESCO. French foreign minister Dumas called Nagobads-Ābols to apologize for his absence, but most of the French European Affairs Department staff were present.[46] These Independence Day celebrations, with participation of foreign dignitaries, were significant for countries that were not actually independent. The symbolic act of attending a reception became a political statement affirming that the Baltic countries were seen and their situation recognized as exceptional and problematic. However, as Estonian diaspora activists noted, "nobody from the American delegation showed up."[47]

The Paris summit had clearly shown that Western willingness to give treatment reserved for sovereign states to the Baltic countries had its limits, and that those limits were largely determined by the necessity of maintaining good relations with the USSR. For the French, the exclusion of the Balts from the summit was an unpleasant incident, while a Soviet departure from Paris would have been a diplomatic catastrophe, as it would have jeopardized the signature of the Paris Charter, the Conventional Armed Forces in Europe Treaty, and US attempts to gain Soviet support for a military UN-approved intervention against Iraq.

The question that remains unanswered and was puzzling for actors at the time is why the USSR gave its agreement to the Baltic participation and then withdrew it just before the summit. The French explained this sudden change as an intentional or accidental miscommunication on the Soviet side: the Soviet ambassador in Vienna might, they suggested, have made a decision that was then not properly communicated to the minister, or the minister might have agreed to the Baltic presence without the president's consent.[48] Meanwhile, the Balts saw this as an intentional Soviet attempt to humiliate them and to test Western resolve. On November 22, the diplomatic advisor of Lithuanian president Landsbergis called the French Ministry of Foreign Affairs to express Lithuanian disappointment. "The solution found is the worst possible signal that one could send to Gorbachev. Now he knows, if he ever doubted that his hands in the Baltics are free and that he can soon apply direct presidential rule here."[49]

Indeed, at the time of the Paris summit, the tensions between the Balts and Moscow started to increase again.

THE RISE OF TENSIONS IN BALTIC-SOVIET RELATIONS AFTER THE PARIS SUMMIT

The negotiations that were supposed to start in the summer of 1990 between the USSR and Lithuania, Latvia, and Estonia failed to bring any solution to the Baltic problem. While the Baltic side had come to the table with a clear goal of negotiating independence, the Soviet side had no mandate to discuss secession. In August, Moscow had finally started talks with twelve Soviet republics about the text of the new Union Treaty and tried to turn negotiations with the Baltic countries into similar discussions about the future of republic-center relations. While this approach might have worked in 1988, in 1990 remaining in the Union was not an option for Vilnius, Riga, and Tallinn, and the negotiations broke off in the fall.[50]

On November 17, just before the Paris summit, the Supreme Soviet of the USSR approved several of Gorbachev's initiatives regarding the restructuring of the USSR, including the creation of a new Federation Council—a chief executive body that would assemble the heads of all fifteen republics. The same day, the Baltic countries announced they would not participate in the work of the Federation Council, as they intended to leave the Soviet Union, not to reform it. On November 23, Gorbachev presented the new Union Treaty to the public. The project proposed to reform the relations between the center and the republics, allowing them to have more autonomy in the economic domain and more control over their territories. But it still retained the supremacy of federal laws over republic laws and Moscow's exclusive control over military affairs and foreign policy. The Baltic states, along with Georgia, refused to participate in the negotiations.

This new wave of tensions between Baltic countries and Moscow emerged in the context of a wider change in Gorbachev's policies that started in November 1990 and has been labeled "Gorbachev's shift to the right."[51] Since the early years of Perestroika, various political forces such as Gorbachev's liberal advisors, Yeltsin's Russian democrats, and Soviet conservatives had competed to define not just the political course but the very identity of the country, putting Gorbachev under increasing political pressure. In the autumn of 1990, the Soviet president was fighting for his political survival. Being caught between the radical Russian democrats and the Baltic independence movements on one side, and the conservative wing on the other, Gorbachev chose to make a tactical retreat and temporary concede to those who represented the most powerful threat—the Party, the military, and the KGB.[52]

According to French diplomats, during the first week of December, a meeting of the recently created Soviet Defense Council took place. There the liberal elements of the presidential entourage (Shevardnadze, Yakovlev, and Bakatin) were disowned.[53] Indeed the spectacular resignation by Eduard Shevardnadze on December 20 was preceded by other important changes in the Soviet leadership. With deep concern, the Baltic states observed the removal of liberal Vadim Bakatin, with whom they had good relations, from the position of minister of internal affairs.[54] Their anxiety increased with the appointment of the former chief of the Latvian KGB, Boris Pugo, to that function, and the designation of Colonel Boris Gromov as his deputy.[55]

Since the summer of 1990, the conservatives had been pushing Gorbachev to restore order in the rebellious republics by declaring a state of emergency and imposing direct presidential rule.[56] When in December all the key security institutions—Ministry of Defense, Ministry of Interior, and the KGB—had fallen under the control the conservatives, the Balts started to fear that Soviet forces might try to destabilize the situation in their republics, in order to declare a state of emergency. Initially it seemed that the first target of these attempts would be Latvia.[57] In late November, the conservative Latvian and Russian communists created a National Salvation Committee that joined forces with Latvian Interferon and called for the introduction of direct presidential rule.[58] In December several bombs exploded in Latvia, increasing the distrust between pro- and anti-independence forces.[59] In this context the local leadership "did everything possible to ensure that civil resistance would be entirely non-violent."[60] On December 13, Tautas Fronte issued the so-called instructions for the x hour, calling the population to civil disobedience in the case that direct presidential rule was imposed.[61] In late December the Latvian deputy chairman of the Supreme Soviet told US diplomat George Krol that "If force is not used against us we will certainly achieve our goals. But if force is used, then we are going to be thrown back so far into totalitarianism that we will not be able to find our way out again."[62]

The developments in the Baltics did not go unnoticed in the West. By the end of November, a report was circulated in the White House regarding the possibility of selective martial law in the USSR.[63] Uncertainty about how to understand the developments in the Soviet Union was a significant problem for the Bush administration in late 1990s. By mid-December the CIA argued that a serious turn to the right had taken place. The Bureau of Intelligence and Research rejected this idea, while the NSC spoke about a "creeping crackdown" taking place in the Soviet Union.[64] One State Department report argued that the United States had to be careful not to overreact, and not to take each alarming statement by one of the fifteen republics as the beginning of a large-scale crisis.[65] Another internally circulated document pointed out that in the case of a Soviet crackdown the United States might not immediately be able to decide whether it was a tactical diversion or a long-term shift in the Soviet policy.[66] By mid-December, senior officials from various government agencies (NSC, State Department, Joint Chiefs of Staff, CIA, White House) agreed to meet regularly to share their information about the deteriorating political situation in the USSR.[67] On December 21, Brent Scowcroft advised the president that "at this time of uncertainty" the country should send strong signals to Moscow that United States would not accept the use of force in the Baltics, or in "the Soviet Union proper."[68]

Once again, the president was very reluctant to put too much pressure on the USSR. During their November meeting in Paris, Bush and Gorbachev had agreed on a UN resolution that would set a deadline for Iraq to withdraw from Kuwait. On November 29, Resolution 678 was approved, giving Iraq until January 15, 1991, to leave the occupied territories. As the deadline was approaching and the international alliance led by the United States was preparing for war, the administration was trying not to complicate its relations with the USSR. Soviet consent to the military intervention was crucial for its legitimacy, but extremely unpopular among Soviet conservatives, who saw it as the last step toward the loss of Soviet superpower status. On December 12, to reward Soviet support for the upcoming war and to reinforce Gorbachev's position, Bush temporarily waived the Jackson-Vanik Amendment, making possible the release of $1 billion in Commodity Credit Corporation (CCC) credit guarantees and $300 million in export-import bank credits for the purchase of US goods.[69] The president also offered technical assistance to improve food distribution and $5 million under the International Disaster Relief Program and proposed that the Soviet Union be given "special association" with the International Monetary Fund and the World Bank.[70]

On December 31, National Security Advisor Brent Scowcroft urged President Bush not to convey New Year's greetings to Gorbachev over the phone, since in the case of a Soviet crackdown this call "would not look too great."[71] The president, however, went ahead, called his Soviet counterpart, and did not mention the Baltic situation during the conversation.[72]

As the UN deadline for Iraq approached, tensions continued to escalate in the Baltics. The Press House in Riga, where the major republican newspapers were printed, was seized by the Special Forces of the Soviet Interior Ministry on January 2. On the next day, Lithuania's pro-independence Communist Party buildings were invaded by the same special forces. On January 7, Soviet interior minister Yazov announced the arrival of additional troops in the Baltics to reinforce the draft for the Soviet army. At the same time, Soviet paratroopers were deployed in Ukraine, Moldova, Georgia, and Armenia. On January 8, the three Baltic states released a joint statement indicating that the real purpose of the Soviet army movements was to prepare for the crackdown on the Baltics and asking for international help.[73]

Meanwhile, a governmental crisis erupted in Lithuania: Prime Minister Prunskienė resigned over a dispute with the parliament concerning food prices. Anatol Lieven has argued that this internal problem led the Soviet government to shift the destabilization campaign from Latvia to Lithuania.[74] Indeed, on January 10, Mikhail Gorbachev called for full and immediate restoration of the Soviet constitution in Lithuania.[75] The Soviet president insisted that, if Vilnius failed to yield to this demand, a National Salvation Committee—similar to the one that already existed in Latvia—would be created to take over power in the Lithuanian SSR.

Ambassador Matlock reported that day that there was a real danger of bloodshed in the Baltic region and urged George Bush to send a letter to Mikhail Gorbachev.[76] But the president decided not to act. On January 11, Gorbachev himself called the White House. Scowcroft convinced the president of the need to mention the Baltic States, but Gorbachev actually preempted him. When Bush expressed his hope that force would not be used against the Baltic countries, Gorbachev launched into a monologue, from which the American side understood that the Soviets were actually non-committal on this question.[77] Bush did not insist and turned instead to questions concerning the upcoming Gulf War. When journalists later asked the president if, during the call, he had addressed the crackdown in the Baltics, Bush tried to downplay the seriousness of the conversation, explaining that: "There was not great discussion of that."[78]

On January 12 a dramatic Federation Council meeting took place in Moscow. Even though the Baltic states usually did not take part in the work of the council, this time it was attended by Estonian prime minister Savisaar, Chairman of Latvian Supreme Soviet Gorbunovs, Latvian prime minister Godmanis, and the permanent representative of Lithuanian government in Moscow Egidijus Bičkauskas. The session was opened by Interior Minister Pugo, who painted a bleak picture of Lithuania on a brink of total chaos and hinted at the need to establish direct presidential rule. He was supported by the Soviet hardliners such Defense Minister Yazov, his deputy Valentin Varennikov, and the head of the KGB Vladimir Kryuchkov. Meanwhile, Baltic officials and Yeltsin opposed this initiative, argued that Pugo's report was a distortion of reality, blamed Kremlin for the failed negotiations with the Baltic countries, and called for a peaceful solution.[79] They were supported by Moldova, which often rallied with the Balts and Armenia, but also by the more conservative Central Asian leaders Islam Karimov and Nursultan Nazarbayev. While the attitudes of these officials toward Baltic independence project varied, none of them wanted to create a precedent of direct presidential rule and legitimize the use of force against one of the republics. In the end, it was agreed that a special commission of the Federal Council would be sent to Vilnius to assess and de-escalate the situation.

Just a couple of hours after the meeting ended, Soviet troops killed fourteen civilians in Vilnius.

On the evening of January 12, 1991, Soviet forces from the KGB special unit Alpha and Pskov Airborne Division advanced toward the broadcasting tower in Vilnius. After arriving at the building, they were faced with hundreds of unarmed people who had come to defend it. After a brief hesitation, the tanks started to move through the crowd, and the soldiers opened fire. Fourteen people were killed, more than 100 were wounded, and the TV tower was taken by force. The same night Soviet troops seized the Lithuanian radio and telegraph building.

In the early hours of January 13, Baltic independence movements—Rahvarinne, Tautas Fronte, and Sąjūdis—called citizens of the three republics to defend the freely elected parliaments. During the day, thousands of volunteers from the countryside arrived in the capitals. That night, barricades were built around key buildings in the three cities. For a week, people remained at the barricades day and night, taking turns to sleep in churches and schools. Soviet troops continued tactics of harassment without undertaking massive attacks. On January 20, Soviet Interior Ministry's Special Purpose Mobile Unit (OMON) attacked the Latvian Ministry of Interior while Gorbunovs was dining with the marshal of Polish Sejm in a restaurant across the street.[80] Five people were killed and eleven injured.

The use of force against civilians was a breach of one of Perestroika's core principles: violence should not be seen as solution to either international or domestic problems.[81] While it had already been carried out twice during Gorbachev's tenure—in Tbilisi in 1989 and in Baku in 1990—the attack in the Baltics seemed to cross a new red line. As late as December 1990, Gorbachev himself had told Georgy Shakhnazarov that the use of "forceful methods" would be the "the end of everything" and that he would rather resign than resort to violence.[82] Shaknazarov had agreed that it indeed would be the "the betrayal of the very idea for which we started all this."[83]

Gorbachev always rejected any accusation of participation in the decision-making behind the use of force against civilians in the Baltics, but the question of his complicity has long been debated by historians.[84] In his memoirs Gorbachev seems to be reducing the problem of his involvement to the question of whether he knew that a decision was made to take the Vilnius TV tower by force, claims to have known nothing, and blames "the power ministries" (Defense and Interior) and KGB for conspiring behind his back.[85]

However, the attack on the TV tower was part of a larger plan to reduce the agency of Baltic governments and destabilize the situation to the point that imposition of direct presidential rule might appear justified. Indeed, according to the commander of the Alpha unit that operated in Vilnius during the night of January 13, the order to seize the Lithuanian TV tower came from the head of the KGB Vladimir Kryuchkov.[86] In the Latvian case both the commander of Riga OMON and the investigator who later worked on their crimes have told journalists that during 1991 the group took orders directly from the Soviet interior minister Boris Pugo.[87] Lithuanian court rulings of 2020 have pointed to the cooperation between the Soviet Defense Ministry, Soviet Interior Ministry, and the KGB.[88] The Gorbachev Foundation document collection "Soyuz mozhno bylo sokhranit" reveals that in December 1990 Pugo and Kryuchkov ordered the KGB to work on "the possibilities to introduce state of emergency" in the country.[89] According to the Lithuanian investigation around the same time, Yazov established headquarters to coordinate and command a military takeover in Vilnius.[90]

Was the Soviet president oblivious to these preparations? Gorbachev admits having been informed by Yazov, Kryuchkov, and Pugo that they had taken measures for the introduction of the presidential rule in Lithuania but claims that these plans were made only to stop a potential local outbreak of violence.[91] However, Kryuchkov in his memoirs has written that all the preparations were carried out under Gorbachev's orders and the president himself authorized the use of force on January 10, 1991.[92] The credibility of Kryuchkov's account can be questioned due to his animosity toward Gorbachev, and the overall tendentious tone of his account. Yet, Gorbachev did escalate the crisis by approving deployment of additional troops in the Baltics on January 7 and by pressuring the Lithuanian parliament to revoke its independence declaration on the 10th.[93] Furthermore, while it is not fully known what Gorbachev did or did not do before and during the attack on the TV tower, it is very well known what he did or did not do after it. For a week between January 13 and January 20, the Soviet president did not condemn the use of force against civilians, did not order an investigation, took no steps to deescalate the situation, and avoided his liberal advisors and the Baltic leadership.[94] The reasons behind this shift can be understood only in the context of Gorbachev's turn to right during the winter of 1990–1991. The rapprochement with the hardliners led to an opening toward their long-standing request for a crackdown in the Baltics and, when they made their move, Gorbachev waited to see what it would bring. It turned out that the use of force brought not only civil resistance in the Baltic countries but also domestic and international outrage.

The first to protest against the events in Vilnius were people from Gorbachev's own liberal circle. Their outrage stemmed from both the feeling that the attack in the Baltics was a betrayal of Perestroika and the realization that they had lost influence over the decision-making processes in the USSR. Only very limited information about what had happened in the Baltics was shared with them and, during the first week after the shooting in Vilnius, Gorbachev was ignoring their pleas to de-escalate the situation.[95]

On January 14, the Soviet president gave a speech before the Supreme Soviet about the events in Vilnius blaming Lithuanians for the bloodshed. His diplomatic aide Chernyaev found the discourse "pathetic, inarticulate and sickening."[96] The previous day Mavriks Vulfsons, Latvian deputy of the USSR Congress of People's Deputies, had called him asking to help the Balts. However, the liberal circle was unable to influence the president. The head of the presidential press service, Vitaly Ignatenko, and Chairman of the Supreme Soviet Yevgeny Primakov tried to convince Gorbachev "to go to Vilnius, lay a wreath and meet the people." Their attempts were unsuccessful.[97]

The chagrin of Gorbachev's closest liberal circle was profound. Alexander Yakovlev, according to his own memoirs, was hospitalized.[98] His colleagues who had worked for the implementation of Perestroika such as Primakov and Ignatenko tried to disassociate themselves from the president. Andrei Grachev, who had been appointed as head of the president's International Department, refused to accept the position.[99] In a letter (that in the end was never sent) to Gorbachev, Chernyaev wrote that he felt the "same painful shame" that he had felt under Brezhnev and Chernenko.[100]

The liberal City Soviet of Leningrad called on the president "to stop the use of military force in Lithuania, remove the USSR Minister of Defense and the Commander of the Baltic Military District from their posts, apologize to the legitimate government of Lithuania and the Lithuanian people, and immediately begin talks with the Lithuanian government."[101] The Presidium of the Moldovan and Ukrainian Supreme Soviets issued statements supporting Lithuania.[102] Patriarch Alexy II of Moscow, who was born in Estonia, declared that use of force in Lithuania was a major political mistake and a sin, while arguing that mistakes were made on "both sides."[103] On January 14, the liberal newspaper *Moskovskiye novosti* was printed with black borders and its editorial interpreted the use of force in the Baltics as a sign of the end of the democratization of the USSR: "We are mourning the victims in the Baltic republics, but the mourning is not for the dead alone. On the bloody Sunday of January 13 in Vilnius, democracy was shot down."[104]

On January 16, around eighty people whose names had been associated with the democratic forces of the Soviet Union made a joint statement expressing their outrage about the president's unwillingness to take a stance against Soviet military action in the Baltics. Among others, the document signatories were: journalist Alexander Bovin, economist Nikolai Shmelev, filmmakers Elem Klimov and Tengiz Abuladze, sociologist Tatyana Zaslavskaya, Moscow mayor Gavriil Popov, and stage and film director Mark Zakharov. The main message of the statement warned that Gorbachev had abandoned Perestroika:

All this time we have supported the president, sometimes closing our eyes on the inconsistencies of his policies. We hoped that he would support democracy, that he would preserve his loyalty to the presidential oath. However, the crime committed in Vilnius was denounced neither by the president nor by the Supreme Soviet of the USSR. After this, we can no longer deceive ourselves. The takeover has already begun. If it succeeds, then camps, repressions, fear, hunger, and destruction will once again await us. Furthermore, our country will again be cut off from the rest of humanity by an iron curtain and will become a nuclear scarecrow for the whole world.[105]

This disappointment and outrage were not limited to political elites. During the crisis Gorbachev received telegrams from concerned Soviet citizens not only in the Baltics but also in Armenia, Georgia, Russia, and Ukraine, condemning the use of force.[106] On January 14 in Riga more than 600,000 people staged a rally to express solidarity with Lithuania. The same day 6,000 people gathered in Leningrad; a crowd of 4,000 people paraded through the Red Square, shouting "Shame!," "Down with the Murderers!," and 'Down with the Nobel Prize Winner!"; tens of thousands also demonstrated in Lviv, Tbilisi, and Kishinev. On January 20, one of the most massive demonstrations by civil society in the USSR took place in Moscow.

The chairman of the Russian Supreme Soviet Boris Yeltsin flew to Tallinn to show his support for the Baltics on January 14. He called upon Russian soldiers deployed in the Baltic republics to disobey orders and not to shoot civilians. Yeltsin supported the leaders of the three Baltic countries in a joint statement inviting the secretary-general of the United Nations to convene an international conference to resolve the Baltic question.[107] On January 19, arguing that the events in Vilnius might be the beginning of a broader crackdown, Yeltsin called for Gorbachev's resignation.[108]

The use of force in the Baltic republics was at odds not only with domestic but also with international expectations of how the *new* Soviet Union should treat its own citizens. The apparent end of Perestroika was the central narrative in both the US and European media. The dramatic wording used by journalists in the United States, the UK, France, Germany, the Nordic countries, and Poland when writing about the situation in the Soviet Union conveyed the sense of an imminent crisis, and this shaped public opinion and put pressure on decision makers.[109] Roger Steel in the *Guardian* wrote that "the hopes for glasnost have collapsed"; *Le Monde* concluded that Perestroika had received its coup de grâce; and the *Wall Street Journal* heralded the "bloody end of Perestroika."[110] For the Swedish *Aftonbladet*, Perestroika had died in "the bloodbath of Vilnius," and reports in the *New York Times* likewise suggested that the new post–Cold War world order had been killed in the street of Vilnius.[111] A lead editorial in the *Times* of London discussed the eventual need for the West "to revive and redefine George Kennan's doctrine of containment."[112] Even in countries like Finland and Germany, where the governments were trying to downplay the seriousness of the Vilnius events, the press was using the strongest terms possible to describe a perceived Soviet return to backwardness and totalitarianism. A columnist for the conservative *Frankfurter Allgemeine Zeitung* argued that the USSR was turning back to Stalinism, and the main Finnish newspaper, *Helsingin Sanomat*, warned that Moscow was going "back to the Middle Ages."[113] The fact that force had been used against unarmed civilians was certainly troubling for the West. Since the eighteenth century, the renunciation of wanton violence against peaceful protests has been crucial for the self-perception of the enlightened modern state and society, as well as for its definition of sameness and otherness.[114] The consolidation of the human rights discourse and Cold War narratives reinforced this trend. The new "civilized" Soviet Union was expected to uphold human rights and norms and turn away from the violent practices of its totalitarian past. When force was used against unarmed civilians, German and Finnish journalists explicitly underlined Soviet otherness, qualifying Soviet actions in Vilnius as non-European.[115] Meanwhile in France, *Le Monde* published an opinion piece by Czesław Miłosz pointing at the "Europeanness" of the Baltic countries and insisting that "they have the right to expect that they are recognized as sovereign members of the community of European nations."[116]

At the same time, Western relationships with state violence have always been ambivalent. While wanton violence has mostly been seen as barbaric and uncivilized, controlled use of state violence often is being perceived as justified.[117] The criteria for defining just and unjust violence are of course subjective, arbitrary, and rooted in the subjective understanding of the outside watcher. The shootings in Vilnius and Riga were not the first time that force had been used against civilians under Gorbachev. A still unknown number of people were killed in Alma-Ata in December 1986, when Kazahs protested against the appointment of Gennady Kolbin as the republic's first secretary. The true number of victims is debated until this day, but at the time the official reports of two deaths did not raise any substantial reactions in the West. On April 9, 1989, a demonstration in Tbilisi was dispersed by force, leaving 20 dead and more than 100 injured. In January 1990 during the crackdown in Baku, at least 140 people were killed. In both cases domestic and international publics were cautious in their reactions and even supported Gorbachev. On the one hand, the circumstances on the ground in the Baltics and Caucasus did differ: local ethnic violence preceded the Soviet crackdown in Baku, and local communist authorities were actively involved in the use of force in Tbilisi.[118] On the other hand, both the domestic and international attitudes were also shaped by Western and Soviet perceptions of these regions. The Baltics and the Caucasus were important Soviet tourist destinations. However, a trip to the Baltics was perceived as an experience in the Soviet West whereas a trip to Caucasus was a journey to the orientalized Soviet exoticism.[119] In other words, societal responses to violence were also rooted in ethnic prejudices and Soviet/Russian orientalism: use of force in the "orderly" and "civilized" Western republics had stronger echoes than in the "wild" East. The belief that the Baltic countries were more "civilized" than other Soviet regions was shared at the highest levels of Soviet and republic leadership. During the dramatic January 12 Federation Council meeting, Uzbek leader Karimov opposed the use of force against Lithuania, arguing, "If the events in the Baltics were transferred to our region, there would be a huge number of victims. This is an indicator of the difference. There is a certain culture, political consciousness in the Baltics."[120] These Soviet ethnic hierarchies were not only internalized but also exported. For example, on March 20, 1990, Shevardnadze told Bush that his people (the Georgians) were "very different from the Baltic people" and that unlike Lithuanians they would "probably attack the garrisons."[121] At the same time, both Baltic and Caucasian as well as Central Asian nations for the Western publics were what Czechs and Slovaks had been to the British prime minister Neville Chamberlain in the 1930s "little known people quarrelling in faraway countries"; they lacked visibility on the international scene and their histories were little known in the West. Thus, Western perceptions of them were often constructed on the go from whatever snippets of news appeared in the media. The ongoing Nagorno-Karabakh conflict reinforced the image of the violent "East" and, in the eyes of many, legitimized the state violence in the region. The Baltic situation was better not only because of the non-recognition policy that distinguished Estonia, Latvia, and Lithuania from the other twelve republics, but also because until January 1991 the Baltic independence struggle had been entirely non-violent.[122] Furthermore, the Baltic geographical situation and history situated them in the liminal zone between the Soviet other and the European self, thus generating more compassion and visibility internationality.

EUROPEAN OUTRAGE

The strongest reaction to the Soviet use of force came from the countries that for historical reasons were able to emotionally identify with the Balts. A sense of sameness, rooted in a shared fear of the Soviet other, and a shared cultural heritage were the driving forces behind civil-society reactions in Eastern and Northern Europe.

Small demonstrations, from a few dozen to hundreds of people, took place in Sofia and Oslo. More extensive demonstrations were staged in the Czech and Slovak Federative Republic, where several thousand people marched in the streets of Prague on January 13 and 14.[123] In Finland, the Baltic question was particularly sensitive because of the discrepancy between public sympathy for the linguistically and culturally close Estonia, and the government's strategy of keeping a neutral position vis-à-vis "Soviet internal problems." In Helsinki between 300 and 400 people marched from the Soviet embassy to the president's palace, calling for President Koivisto to resign.[124] In Denmark, which over the previous months had emerged as one of the main advocates for Baltic independence, two of the country's biggest newspapers, the center-left *Politiken* and the conservative *Berlingske Tidende*, called their readers to a jointly organized protest in support of the Baltic states.[125] The event assembled between 15,000 and 20,000 people. The Swedish tabloid *Expressen* urged its readers to write to the Soviet president and ask him to give Sweden's neighbors "their national freedom back."[126] In Sweden, where there was a significant Baltic community, smaller demonstrations had already been held in Stockholm over several months, but after the shootings in Vilnius, up to 5,000 people assembled, including the Swedish, Latvian, and Estonian ministers of foreign affairs.[127] On the morning of January 13, the heads of Latvian and Estonian diplomacy; the deputy speaker of the Latvian Supreme Soviet; the leader of Tautas Fronte, Dainis Īvāns; and the deputy speaker of the Lithuanian Supreme Soviet, Bronius Kuzmickas, arrived in Sweden with authority to create governments in exile. They were received by the Swedish foreign minister, Sten Andersson, who offered financial help for their stay in the West during the crisis. After having held a meeting to coordinate their actions, the foreign ministers left for a tour around Europe while the deputy speakers made their way to the United States.[128]

Meanwhile, the Lithuanian minister Algirdas Saudargas headed to Poland, where he was warmly welcomed by the parliament. It was in Poland that the most massive demonstration outside the Soviet Union took place. As the German press noted, the Soviet embassy in Warsaw and its consulates in Gdańsk and Kraków were constantly besieged by protesters.[129] In the days after January 13, demonstrations involving 15,000 people took place in all the most prominent Polish cities, marking not only Polish support to the Baltic nations but also a step toward a historic reconciliation between Poland and Lithuania.[130] In an act of solidarity, a Polish parliamentary delegation joined their Lithuanian colleagues in the besieged parliament building and declared themselves ready to die by their side.[131] A group of Swedish lawmakers traveled to Vilnius, Riga, and Tallinn and met with their Baltic counterparts. The Icelandic minister of foreign affairs, Jón Baldvin Hannibalsson, as well as the Swedish deputy minister of foreign affairs, visited the Baltic capitals during "the weeks of barricades" and expressed their support for the Lithuanian, Latvian, and Estonian causes. The prime ministers of all the Scandinavian countries, separately and in joint statements, asked the Soviet Union to stop the use of force in the Baltics and warned that suspension of aid could be a possible outcome of the failure to do so. Sweden's prime minister went even further and announced that Soviet actions in the Baltics cast doubt on peace and détente in Europe in general.[132]

Beyond these countries, the Baltic cause was supported by Hungary, the Czech and Slovak Federative Republic, the UK, and Canada, all actively expressing their outrage at Soviet actions. Canada gave a very concrete warning, declaring that it was going to "reconsider all aspects of its relations with the USSR, including its credit line of nearly a billion dollars."[133] Prague called upon Hungary and Poland to take joint action in leaving the Warsaw Pact.[134] Immediately after the events in Vilnius, Foreign Secretary Douglas Hurd announced that the UK had to "consider the whole of our relationship with the USSR and how and under what conditions they can be preserved."[135] Speaking for the EC, the foreign minister of Luxembourg stated explicitly that further aid to Moscow was conditional on "the continuation of Perestroika and the democratization of the Soviet Union," implying that the use of force in Vilnius had put Soviet commitment to Perestroika reforms in question.[136]

In this context, not only the United States but also France and Germany initially appeared to be more cautious than their partners. The Baltic question was not crucial for Mitterrand, who was interested in good long-term relations with the USSR, and his main ally Kohl was trying to downplay the importance of the Vilnius events.[137] Soviet interests were the absolute priority for Bonn. Kohl both trusted Gorbachev and publicly insisted that the Soviet president had not personally ordered the attacks.[138] Nonetheless, a joint statement was issued by French foreign minister Dumas and German foreign minister Genscher condemning the "blow against democracy, law and the Charter of Paris for a New Europe."[139] However, according to the Soviet ambassador in Paris, Yuri Dubinin, Roland Dumas later tried to downplay the importance of the declaration: "He believed that it was necessary to call me to explain: 'We were not able not to do this.'"[140] Dubinin also recalls that on January 24, the French president told him that France had been trying to calm the reactions of some of its European partners. In January, however, even Mitterrand wrote a letter to Gorbachev, urging him to start a constructive dialogue with the Baltic republics.[141]

The increasingly harsh European reactions to the Baltic crisis put the White House in a complicated position. On the one hand, it had to preserve overall relations with USSR. But on the other hand, it risked losing its credibility and, as Condoleezza Rice put it, would "cede the high ground" to Congress.[142]

AMERICAN HESITATIONS

After the killings in Vilnius on January 13, French diplomats in Washington reported to Paris that the first US official reactions to the new Lithuanian crisis had been surprisingly strong and that a new and important, but as yet undefined, change had taken place in US-Soviet relations.[143] In reality, the US administration was maneuvering between condemning the Soviet actions in Vilnius and pursuing Soviet-US dialogue on the Gulf War. The task was complex. Initially the strategy was to assign the harshly worded conversations to Baker, while Bush maintained his usual friendly tone with Gorbachev. On January 15, the secretary of state called the new Soviet minister of foreign affairs, Alexander Bessmertnykh, and warned him that "our ability to pursue our new relationship depends on your government upholding the principles of Perestroika" and "if you do not get something done Sasha, this will be the end of the whole thing."[144] A few days later, White House Chief of Staff John Sununu announced that the summit initially scheduled for February might be canceled because of the events in the Baltics.[145] At the same time, when the Soviet president himself called the White House on January 18, Bush openly told him that he had "really empathized" with Gorbachev during the week.[146] The only "pressure" that the American president put on Gorbachev was the phrase: "We are so hopeful that the Baltic situation could be resolved peacefully."[147] The rest of the conversation was devoted to the Gulf, as the president was very reluctant to do anything that might be perceived as attempts to "punish" Gorbachev.[148]

After the January 13 shootings in Vilnius, the White House had to face direct pressure from Congress and the Baltic diaspora to take a stronger stand on the Baltic question. Meanwhile, the press was setting the tone for a harsh debate about the future of US-Soviet relations. The *Wall Street Journal* directly blamed Gorbachev for the killings in Lithuania, calling the Vilnius events "a peace laureate's putsch."[149] *USA Today* pointed out that the Soviet president had "veered dangerously off the path to democracy,"[150] and the *Los Angeles Daily News* announced the end of "Gorbymania" in the West.[151] On a similar track, the *New York Times* columnist William Safire argued that if necessary Gorbachev would be ready to "crush not only the independence movements in the captive nations but the reformers inside the republics"[152] Meanwhile, Mary McGrory asked in the columns of the *Washington Post*: "But does Gorbachev want to throw away his reputation, tarnish his Nobel Peace Prize, lose the respect and trust of the West by sending tanks against unarmed people? Can't he think of something else?"[153]

Since the unilateral Lithuanian proclamation of independence on March 11, 1990, essential differences had emerged between Congress and the White House in their attitudes regarding the Baltic question. While the administration thought that Baltic independence could be achieved only with full Soviet consent, an active and visible part of Congress considered that, if the Soviets did not respect Baltic rights to self-determination, Lithuanian independence could and should be imposed on them.

During the month of January, legislative initiatives regarding the Baltic situation flourished. Several pieces of legislation were proposed regarding possible sanctions against the USSR. Other initiatives concerned a possible discussion of the situation at international organizations such as the United Nations, condemnation of Soviet actions, support for Baltic independence, and providing humanitarian aid to Lithuania.[154] However, only two of the initiatives submitted to the US Congress after January 13 were approved: Senate Resolution 14 and House Resolution 40 calling the president to proceed to economic sanctions against the USSR.[155]

During January 1991 more than 200 speeches on the Baltic question were made in Congress, about three times more than in March 1990, when Lithuanian independence was proclaimed. In January 1991, as in spring 1990, among the most active members of Congress supporting the Baltic cause represented Illinois, California, Connecticut, and New York. Furthermore, Republican and Democrat anti-communists such as Jesse Helms (North Carolina), Robert Byrd (West Virginia), and Don Ritter (Pennsylvania) seized the opportunity to criticize Gorbachev. At the same time, dozens of members of Congress with no previous record of a strong commitment to Baltic independence rose to condemn the Soviet actions. Their activity can be explained both by genuine distress in the face of the use of force against civilians and as an attempt to gain visibility by discussing a sensitive issue that was making the international headlines.

Furthermore, many members of Congress were pushed to act on the Baltic issue not only by their Baltic American constituents but also by both conservative and human rights support groups. As President Bush later explained to the Soviet foreign minister, during the crisis he had received a letter from conservative activist and commentator Paul Weyrich warning the White House that he had "never seen the conservative movement more united than in the case of the Baltic States." In the same conversation, Bush insisted that: "Most of these people didn't believe in dialogue with the USSR, to begin with. But this is broader and deeper than I thought. . . . On the left, some in the human rights community, who wouldn't join with the right except on this are also excited."[156]

On January 22 National Security Advisor Brent Scowcroft met with the president of the American Latvian Association Valdis Pavlovskis, Asta Banionis from the Lithuanian American Committee, and Mari-Ann Rikken from the Estonian American National Committee.[157] The meeting was rather tense from the beginning, as the Baltic activists accused the administration of having turned a blind eye to the Baltics. In the middle of the conversation, President Bush suddenly joined the group to express his support for the Baltic cause. This, however, did not improve the atmosphere. The meeting ended with a clash between the president and the Baltic Americans, with Rikken accusing Bush of appeasement, and the president raising his voice and asking her "not to use this word."[158]

However, after the killings in Riga on January 20, the mood inside the Bush administration started to change. The reasons for these changes were summarized in a memorandum written by Condoleezza Rice to Brent Scowcroft. Rice called for a stronger US reaction regarding the situation in the Baltic, arguing that, first, the use of force meant that Perestroika was in danger and, second, that the White House risked losing its credibility by letting both the Europeans and Congress take a stronger stand on the Baltic question than the president did. According to Rice, the Baltic story was just a sign of a much deeper crisis in the Soviet Union: the central government's shift toward the right. Thus, the senior director of Soviet and East European affairs urged the administration to abandon the "any Gorbachev is better than the alternative" logic and to focus on keeping the Soviet president committed to Perestroika. "Our goal must be," she explained, "to use what leverage we have to persuade him not to commit suicide through a Faustian bargain with forces on the right."[159] For the first time, Rice invited the president to consider that there might be other alternatives to Gorbachev besides Yeltsin, namely the democratically minded men from his circle: Yakovlev, Shevardnadze, and Bakatin.

Though he was far from willing to consider such a drastic option, Bush accepted the need to increase pressures on the Soviet president. Concerned about both the stability of Gorbachev's power and Soviet positions regarding the Gulf Crisis, Bush preferred to try a personal approach before exercising public pressure. On January 23, 1991, he wrote a letter to Gorbachev. In this very carefully worded document, the administration tried to balance warnings about possible consequences of Soviet actions in the Baltics, with reassurances of the US desire to preserve good relations with the USSR in the long term. The president drew Gorbachev's attention to the restraint his administration had shown and the internal pressures he personally had faced, before proceeding to warn his Soviet counterpart that "unless positive steps toward peaceful resolutions of the conflict with the Baltic leaders are taken," the United States would proceed to economic sanctions, freezing export-import credit guarantees, commodity credit corporation guarantees, support for special associate status for the Soviet Union in the IMF and World Bank, and most of its technical assistance programs.[160]

On a more positive note, the president then assured Gorbachev that he did not underestimate the difficulties the Soviet president was facing, that "nobody wanted the disintegration of the USSR," and promised to do everything in his power to preserve US-Soviet relations in this "difficult period." At the end of the letter Bush, however, reminded Gorbachev that use of force was incompatible with Perestroika: "Mikhail, I cannot help but recall that you yourself told me that you personally could not sanction the use of force in the Baltic States because it would mean the end of Perestroika. . . . I urge you to turn back now to a course of negotiations and dialogue and to take concrete steps to prevent the further use of force and intimidation against the Baltic peoples and their elected leaders."[161]

The day before Bush's letter was sent to Moscow, Canada suspended its offer of technical assistance and a $150 million line of credit to the Soviet Union.[162] On January 23, the European Parliament blocked a $1 billion European Community food-aid package for the Soviet Union. The EC suspended a high-level meeting with Soviet trade officials scheduled for the same week and announced that it would temporarily halt the execution of a $550 million technical assistance agreement with Moscow, due to the latest violence in Latvia.[163]

By the end of January, the Soviets started to backtrack in the Baltic states, mostly because of internal factors: the outrage of civil society, the support of Yeltsin and other Russian democrats for the Baltic cause, and the unwillingness of the Soviet military to get involved in "internal policing."[164] At the same time, international reactions did have an impact on the Soviet leadership. If the Soviet forces behind the attacks had hoped the international community would be too focused on the Gulf War to pay substantial attention to what was happening in the Baltic republics, they were mistaken. On January 14 the Vilnius events dominated front-page headlines across Europe and North America.[165] According to *USA Today*, over the weekend of January 12–13, news broadcasts in the United States split their coverage fairly evenly between the upcoming Gulf War and the events in Lithuania.[166] After January 13, more than 160 foreign journalists were in Riga and Vilnius providing daily coverage for their news outlets.[167] This complicated the task of the Soviet hardliners: armed seizures of the government and parliament buildings in Vilnius, Riga, and Tallinn would require the shooting of civilians standing on the barricades, under the watchful eyes of the Western press.

In the period between January 13 and January 31, Gorbachev and the Soviet Foreign Service changed their communication strategy on the Baltic situation. Initially, to the great surprise of the Soviet president's diplomatic aide, it seemed that, during the first days after the shootings in Vilnius, Gorbachev had not noticed the extent of foreign indignation.[168] On January 13, Deputy Foreign Minister Anatoly Kovalev delivered a message from Gorbachev to the US, French, German, Italian, British and Finnish ambassadors stating that the situation in Lithuania was unstable because of the Lithuanian governmental crisis and unbearable provocation against the Soviet military and their families.[169] It also expressed the intent to work with the new National Salvation Committee and called the Lithuanian parliament and government the "old authorities." While the American ambassador noticed Kovalev's "trembling hands," the French ambassador perceived his explanations as a return to Soviet hypocrisy and a sign of Gorbachev's deep embarrassment.[170] Embarrassed or not, Gorbachev was avoiding addressing the fact that fourteen people had been killed the previous night and attempting to legitimize the National Salvation Committee.

After the shootings in Riga, Gorbachev's attitude started to shift. On January 21, Gorbachev met with the chairman of Estonian Supreme Soviet, and the day after with both Gorbunovs and the leader of Latvian communist hardliners. On January 22, Primakov, Ignatenko, and Chernyaev persuaded the president to let them prepare a speech for him to deliver before the Supreme Council. Even though Gorbachev did not read the text as written, he used it as a draft and publicly dissociated himself from the killings in the Baltics.[171] The same day in Paris, the minister counsellor from the Soviet embassy met with the deputy director of the European affairs division at the French Foreign Ministry and, "visibly embarrassed," according to the French diplomat, delivered a document that denied Moscow's responsibility in the shootings.[172]

On January 23, US Ambassador Jack Matlock handed Bush's letter to the Soviet president. In his response, Gorbachev claimed that the country was on the brink of civil war and that he had to do everything to avoid it— "even things that might be inexplicable."[173] On January 26 the new Soviet foreign minister Alexander Bessmertnykh arrived in Washington, having left the position of Soviet ambassador to the United States only two weeks earlier. Traveling to Moscow overnight from January 13 to 14, he had seen the first shocking pictures from Vilnius while changing planes in London and brought to Gorbachev British newspapers with photos of Soviet tanks crushing civilians in Vilnius.[174] When he returned in Washington with Gorbachev's answer to Bush's letter, Bessmertnykh immediately met with Secretary of State Baker. According to Talbott and Beschloss, this conversation convinced the Soviet foreign minister that the US administration needed tangible proof that the situation in the Baltics was improving, in order to resist calls at home for sanctions.[175]

Two days later, on January 28, Bessmertnykh was received by President Bush and conveyed to him Gorbachev's promise that Soviet forces deployed in the Baltics in early January were going to be withdrawn. The meeting between the US president and Soviet foreign minister lasted forty-five minutes and was entirely devoted to the Baltic countries. The words Bush used were much harsher than in his letter to Gorbachev. The Soviet minister divided his explanation on the Baltics into two parts, first speaking freely without notes and then reading parts of Gorbachev's letter. There was a significant difference between the minister's perception and Gorbachev's explanation. While both portrayed the violence as an unfortunate accident, Bessmertnykh acknowledged the Soviet share of responsibility, while the sections that the minster read from Gorbachev's letter directly blamed the "irresponsible Baltic leaders" who were "organizing harassment of national minorities."[176]

In response, Bush launched into a longer monologue, warning the Soviet Union that if progress was not made in the Baltics, US-Soviet relations "would be in peril," and stressed the pressures he was facing at home:

> We are doing our best to stay on track here, but I am becoming a minority at this point. . . . I am sure Gorbachev knows how strongly we feel about use of force. . . . We don't have much time. The sooner you find visible ways to show things are changing for the better. I am not making this up. I don't want you to underestimate the feeling. You must find a way to be flexible on the constitution. I do not want to see this relationship fall apart.[177]

Baker reinforced the president's argument, saying that he did not know how much time "we will have before we have to do something."[178] At this point, Bessmertnykh tried to change the topic and implicitly reminded the Americans that they needed Soviet cooperation for other matters, but Bush and Baker refused to play his game. When Bessmertnykh mentioned the Strategic Arms Reduction Treaty, Bush cut him short saying that he did not perceive START as a favor to anyone. The Soviet foreign minister then invoked the need to address the settlement in the Middle East and even made a historical reference to the year 1943 "when Germans were at Stalingrad." Baker avoided the Gulf War topic by expressing his hopes that withdrawal of forces from the Baltics would minimize the chances of any further "accident," and the president then concluded the conversation.

A few hours after the meeting, Bessmertnykh told journalists in Washington that some army units would be withdrawn to allow a resumption of talks between Moscow and the secessionist governments of Soviet Lithuania, Latvia, and Estonia. On January 31, a spokesman for Gorbachev confirmed that Soviet troops "have either left the region or are about to do so."[179]

The reasons for the Soviet retreat in the Baltics were twofold. First, Soviet internal dynamics pressured Gorbachev to distance himself from the forces that were carrying out the operation in the Baltics. At the same time, Western reactions, limited as they were, had an impact on Gorbachev. In a letter sent to Mitterrand, Gorbachev complained that Western reactions to the events in the Baltics reminded him of the "worst moments of the cold war."[180] The message shows that he had taken seriously Western threats to slow down economic cooperation and aid.[181] The Soviet president warned that such an action would be an "unforgivable historical mistake," and asked Mitterrand to use his influence on the international stage to help him.[182] In a similar letter sent to Finnish president Mauno Koivisto, Gorbachev blamed the international press for "one-sided, biased and outright irresponsible interpretation of the events" and accused Nordic countries (except Finland) of "encouraging disruptive forces in the USSR."[183]

According to Chernyaev, the Soviet president expressed a similar disappointment about Western attitudes while talking with the foreign ministers of Italy, Luxembourg, and the Netherlands[184] on February 16: "They came to preach to Gorbachev about democracy and the Charter of Paris. But they got a counter-attack: are they not ashamed for believing that Gorbachev betrayed Perestroika?!"[185]

As Andrei Grachev noted, in Gorbachev's perception, foreign policy and internal politics were two separate domains in which different kinds of action could be pursued.[186] In other words, Gorbachev believed that, as long as his foreign policy stayed the way it had been during recent years, nobody would question his commitment to Perestroika. This assumption turned out to be wrong—his shift in domestic policies made the West anxious about the overall future of the reform movement.

By early February 1991, additional Soviet troops had left the Baltic countries. The elected Lithuanian, Latvian, and Estonian governments continued their work, and the citizens left the barricades. Another Baltic crisis was over, though without resolution to the Baltic question. However, unlike spring 1990, the January 1991 events ended with a relative victory for the Balts: they had been able to hold their ground during the standoff with Soviet forces, and the West had started to doubt Gorbachev.

CHAPTER 5

The Rise of the Republics, the Fall of the Center

The Baltic Exception and the Collapse of the USSR

> We recognized the integrity of the Soviet Union within certain boundaries in 1933, and we do not want to encourage its breakup. Sooner or later, we will have to say it.
> —Brent Scowcroft to President Bush, February 1991

In early August 1991, Ojārs Kalniņš, information coordinator at the Latvian legation in Washington, left for vacation and jokingly asked his colleague at the foreign ministry in Riga "not to liberate Latvia" while he was on holiday.[1] A little more than a month later Latvia, as well as Estonia and Lithuania, were free and internationally recognized states. One of the first countries to recognize the restoration of Baltic independence was Denmark. Years later, Estonian foreign minister Lennart Meri remembered that as he and his Latvian and Lithuanian counterparts were entering the Danish royal palace to meet Queen Margrethe II, he was moved to tears by the suddenness of the change in the fortune of his country.[2] The change was indeed sudden and monumental: Soviet rule in the Baltic states that had lasted almost fifty years was over in ten days. The international community that had cautioned Baltic states to slow down their drive for independence rushed to grant them recognition.

The August putsch has often been seen as some sort of *deus ex machina*, which resolved the Baltic problem by dismantling the USSR. Indeed, the failed coup accelerated the already ongoing power diffusion in the USSR.

Politics of Uncertainty. Una Bergmane, Oxford University Press. © Oxford University Press 2023.
DOI: 10.1093/oso/9780197578346.003.0006

It empowered the republics and Baltic ally Boris Yeltsin and weakened the center institutions and Mikhail Gorbachev.

However, while the failed coup deeply shook the USSR, it did not destroy it. Of all twelve Soviet republics that had declared independence, only Lithuania, Latvia, and Estonia were recognized by the international community immediately after the putsch. In late August, political rivals Mikhail Gorbachev and Boris Yeltsin joined forces to preserve the Union, and at least ten of the Soviet republics seemed willing to go along with these efforts.[3]

This chapter analyzes the reasons and circumstances that led the international community, Yeltsin, and Gorbachev to recognize Baltic independence three months before the collapse of the USSR, and how this recognition impacted the already loosening union.

SOVIET POWER STRUGGLES AND AMERICAN UNCERTAINTY

After the bloodshed in Vilnius and Riga in January 1991, it had become clear to Moscow that imposing central will on the rebellious Soviet republics would require massive use of force.[4] This was not a valid option for Mikhail Gorbachev, not only because of his personal reluctance toward violence but also because the January crisis had shown that the use of force would be very costly in terms of international financial and moral support. At the same time, the Soviet economy was in serious difficulty and the country was suffering from an acute crisis of multiple sovereignties: Baltic governments organized referendums on independence, Yeltsin's influence in the USSR was quickly rising, and other Soviet republics—notably Georgia, Armenia, and Moldova, and even Ukraine—had become more and more defiant toward the central authorities.

The White House followed these developments with deep concern. As the economic and political crisis in the USSR deepened, US agencies had produced one concerning report after another envisaging possible scenarios of the Soviet future such as civil war, riots by Soviet soldiers in East Germany, consumer riots in the USSR, large-scale ethnic violence, anarchy, political crackdown, military crackdown, nuclear accidents, loss of control over atomic weapons, return to authoritarianism, Gorbachev's removal by conservatives, Gorbachev's removal by liberals, or Gorbachev's death.[5] However, the possibility of some sort of Soviet disaster in the future weighed less on American decision makers than did the existing ambiguity and uncertainty. The multitude of actors, the changing power dynamics, Gorbachev's swings between the left and the right, the transformation of center-periphery relations, the emergence of more and more powerful republics, reports of sporadic violence: all these factors made the Soviet situation confusing, difficult to rationalize, and hard to deal with. As Brent Scowcroft pointed out in February: "Were the conflict in the Soviet Union to result in an outright victory of democratic forces or full-scale and successful repression by reactionaries, we would at least know the kind of Soviet Union with which we were dealing."[6] Yet this definite victory of one Soviet faction over another did not seem to be in sight. In the same report, the national security advisor argued, that despite the pre-revolutionary state of the Soviet Union, the resolution of the Soviet future might not be quick, but rather "slow and messy," leaving the USSR in a long period of chaos and deprivation. He concluded that in this context it was going to be a monumental task for the United States to handle US-Soviet relations successfully.[7]

Two of the main challenges the White House had to face when shaping policy toward the Soviet Union were the emergence of more and more powerful republics and the bitter rivalry between Boris Yeltsin and Mikhail Gorbachev.

Starting from at least August 1990, various US officials or agencies advised the president to intensify American contacts with Soviet actors other than Gorbachev. In August 1990, the US ambassador in Moscow had sent a long telegram urging Washington to anticipate general Soviet disintegration and to establish a permanent presence in the Soviet republics.[8] At the time, the NSC had judged the ambassador's views alarmist but agreed that Gorbachev's days might be numbered and that the United States should cautiously establish contacts with the republics.[9] However, in January 1991 after the shooting in Vilnius and Riga, NSC Condoleezza Rice urged her superiors to envisage supporting potential Gorbachev alternatives, such as Bakatin or Shevardnadze.[10] In spring 1991, both Matlock and the CIA tried to push the Bush administration to strengthen its links with Boris Yeltsin.[11] Meanwhile, Scowcroft was skeptical about more profound engagement with Yeltsin or Soviet reformers in general. In his view, Washington had to stay out of Soviet internal power struggles. The window of opportunity to advance the Soviet-US agenda was closing and American efforts had to be focused on arms negotiations.[12]

In sum, in spring 1991 George Bush was in a problematic situation where the changing power dynamics in the USSR pushed him toward extending contacts with additional Soviet actors, but the logic of international relations made him unwilling to undermine the man in charge of centralized Soviet foreign policy. In June 1991, a week after being elected the president of RSFSR, Yeltsin was received by Bush at the White House and the general mood of the meeting was reserved but cordial. At the very beginning of their conversation Bush made it clear to Yeltsin that the US priority was the Soviet, not the Russian, president. "I am the US President, and Gorbachev is the USSR President, and so we will deal with each other," the president stated: "We will not do anything to undermine him."[13] During the conversation, Yeltsin was eager to highlight the differences between him and Gorbachev, insisting on his willingness "to let the Baltic states go." "But it is clear that Georgia and the three Baltic republics will leave the Union," he stated, "It is my firm opinion that it would not be worth using force to keep them in the Union. They are entitled to withdraw and not be chained to the Union."[14] Bush expressed his admiration for this stand, yet the next day during a phone conversation with Gorbachev he told the Soviet president "we made it very clear that you are our man."[15]

The Baltic question was another element that complicated the Bush administration's attempts to navigate Soviet power struggles without harming US-Soviet relations. If any, even limited, efforts were to be made to extend US relations with other Soviet actors, Gorbachev had to be reassured that this was not done to undermine him or to destroy the Soviet Union. However, it was hard to reassure the Soviet president while supporting the independence of Estonia, Latvia, and Lithuania, which in Gorbachev's eyes were Soviet republics just like the others. In his report Scowcroft argued that the United States should make a clear distinction between the Baltic states and other Soviet republics by pointing out that Washington recognized the USSR with its 1933 borders—and these did not include the Baltic states. "We do not want to encourage its breakup," he concluded.[16] Yet this approach was bound to upset other Soviet republics and their American diasporas. When on March 17, 1991, James Baker stated this exact idea on ABC's "This Week with David Brinkley," the Ukrainian Congress Committee of America sent an angry letter to the White House insisting that their independence struggle was not less legitimate than that of the Baltic states.[17]

In reality, there was an ever-deepening difference between the international status of the Baltic countries and that of other Soviet republics, which became particularly visible after the January bloodshed.

ALL SHORT OF INDEPENDENCE: THE BALTIC SITUATION IN SPRING 1991

Following the failed Soviet crackdown in the Baltic in spring 1991, several members of the international community started to strengthen their bilateral relations with Estonia, Latvia, and Lithuania. After his trip to Vilnius, Riga, and Tallinn, that took place at the time of the Soviet attack on the Latvian Interior Ministry, Icelandic foreign minister Jón Baldvin Hannibalsson promised to establish diplomatic relations "as soon as possible."[18] His stand was supported by Iceland's parliament, which, in an ambiguous move, recognized Lithuanian independence in February 1991 but postponed the establishment of diplomatic relations.[19] The USSR responded by recalling its ambassador from Reykjavík.[20] Between February and March 1991, Denmark concluded cooperation treaties with the three Baltic countries.[21] The Soviet side summoned the Danish ambassador and explained that these actions damaged Soviet-Danish relations.[22] Germany also seemed to soften its "Gorbachev first" policy, as, on January 29, Genscher promised Meri that the Baltic states would be allowed to participate in the CSCE meeting scheduled for June in Berlin.[23] Meanwhile, in France, Latvian and Lithuanian leaders who visited Paris in May and June respectively were received with red carpets and guards of honor like heads of recognized states.[24] These symbolic gestures were at the same time political statements that distinguished Baltic republics from the rest of the Union and increased Baltic visibility on the international stage.

The aftermath of the Vilnius bloodshed was also marked by an intensification of parliamentary diplomacy among the Baltic neighbors: groups of Swedish, Danish, Dutch, French, and Polish legislators, led by the speakers of their parliaments, arrived in Vilnius, Riga, and Tallinn in January and February.[25] Members of the US Helsinki Commission traveled to the Baltic countries in February, and another delegation arrived in April.[26] At the same time the United States saw yet another increase in the number of legislative initiatives related to the Baltic states: calling for diplomatic recognition of the Baltic states, opening of US trade offices or cultural centers in the Baltic capitals, an increase of US humanitarian aid to the Baltic countries, the withdrawal of trade benefits from the USSR, and appointment of a special US envoy to facilitate Baltic-Soviet negotiations.[27]

After January 1991, the US diplomatic presence in the Baltic countries became almost constant, as at least one diplomat from the consulate in Leningrad was constantly dispatched to one of the Baltic capitals.[28] However, the only country with an official diplomatic representation in the Baltic states was Sweden, which in March 1991 opened consulates in Riga and Tallinn.[29] Sweden was one of the few countries that recognized the annexation of the Baltic states after the Second World War, so the consulate in Riga was a consulate in the Latvian SSR, not in the Republic of Latvia. For countries that practiced the non-recognition policy, the situation was much more complicated, as they had to find a formula that would recognize neither the annexation nor the re-establishment of independence. Denmark, Norway, and Sweden had helped the Balts to establish their "information bureaus" in Copenhagen, Oslo, and Stockholm, and Denmark had opened its own cultural center in Riga in August 1990.[30]

The United States had initially been very cautious regarding the institutionalization of its presence in the Baltic countries, by opening Baltic representations, but after the January attacks its attitude gradually changed, and it started to look for a possibility to deepen relations with the Baltic countries.[31] On March 15, 1991, Secretary of State Baker met with the Soviet foreign minister, Bessmertnykh, and discussed the possible creation of a US office in Riga. It was planned that, in the case of Soviet acceptance of the project, it would be officially announced that the creation of the office would mean neither recognition nor a deviation from the non-recognition policy.[32] The same day he also met with Gorbachev and, according to the Soviet president, used carefully chosen words to express US concerns about developments in the USSR: "Recently I was talking with President Bush, and we both came to the conclusion that your place in history is assured if you don't change course. All your enormous achievements will go down in history if you do not turn back. This is one of the main reasons why we don't believe there to be that kind of turnabout."[33] However, according to Beschloss and Talbott, Baker was much more direct and spoke about the "chilling effect" that "recent developments" in the USSR were having on Soviet-US relations.[34] The transcript of the conversation published in the collected works of Mikhail Gorbachev shows that Baker did try to push Gorbachev toward acceptance of the Baltic independence, arguing that the USSR would be better off with three neutral little Finlands at its borders than "what you have now," that is, three defiant republics.[35]

Another question that the United States discussed with the Balts after the January crackdown was that of economic aid no longer going through Moscow but arriving directly in the Baltic countries. On February 6, 1991, the White House announced that it would send medical aid directly to the Baltic states and that the US Agency for International Development (AID) would pay for the shipment of medical supplies donated by private American sources. On February 27, 1991, the first such shipment of medical supplies was sent to the "Baltics and the victims of the Chernobyl nuclear accident in Ukraine."[36] The Soviet conservative newspaper *Pravda* saw this move as a dangerous shift in US-Soviet relations, explaining that "Washington has crossed a kind of political Rubicon beyond which a new complication in Soviet-American relations can be expected without doubt."[37]

On April 25, Curtis Kamman, deputy assistant secretary for Europe, spoke at the European Affairs Subcommittee of the Senate Foreign

Relations Committee about the possibility of giving financial aid directly to the Baltic republics as part of the designated assistance to Eastern Europe, rather than to the USSR. Ojārs Kalniņš wrote to his government in Riga that in his view the United States was starting "to distinguish more and more the Baltic states from the USSR."[38]

Yet the American engagement with the Baltic states had its limits. When Lithuanian acting president Landsbergis, as well as the Estonian and Latvian prime ministers, came to Washington in May to attend the hearings of the Congress Helsinki Commission and requested a meeting with the US president, National Security Council staffer Nicholas Burns advised Brent Scowcroft to handle the meeting carefully in order to "avoid the impression that the US was taking a more active role in the resolution of the Baltic problem."[39]

While the official transcript of the Baltic meeting with Bush can't be found in the George Bush Presidential library, the account given by Estonian prime minister Savisaar shows that the Americans actually attempted to push the Baltic countries on a track that would be acceptable for Gorbachev, just as in March when they had tried to make Baltic independence appealing to Gorbachev by projecting the image on "three little Finlands." At first Bush carefully inquired about the state of negotiations with the USSR and, when his guests responded that the talks were not producing any meaningful results, Baker suggested that they consider following the Soviet secession law.[40] This of course was unacceptable for the Estonians, Latvians, and Lithuanians, who claimed not to be bound by the Soviet constitution. After the meeting with President Bush, the three Baltic leaders made a joint statement in which they praised Icelandic and Danish support, called the international community to treat them as independent states, and asked for the establishment or re-establishment of diplomatic relations.[41]

By spring 1991, it seemed that Estonia, Latvia, and Lithuania had reached the limits of what was possible in their engagement with the international community. Their officials were received at the highest level in Western capitals; the killing of their citizens by the Soviet forces had provoked international outrage; they had managed to gain international visibility; and nobody in the West contested that in principle their claims for independence were legitimate. Yet, in practice, none of these seemed to bring to the Baltic countries what they were actually looking for—international recognition or at least the active involvement of the international community in their negotiations with the Soviet Union. Since 1989, the Estonian, Latvian, and Lithuanian leadership had looked for an international solution to their situation.[42] However, in the spring of 1991 it occurred to them that the decisive support for their independence actually could come from inside the Soviet Union.

THE BALTIC ALLIANCE WITH BORIS YELTSIN

During the spring and summer 1991, several developments in the USSR worked in favor of the Baltic countries. The first and most important one was the steadily growing influence of Boris Yeltsin.

Baltic links with Russian democratic circles dated back to 1989, when Baltic deputies worked side by side with Russian representatives at the Soviet Congress of People's Deputies, sharing the goal of increasing the republics' autonomy from the center and introducing elements of a market economy in the Soviet system. While some leading Russian Democrats such as Yelena Bonner and Lev Ponomaryov supported Baltic independence because they supported the breakup of USSR, Yeltsin saw the Baltic case as an exception in the Soviet context.[43] In early 1991, Yeltsin was not looking for an independent Russia or for the possibility of destroying the USSR, but he accepted the possible independence of the Baltic states, which in his opinion did not mean the end of the Union between the other Soviet republics.

The United States' reserved attitude toward the Russian leader was one of the reasons for his rapprochement with the Baltic states. While Yeltsin himself was often perceived internationally merely as Gorbachev's rival, his alliance with the Baltic republics was useful in strengthening his international prestige and his access to world leaders. For example, in the summer of 1990, when the Latvian prime minister Godmanis visited Washington, Yeltsin asked him to tell James Baker that Russia would soon be a "sovereign state" and would like to establish direct contact with the US government.[44]

After the crisis in the spring, Boris Yeltsin met with his Baltic counterparts Vytautas Landsbergis, Anatolijs Gorbunovs, and Arnold Rüütel in the Latvian sea resort of Jurmala on July 27, 1990. The meeting resulted in the decision to start preparations for bilateral interstate treaties between each of the three Baltic republics and the Russian Federation. This move can be seen not only as Yeltsin's attempt to weaken Gorbachev's position or to obtain leverage over him, but also as an effort to improve his own image, by showing himself more ready to redefine the relations between the center and the republics than the Soviet president.[45] Yeltsin had stood by the Baltic countries and openly criticized the Soviet president in January and signed cooperation treaties with Estonia and

Latvia, in which the parties recognized each other as sovereign subjects of international law.[46]

While the Balts, with Yeltsin's support and Western backing, had endured the "week of barricades," Yeltsin achieved a significant victory over the conservatives and over Gorbachev himself. In March 1991, the Communist Party of the Russian SFSR announced that it would seek the removal of Yeltsin from the position of chairman of the Supreme Soviet of the RSFSR. Soviet prime minister Valentin Pavlov backed this attempt by instructing the Soviet government to ban all demonstrations in Moscow between March 26 and April 16. However, on March 28, between 120,000 and 150,000 people marched in the streets of the Soviet capital in support of Yeltsin, openly defying the central government.[47] The CP attempts to remove him from office failed, and the Supreme Soviet of the USSR overruled the governmental decree banning the demonstrations.

As the standoff between Russian and Soviet presidents reached its peak, the Balts threw their full support behind Yeltsin. Deeply disappointed by Gorbachev's attitude toward the killings in Vilnius and Riga, the Baltic leaders pinned their hopes on his rival. When in May 1991, a member of the US Congress asked Vytautas Landsbergis: "How can the US help you?" he answered: "Give your support to Yeltsin."[48] On July 29, 1991, Boris Yeltsin took a step further in his support for Baltic independence by concluding a treaty with Lithuania that was more detailed than the Estonian and Latvian treaties and balanced on the edge of recognition of independence and admitted the illegality of 1940 annexation.[49]

While Yeltsin moved ever closer to a recognition of Baltic independence, the legitimacy of Estonian, Latvian, and Lithuanian claims was reinforced by independence referendums that took place in February and March 1991.

REFERENDUMS OF SPRING 1991

The question of possible referendums in the Baltic states had been raised back in spring 1990 by the US administration during its contacts with both the Lithuanian and the Soviet leadership.[50] At the time this idea, strongly backed by Condoleezza Rice, deeply distressed the Latvian American diaspora community, since in their view a referendum in Lithuania would lead to a referendum in Latvia, where it was feared that the results could be disastrous for the independence project given the changed demographics there.[51] In Lithuania, the ethnic situation was more homogeneous, with almost 80 percent of ethnic Lithuanians in 1989. However, Vilnius was also unwilling to conduct a referendum, stating that the declaration of independence of March 11 was final and needed no further approval. At the same time, in late November Gorbachev proposed holding a referendum on the maintenance of the renewed Union. This move put the Baltic countries in a complicated position: unwilling to sign the Union Treaty, they were also reluctant to participate in the referendum that was supposed to endorse it and consequently risked appearing reluctant to give a voice to their own populations.

On January 16, amid the January crisis and the same day that the USSR Supreme Soviet scheduled the Soviet referendum for March 18, the Lithuanian parliament voted to hold their referendum, separate from the USSR. The poll took place on February 9 and resulted in an overwhelming victory for the independence project: 90.5 percent of voters voted for it, with a turnout of 84.4 percent. The referendum, which was observed by lawmakers from Czechoslovakia and Poland as well as a delegation from CSCE, was recognized as legitimate by the international community and received a warm response from northern Europe and the former Eastern bloc. Václav Havel called the referendum results the "expression of the authentic will of the Lithuanian nation."[52] A poll conducted in Denmark showed that after the referendum, 69 percent of Danes wanted to see the establishment of diplomatic relations with Lithuania.[53] The Polish press celebrated the Lithuanian choice and was already planning future relations between Poland and independent Lithuania.[54]

In this situation, the Estonian and Latvian governments were left with little choice and scheduled their own referendums for March 3. As Gorbunovs told Latvian Supreme Soviet on January 23, the referendum was not only a tool for democratic legitimization of the independence project but also a test for society's capacity to rally around a common vision of the future. Both Latvian and Estonian referendums were unofficially monitored by European and American observers. American diplomats from Leningrad were present in Riga and Tallinn, as well as staff members of the Congress Helsinki Commission.[55]

The results of the Estonian and Latvian referendums surprised both Gorbachev and the West, as well as the Balts themselves.[56] In Estonia, 77.8 percent voted for independence, with a turnout of 82.8 percent. In Latvia, 73.7 percent were in favor of independence, with a participation rate of 87.6 percent. Such results would not have been possible without the vote of the Russian-speaking population. The question of the rights of the Russian minority in the Baltic countries would return to the international agenda during the 1990s with a new force, but in 1991, as one French official pointed out, "the argument lost its validity in the face of an undeniable reality—most of the Baltic Russians supported Baltic independence."[57]

The reasons for this support have been underexamined. The main driver of the Baltic independence movements certainly was Estonian, Latvian, and Lithuanian nationalism rooted in an ethno-cultural and not civic perception of the nation. As political scientist Ammon Cheskin has noted when analyzing the Latvian case, from the viewpoint of Tautas Fronte, ethnic Latvians were the core nation of Latvia, while other ethnic groups were representatives of their own ethnicities, who were supposed to support the independence project and democratization, without ever being assimilated in to the core nation.[58] At the same time, the independence project dealt with questions that were important to all inhabitants of the Baltic states, such as the economy, the rule of law, democracy, and the environment and carried a promise of a European/Western future that went beyond the national framework.[59] While calls for restrictive citizenships laws coming from Latvian and Estonian right-wing movements worried the Soviet-era Russian-speaking migrants, the much more moderate discourse of Rahvarinne and Tautas Fronte eventually made the independence project acceptable. Furthermore, the first part of 1991 saw a general rise of intense criticism and rejection of the Soviet state by Russians living in the Russian SFSR. In this period, Russians were becoming alienated from the state with which in the past they had identified.[60] This process had an impact also on Russians living in the Baltic countries, making them less likely to oppose Estonian and Latvian independence.

While the referendums in the Baltic countries significantly contributed to the legitimacy of Baltic claims for independence, the results of all the other Union referendums reinforced Gorbachev's position. The referendum, which officially took place on March 17 in all Soviet republics except the Baltic states, Armenia, Georgia, and Moldova, turned out to be very successful for Gorbachev's plans to maintain a reformed Union. Over all, 80 percent of Soviet citizens living in the participating republics voted in the referendums and 76 percent answered positively when asked: "Do you consider necessary the preservation of the Union of Soviet Socialist Republics as a renewed federation of equal sovereign republics in which the rights and freedom of an individual of any nationality will be fully guaranteed?"[61]

The highest support (97.9%) came from the Turkmen SSR, which also had the highest turnout in the USSR (97.7%), while relatively the most reluctant was the Ukrainian SSR and the Russian SFR, with around 30 percent voting against the preservation of the Union.[62] At the same time, in Russia voters backed the creation of the post of president in the republic. This was an important victory for Yeltsin, who would be elected president of the RSFSR on June 12, 1991.

Initially, it seemed that the positive outcome of the all-Union referendum would allow Gorbachev to ease his stand on the Baltic question. On April 18, the Soviet president stated that only the republics that had taken part in the March 17 referendum would participate in meetings on the new Union Treaty scheduled for April 23. The Estonian Foreign Ministry immediately greeted the statement as an acceptance of Baltic refusal to participate in any debates on a common Soviet future.[63] During the gathering it was announced that nine Soviet republics and the central authorities would start negotiating the draft of the Union Treaty. The agreement between the center and the nine governments stated that participation in negotiations was voluntary, implicitly admitting that Baltic countries, Georgia, Moldova, and Armenia could not be part of them. At the same time, it was indicated that all republics refusing to sign the treaty would have to pay world market prices for goods imported from signatory republics.

Even though the 9 + 1 agreement of April 23 seemed to send a positive message for the Baltic countries, the US diplomat who in early May visited Tallinn, Riga, and Vilnius reported that the mood there was rather grim. "All said they had been unable to find out what the document meant," he wrote to Washington, "and all feared that it might somehow be used against them."[64] At the same time, Baltic officials found that there were grounds for hope and declared themselves to be ready to pay for goods imported from other Soviet republics at the same price that any foreign country would pay. As Estonian government official Endel Lippmaa put it: "Of course we want to think that this is the de facto recognition of our right to independence, but we need more concrete signs from Moscow over time. And certainly, we are also ready to trade in hard currency if that is absolutely necessary."[65] As the nine Soviet republics started negotiations with the center, parallel talks were carried out with the Baltic republics.

A NEW ROUND OF FAILED NEGOTIATIONS

After the January events, Gorbachev kept the promises made to his CSCE partner states and appointed the USSR deputy prime minister to lead a negotiating team with the Baltic states. The Baltic countries prepared their own delegations. The head of the Estonians was Ülo Nugis, speaker of the parliament; the Latvian team was led by the deputy prime minister, Ilmārs Bišers; and the Lithuanian one by Landsbergis himself. The United States endorsed the negotiation process, and James Baker urged the Baltic countries to start the discussions with the USSR without any preconditions or definitions of independence as their ultimate goal.[66] At the same time, other US officials such as Scowcroft were rather pessimistic regarding the Soviet aims. At the end of March, Scowcroft wrote to the president that even if there were reasons for hope, Gorbachev in his view was still committed to obtaining Baltic signatures on the Union Treaty.[67] Balts were equally skeptical about the possible outcome of the talks. On May 17, a US diplomat from the consulate in Leningrad reported to Washington that the Baltic leaders were pessimistic about their negotiations with Moscow but more pragmatic "than reported previously."[68] Baltic pragmatism arose from the fear that refusal to negotiate might be badly perceived in the West. In other words, as the CIA rightly concluded, the Baltic leaders pursued the negotiations "in order to avoid being portrayed as intransigent and testing Gorbachev's professed desire for a political solution."[69]

According to the information released by the Latvian government, the first round of talks devoted to economic issues was concluded on June 7, and the next one, concerning the "status" of the Latvian Republic and the rights and freedoms of citizens living in Latvia, was to be held in Moscow on July 4 and 5.[70] As member of National Security Council Nick Burns noted to his colleague Ed Hewett, the situation in the Latvian case looked hopeful, whereas there was no progress in Estonian and Lithuanian talks with the USSR.[71] However, in July it appeared that the Soviet side was not willing to go further with Latvia either, as the Soviet delegations kept rescheduling the meetings.[72] By late July, Hewett wrote to Scowcroft that even though some progress had been made in the talks between the Baltic republics and the center, the Baltic countries were "obviously dealing with a very difficult negotiating partner" and indicated that the Soviets and the Balts were still "at odds" regarding the main aims of the negotiations.[73] Swedish diplomat Lars Peter Fredén later mentioned in his memoirs that during the summer of 1991 it was evident that "the negotiations between the Baltic States and the Soviet Union had come to a dead-end, and that Moscow was not interested in finalizing them with a meaningful result."[74]

In other words, that summer nobody was sure if the USSR was seriously considering allowing Estonia, Latvia, and Lithuania to definitely leave the Union. On July 13, the Russian newspaper *Izvestia* published an appeal from the deputies of the Supreme Soviet of the USSR to the deputies of the Supreme Soviets of Armenia, Georgia, Latvia, Lithuania, Moldova, and Estonia, urging them to consider possibly signing of the Union Treaty.[75] According to a CIA report, the situation was still very unstable. From the perspective of the CIA analysts, the Balts were able to pull out of the negotiations if they became "convinced that Gorbachev is not serious about talks" or if he used "pressure tactics." At the same it was indicated that Gorbachev might seriously consider "ousting republic governments by force" if the Balts continued to refuse to respect the secession law.[76]

Indeed, limited violence and tactics of intimidation returned to the Baltics in the late spring of 1991. Starting in May 1991, the Riga OMON group, acting under the orders of Interior Minister Pugo, attacked and harassed Baltic border guards.[77] On June 4, Soviet prosecutor general Nikolai Trubin presented a report on the January events in Vilnius that denied any responsibility on part of the Soviet military or law enforcement authorities. The same day, Soviet soldiers entered Vilnius in armed vehicles, which led several hundreds of peoples to gather around the parliament building to protect it against an eventual attack. On June 27, Lithuanian telecommunication facilities were taken by OMON. On July 31, seven Lithuanian border guards were killed "execution-style" at the Medininkai customs post on the Lithuanian-Byelorussian border by Riga OMON group. Although Interior Minister Boris Pugo stated that he did not have control over OMON forces, the previous interior minister Bakatin argued that Pugo had full and exclusive control over OMON.[78]

Against this backdrop, the Baltic states started to look again for outside help. By the end of July, Chairman of the Estonian Supreme Soviet Rüütel told the US consul in Leningrad that Estonian talks with Moscow were going nowhere, and thus Estonians would welcome stronger US pressure on the USSR.[79] Already after the June 3 events, US Ambassador in Moscow Jack Matlock had warned the White House that "there was a real danger of bloodshed" in the Baltics and urged Bush to send another letter to Gorbachev.[80] In the meantime, the White House was preoccupied with in the challenging task of preparing the upcoming Moscow summit, scheduled for late July.

THE LAST SUMMIT

In July 1991, George Bush traveled to the Soviet Union to meet Mikhail Gorbachev. The trip, which turned to be the last visit of an American president to the Soviet Union, reflected all the ambiguities and difficulties of the American effort to navigate the muddy waters of the Soviet internal situation while advancing on the Soviet-American international agenda. A key milestone was reached by signing the START treaty, thus getting one more thing before the perceived window of opportunity closed. In Kyiv, Bush upset Union republics by delivering a speech in support for the integrity of the USSR. In Moscow he insisted that the United States wanted to see a strong and economically powerful Soviet Union, yet no economic aid was given to the USSR. When it came to the Baltic question the president affirmed once again his commitment to Estonian, Latvian, and Lithuanian independence, while back in Washington the White House was pushing through the Congress a Soviet-American trade treaty that was upsetting for the Baltic countries for various reasons.

The summit took place in the context of rising American concerns about the stability of Gorbachev's power. Already, during Yeltsin's visit to Washington on June 20, rumors that circulated in Moscow had reached the White House. That day the democratically minded major of Moscow, Gavriil Popov, informed the US ambassador that Prime Minister Pavlov, KGB Chief Kryuchkov, and Defense Minister Yazov were organizing a coup against Gorbachev. The White House decided to warn the Soviet leadership. Bush talked with Yeltsin, and Matlock met with Gorbachev. While both Yeltsin and Gorbachev reassured the Americans that the rumors about the coup were unfounded, the incident increased Bush's concern about Gorbachev's future.

At the same time, the US willingness to help the USSR had its limits. In March 1991, Gorbachev had asked for $1.5 billion in grain credits. In his memoirs, Bush mentions that he was reluctant to provide this assistance because of the situation in the Baltics, problems related to the Strategic Arms Reduction and the Conventional Armed Forces in Europe treaties, and lack of necessary reforms in the Soviet economy. Even if by early May the White House finally agreed to proceed with the grain credits, Bush was not willing to commit the country to large-scale financial assistance.[81]

Economic aid to USSR was discussed at the G7 meeting in London on July 16–17. While France and Germany strongly supported Soviet demands, the other partners, including the United States, were more reluctant. The summit ended without any concrete achievements for Gorbachev, despite the Soviets finally compromising on details that had blocked the signature of START. While the Soviet president thanked Mitterrand for his unequivocal position during the summit,[82] his meeting with Bush was tense. The US president in his memoirs writes about the "warm" talks he had with Gorbachev at the US embassy, but the diary of Anatoly Chernyaev and transcripts of the meeting from the Bush Library tell a different story.[83] During the meeting Gorbachev questioned the American commitment to the democratic and market-oriented Soviet Union.[84] Bush, who according to Chernyaev "turned crimson,"[85] explained that he had to "look at everything in light of US interests." He agreed that the USSR needed technical help to implement a market economy and promised to work with his G7 colleagues, but stated: "The best thing that you could do politically is to cut loose on the Baltic and Cuba."[86] According to Bush, he again insisted on Baltic independence during their one-on-one meeting, but Gorbachev responded that the Soviet constitution should be respected and then talked about the complications of independence, eventual compensation (from the Baltic countries to the USSR), and economic interdependence.[87]

After the rather unpleasant meeting in London, the US administration prepared very carefully the president's trip to the USSR, which was initially supposed to take place in February 1991 but was postponed due to the events in the Baltic countries. The main aim of the visit was to sign the START treaty; however, the US administration did not want to frame the meeting as "an arms reduction summit" but instead as the first "post–Cold War summit."[88] It was supposed to "symbolize the change in the focus of the US-Soviet relations from managing superpower conflicts to a new partnership in world affairs."[89] Five goals in addition to the signature of START were set for the meeting. Two of them directly concerned the Baltic countries: the normalization of trade relations and the exploration of US relations with the republics and the center.

The "normalization of trade relations" meant the return to the question of the Soviet-American trade treaty that had been signed during the Washington summit in June 1990 but not submitted to Congress. Bush had linked the submission of the treaty with Soviet laws on Jewish emigration and the beginning of negotiations on Lithuanian independence. In the summer of 1991, the talks were officially ongoing, and on May 20 the Supreme Soviet had voted on a law that eased emigration from the USSR. Thus, the United States seized upon the possibility of somehow contributing to the improvement of the Soviet economy and prepared to submit the treaty to Congress.

The Baltic leadership, as well as their supporters in the US Congress, perceived the treaty as dangerous for the Baltic countries, as it would grant Most Favored Nation status to the USSR, with the inclusion of the Baltic states. Estonia, Latvia, and Lithuania had concluded trade treaties with the United States and received MFN status in 1925/1926. In 1951, Baltic representatives in America had agreed on the suspension of those treaties. Thus, in the Baltic perception, their inclusion in the Soviet MFN status could compromise the non-recognition policy and the idea of the continuity of the Baltic states.

In early July the US consul in Leningrad George Krol met with the Baltic foreign ministers and delivered a message from Curtis Kamman regarding MFN status for the USSR. While the exact content of the message has not been found in archives, documents from the Baltic archives show that Estonians and Lithuanians were not pleased with the US plans. The same day, Lennart Meri, the foreign minister of Estonia, wrote to James Baker stating that the Estonian side was "surprised and confused" by the conversation.[90] The next day Vytautas Landsbergis sent an unusually strongly worded and emotional letter to Washington stating that the planned treaty was a "new agreement between the great states harming a small nation."[91]

The Latvian government was much more open to explorations of the practical benefits of the treaty, and the Ministry of Foreign Affairs even prepared a positive draft response to the White House.[92] However, this letter was never sent, as the Latvian government decided to seek a joint position with the two other Baltic states.[93] On July 26, Riga, Vilnius, and Tallinn sent a joint message to Washington, stating that the Baltic states supported the trade treaty between the USSR and the United States, as it could contribute to the building of the market economy in the Soviet Union. However, the Baltic countries asked to be excluded from the treaty as "this might lead to a gradual recognition of their annexation" and suggested restitution of the treaties of 1920.[94] The United States refused to take this step, as in their eyes it would mean recognition of the Baltic countries, and it was not yet willing to do this.[95]

On July 29, 1991, a meeting was held in the Latvian Representation in Moscow between Latvian and Estonian representatives, the head of the US State Department's Soviet Affairs Department Alexander Vershbow, and First Secretary of the US Embassy in Moscow Judith Mandela. The American side informed the Balts that on July 30 Bush was going to announce the granting of MFN status to the USSR, including the Baltic states. Vershbow underlined that this decision would in no way alter the United States' non-recognition policy and drew his interlocutors' attention to the fact that the United States was going to give $15 million in technical assistance to the "USSR and the Baltic countries," of which $7.5 million was destined for Estonia, Latvia, and Lithuania.[96] The Baltic governments refused the deal and turned toward their supporters in the Senate. On July 31, Democrat Senator Bill Bradley (NJ) introduced a bill calling for reactivation of the MFN trade treaties between the United States and the Baltic states that had been suspended in 1951. As noted by Latvian diplomat Ojārs Kalniņš, all Baltic American organizations supported Bradley's initiative and started to prepare an important lobbying campaign.[97]

While the Baltic governments and their allies in Congress were getting ready to fight what they saw as prioritization of Soviet interests over those of the Baltic countries, the White House was planning to use the Moscow summit to expand US relations with the republics. The other Moscow summit goal that directly concerned the Baltic countries was the "exploration of US relations with the republics and the center." For the Bush administration this meant needing to find a middle way between "showing interest in Soviet republics" and "supporting separatism." Trying to do the first and avoid the second, the Bush administration made one of its most important public relations failures. To underline the importance of the Soviet republics in US policy, Bush visited Ukraine, but refused to meet with leaders of the Ukrainian opposition.[98] During a speech at the Ukrainian Supreme Soviet he stated:

> Yet, freedom is not the same as independence. Americans will not support those who seek independence in order to replace a far-off tyranny with a local despotism. They will not aid those who promote a suicidal nationalism based upon ethnic hatred.[99]

The speech upset the leaders of the Ukrainian Popular Front (*Rukh*). To them, the message was clear: "Bush would not support Ukrainian independence, and its proponents are on their own."[100] The statement was also badly received by the American-Ukrainian community, which supported both the *Rukh* and the idea of Ukrainian independence. Later in August conservative the *New York Times* columnist William Safire sharply criticized Bush "for lecturing Ukrainians against self-determination" and called the address the "Kiev chicken speech."[101] While trying to respond to the critics, White House staff argued that Bush's criticisms of "misuses of freedom" were directed not particularly against Ukraine but toward developments "in all Soviet republics except the Baltic countries."[102]

Indeed, even if the Baltic question was far from being the priority of the summit, George Bush publicly emphasized the special status of Estonia, Latvia, and Lithuania and expressed his support for Baltic self-determination. Upon his arrival in Moscow he listed the Baltic question among the main "differences" between the superpowers, stating: "And yes, we have differences, but this hope can enable us to address our differences—differences over Cuba or the future of the Baltic States or what Japan calls the Northern Territories."[103] On July 30, during his remarks at the Moscow State Institute for International Relations, Bush linked the Baltic question and the question of Kuril Islands:

> In many cases, we face conflicts and quarrels rooted in the world war fought 50 years ago, frozen in place by the long cold war that followed: Disputes like Japan's claim—which we support. . . . Difficult, as well, are questions regarding the future of the Baltic states—Estonia, Latvia, and Lithuania. Today, a new generation of Baltic leaders—democratically elected and reflecting the will of the Baltic peoples—asks a new generation of Soviet leaders to repudiate one

of the darkest legacies of the Stalin era. Surely, men and women of reason and goodwill can find a way to extend freedom to the Baltic peoples.[104]

As noted by Ojārs Kalniņš at the time, the US press exaggerated the importance of Bush's statement on the Baltics, giving the impression that it had a more prominent place in the US-Soviet talks than it actually had.[105] In reality, while willing to remind the USSR about the US stand on the Baltic issue, Bush was not willing to harm Gorbachev by insisting too strongly on it.

On the second day of the summit, while Bush and Gorbachev were discussing negotiations on the Union Treaty at the summer house at Novo-Ogarevo, Bush received a message from the National Security Council about the killings of the Lithuanian border guards at Medininkai. The moment was embarrassing for Gorbachev as he had to learn about developments in his own country from the US president, and he visibly paled, according to Bush. But as noted by historian Serhii Plokhy, the incident suited his narrative about the possibility of Yugoslav-type chaos in the USSR.[106] During his discussion with Bush, he jumped directly from the question of Yugoslavia to that of the USSR, without forgetting to mention the Baltic countries:

> I said that dissolution of the state, even partially, could begin a chain reaction of great danger. There are so many territorial disputes around. Within the Soviet Union, people didn't even notice our internal frontiers. As soon as nationalism appears, they claim borders that are going back to Alexander the Great. Belorussia wanted back the territory given to Lithuania when it joined the Soviet Union. If Lithuania goes, Klaipeda goes too. If it is all given back, what would remain? Eastern Estonia is settled mainly by Russians (Ukrainians too).

At the end of the conversation, he re-insisted on the impossibility of the Balts leaving the Union without respecting the Soviet constitution: "Kohl asked me about self-determination," Gorbachev told Bush: "I said there is no contradiction. We have to keep self-determination within a country in the constitutional framework. This is my attitude to the Baltics."[107]

The conversation was telling as to the state of relations between the Soviet Union and the Baltic countries. Despite the ongoing negotiations and violence in January, Baltic and Soviet positions had not changed since the spring of 1990: Gorbachev wanted the Balts to respect the Soviet constitution, and the Estonians, Latvians, and Lithuanians refused to do so.

Thirty-six days after this conversation, Mikhail Gorbachev would recognize the independence of Estonia, Latvia, and Lithuania without applying the Soviet constitution to the Baltic case.

AUGUST COUP AND THE INTERNATIONAL RECOGNITION
OF THE BALTIC STATES

The coup attempt that took place in the USSR between August 19 and August 21 was the hard-liners' reaction to the threat that the Union Treaty represented to the survival of a centralized Soviet state. At the same time, it was also the expression of their long-term deep dissatisfaction with Gorbachev's policies. In the field of foreign policy, Gorbachev and Shevardnadze were accused of "acting against Soviet interests," "losing" Germany and Eastern Europe, and making "concessions" for arms reduction treaties. In terms of internal politics, Soviet conservatives perceived Perestroika as dangerous because the democratization of the Soviet state not only threatened the integrity of the Union but also undermined the Party's leading role in the country. Among the main plotters were people who had been involved in the January events in the Baltics: KGB chief Kryuchkov, Interior Minister Pugo, and Defense Minister Yazov. All three played key roles in the events, and when the putch failed Pugo committed suicide. Other important plotters were Defense Council Deputy Chairman Oleg Baklanov, Vice President Gennady Yanayev, and Prime Minister Valentin Pavlov. The initial plan was to obtain control over Moscow and Leningrad by increasing military presence in these two cities and then declaring direct presidential rule in the Baltic countries, Moldova, Georgia, and significant Soviet cities.[108] Paradoxically, the coup resulted in the further destabilization of the Soviet empire that it was supposed to save, as the three Baltic republics emerged from the coup as fully independent and internationally recognized states.

Baltic independence was not something that Gorbachev wanted or needed after returning from Crimea. However, both the EC and the United States restored diplomatic relations with the Baltic states before the USSR recognized the independence of its former republics. The EC members were among the first states to make this decisive move; the United States hesitated for more than a week. Both the American hesitation and the European rush to recognition were a reaction to the changing power dynamics in Moscow. At the same time, the final decision to embrace Baltic sovereignty was embedded in a long-established perception that the Baltic republics were a special case in the Soviet context.

The Days of the Coup

The initial American response to the August coup was very cautious. Before his early morning press conference on August 19 (the first day out the putsch), George Bush called two foreign leaders. The first call was placed at 6:42 A.M. to British prime minister John Major, and the second at 6:50 A.M. to the French president. As Bush explained, he aimed to "compare notes" or in other words adjust their positions.[109] Both Bush and Mitterrand agreed that despite the conservative coup, a rise in tensions in USSR-Western relations should be avoided.[110] When Bush spoke with a US journalist at his summer house in Maine he did not explicitly "condemn" the putsch but also expressed his hope that Yanayev would stick to the reforms in the USSR.[111]

However, during the day of August 19, the Bush administration hardened its stand on the Soviet situation. According to historian Serhii Plokhy, a document that arrived at the White House during the day and a CIA report that was presented at a White House meeting convinced the administration that the coup was likely to fail.[112] First in a letter to George Bush that was delivered to the American chargé d'affaires by the foreign minister of Russian SFSR, Andrei Kozyrev, Boris Yeltsin expressed his determination to defend constitutionality in the USSR and urged the United States to call for Gorbachev's return.[113] The letter not only showed the determination of Russian democrats to resist the coup, but also their wish to support Gorbachev. Second, CIA deputy head Richard Kerr presented a report suggesting that the coup was badly organized and its outcome not certain at all. In other words, it became increasingly evident that the takeover might not succeed.

During a deputies committee meeting at 5 P.M. a new, much more strongly worded statement was approved. The text actually condemned the coup and outlined several core principles that the United Sates was going to follow, such as belief in the need to continue the reforms in the USSR, support for elected leaders of the USSR, refusal to legitimize the coup, and opposition to the use of force "in the Baltic republics or against any Republics."[114]

Initially, Bush's concern regarding the Baltic situation during the coup consisted of a fear of repeating what he saw as a significant US failure during the Hungarian uprising in 1956, namely to initiate resistance that it would not be able or willing to back up. On August 19, around 3 P.M. while talking to Dutch prime minister Ruud Lubbers, Bush explained that he wanted to avoid giving the impression of being prepared "to do something in NATO that we really are not prepared to do, such as military action" as "we can end up inciting violence." Talking about the Lithuanian president Landsbergis, Bush said that "this hardliner in Lithuania may end up calling for troops."[115] The same day he wrote in his diary: "At this point, I am worried about the Baltics, we are going to have cries to bring military help from Landsbergis. We hear that Estonia has been taken over by the

Soviet military, that the radio and the TV are now in the control of the Soviet military in Lithuania. And so we have got some big problems that will have enormous impact here at home."[116]

The information that the US president had at hand was not entirely accurate. Estonia had not been taken over by the Soviet military, but the situation in the Baltic states was indeed tense. In the early hours of August 19, the National Salvation Committees reappeared in the public sphere and pledged their allegiance to the coup plotters in Moscow, while Soviet armed vehicles re-entered the Baltic capitals. That day the commander of the Baltic Military District informed the Estonian, Latvian, and Lithuanian governments that he was in charge of the execution of the State Committee's orders in the Baltic region. During the following hours, the Soviet forces seized the Latvian TV and radio buildings as well as Lithuanian TV and radio buildings in Kaunas, the headquarters of the Latvian independence movement, and the Latvian interior ministry and the telecommunication centers in Riga and Vilnius. The Pskov Airborne Division, which had operated during January 13 event in Vilnius, attempted to seize the TV tower in Tallinn but was stopped by Estonian volunteers. In Vilnius, Soviet paratroopers first encircled the parliamentary building on August 19, but faced with a large crowd of civilians, retreated. During the second attempt to seize the building on August 21, one of its Lithuanian guards was killed by the Soviet paratroopers. On August 20, around 11 P.M. local time, the Supreme Soviet of Estonia proclaimed the restoration of full independence. Fourteen hours later, on August 21, George Krol from the US consulate in Leningrad attended a session of the Latvian Supreme Soviet in which Latvian deputies voted for independence, while the Soviet armed vehicles were entering Riga Old Town and drawing near to the parliament building.[117]

On the evening of August 21, the putsch was over. The indecisive and unprepared men in Moscow who led the poorly organized coup were unwilling to take decisive actions such as arresting Yeltsin. Their main challenges besides their own ineptitude were the thousands of people gathered to defend the Russian parliament and the lack of clear support from the Soviet military. While Kryuchkov was initially willing to go through with the operation and attack the Russian White House, officers on the ground refused the orders and as a result Yazov also retreated from the plan.[118]

Lacking popular support and backing from the army, the organizers of the coup rushed back to Crimea to beg for Gorbachev's support. The Soviet president, however, did not receive them, but warmly welcomed a group of Russian Democrats. Anatoly Chernyaev was deeply moved by the scene in the living room of the Crimean *dacha* when the members of the delegation sent by Boris Yeltsin rushed toward the president of USSR to embrace him. "I looked at them," he later wrote in his diary. "Some of them had railed against Gorbachev in the parliament and in the press more than once; they had argued with him, and indignantly protested against him. But now, the misfortune instantly brought to light that they were part of a whole, and that the country needed exactly this whole. I even said while watching this collective joy and embraces: Thus finally the center and Russia have united."[119]

Later that night Gorbachev returned to Moscow. While the conservative attempts to depose him had failed, new problems were about to arise in his relations with the Soviet republics. During the putsch, Boris Yeltsin had increased both his own political capital and the Russian SSR's control over Soviet institutions.

In the standoff between Boris Yeltsin and the State Emergency Committee, Yeltsin's main assets were both his legitimacy as an elected leader and his physical courage. Images of the Russian president standing on a Soviet tank in front of the Russian White House and calling for resistance not only inspired Soviet citizens but also improved Western perceptions of him. At 8 A.M. on August 20, Bush called Yeltsin for the first time. Rather cold and reserved at the beginning of the conversation, the US president opened up after Yeltsin's passionate description of the situation and testimony of the determination of Russian democratic forces. At the end of the conversation, Bush warmly wished Yeltsin "Good luck," congratulated him for his commitment, and promised to pray for him.[120]

While at the international level, the coup increased Yeltsin's legitimacy and popularity, internally it helped him to expand his control over the Union institutions. During the first day of the coup, the Russian president declared all USSR organs of executive power acting on RSFSR territory as being under his authority.[121] Meanwhile, exhausted by the days in captivity, Gorbachev failed to benefit from the fact that the hard-liners' attack had increased his popularity.[122] After his return from Crimea, Gorbachev went home without stopping at the Russian White House, where thousands of people were celebrating his return and their victory.[123]

While Yeltsin's increasing popularity posed a new threat to Gorbachev's power, Estonian and Latvian declarations of independence announced a new standoff in the Baltics. On August 23, Baltic representatives in Moscow had called on the Russian president to recognize the independence that in the Latvian and Estonian cases had been proclaimed only a few days earlier. The same day, Latvian Anatolijs Gorbunovs arrived in Moscow and requested a meeting with Boris Yeltsin, which he agreed to the following day. Interviewed in 2015, Latvian representative in Moscow Jānis Peters remembers that, as Gorbunovs and his advisors entered Yeltsin's office, they encountered a "smiling" Estonian delegation.[124] Indeed, after a brief discussion with Arnold Rüütel, the Russian side had proposed that the Estonians draft a recognition document, and Yeltsin had signed it without any reservations, wishing Estonian Republic "all the best."[125]

Unsure of what had happened between the Estonians and Yeltsin, Gorbunovs proceeded by listing three questions that he wanted to discuss: the removal of Riga OMON from Latvian territory, Yeltsin's attitude toward the "new legal status" of Latvia, and the future of their relations. After a rather lengthy discussion regarding the situation with OMON in Riga and the previous days' events in Moscow, Yeltsin pointed out that the second issue of the agenda was obviously the most important one for Latvians. A copy of the Estonian-drafted declaration was brought into the room, and Yeltsin signed it in front of the baffled Latvian delegation.[126]

In the context of change in the post-coup power dynamics, Yeltsin's recognition of Baltic independence put the international community in a difficult position. Since Lithuania's restoration of independence on March 11, 1990, Vilnius, and later also Riga and Tallinn, had hoped the international community would grant them recognition, thus pushing the USSR to accept Baltic independence as a fait accompli. However, both the United States and Europe had argued that the recognition could come only after the Baltic countries had obtained effective control over their territories and populations, and it was understood that this effective control could be acquired only through negotiations with the Soviet Union.

When the president of the Russian SFSR, empowered by the failed coup, had consented to the restoration of Estonian, Latvian, and Lithuanian statehood, the Western capitals had to come to a decision not only about the future of the Baltic states but also about the future of the Soviet Union. Was it now up to the Russian, not the Soviet, president to grant independence to the Soviet republics? Was this indeed the end of Soviet rule in the Baltics or was Russian recognition just another eccentric gesture by Gorbachev's rival? Was Gorbachev still relevant? Were the Baltic states indeed free to leave the union, or could the Soviet central apparatus still prevent them from doing so?

Even before Yeltsin's decision, small European states had made the move that Vilnius, Riga, and Tallinn had hoped for and recognized the Baltic states without waiting for Soviet consent. On August 22, Iceland became the first country to officially recognize the independence of Latvia, Estonia, and Lithuania. On August 23, the foreign minister of Belgium, Mark Eyskens, announced that he was hoping to re-establish diplomatic relations with the Baltic states and would seek a common EC position on the question.[127] On August 24, EC member Denmark recognized the reestablishment of Baltic independence. The head of Danish diplomacy Uffe Ellemann-Jensen commented on the deep joy and relief of the Danish nation and affirmed Denmark's readiness to provide financial assistance.[128] Over the following twenty-four hours the Baltic States were recognized by Hungary, Argentina, Norway, and Finland.

Meanwhile, other European governments were struggling to reach a decision regarding Baltic independence. In France on August 23, a heated debate took place at Quai d'Orsay. While the director of the European Affairs Department, Jacques Blot, insisted that France should proceed to recognition, other officials such as the secretary-general of the ministry, François Scheer, and the *chef de cabinet du ministre*, Bernard Kessedjian, opposed the idea.[129] In the case of Sweden, the only country with a permanent representative in Baltic capitals, Lars Fredén, the diplomat based in Riga, was actively pushing for recognition, while the central administration in Stockholm was still hesitating.[130] In Germany, Chancellor Kohl was strictly opposed to immediate recognition, but the foreign minister, Hans-Dietrich Genscher, supported it.[131] After Yeltsin's move, Genscher managed to convince Kohl to establish diplomatic relations with the Baltic states. On the afternoon of August 25, French foreign minister Roland Dumas called Mitterrand to ask about possible recognition. At that point, the president left the decision to the minister, responding: "Do as you feel."[132] Thus, the same night Dumas announced on national television that France recognized the re-establishment of the independence of the Baltic states and that a formal declaration would be adopted in an extraordinary meeting of the European Community.

While the European countries one after another proceeded toward the re-establishment of diplomatic relations with Estonia, Latvia, and Lithuania, the debate over who possessed sovereign power in the Baltic republics was not over yet. The situation on the ground was ambiguous. The Estonian, Latvian, and Lithuanian governments had taken control of the local KGB and PC headquarters, but the army and the Union border guards still followed orders from the central authorities in Moscow. An anecdotal incident that took place during the visit of the French foreign minister reveals the confusing nature of the Baltic situation during the last days of August 1991. When Roland Dumas's plane landed in Vilnius, two border guards, one Lithuanian, the other one Soviet, argued for a considerable time about which of them had the right to verify the French minister's passport.[133]

This example of post-coup ambiguities and uncertainties highlights the constitutive aspect of the international recognition of Estonia, Latvia, and Lithuania. Instead of just acknowledging Baltic independence as a by-product of the post-coup Soviet collapse, Boris Yeltsin and the international community consolidated Baltic sovereignty.

However, while European capitals and the Russian president dismissed Gorbachev's views on the Baltic issue as no longer relevant, the White House was still waiting for a sign from the Kremlin.

American Hesitations

Unwilling to undermine or humiliate Gorbachev, George Bush was reluctant to prioritize Yeltsin's decision on the Baltics over Gorbachev's position. On August 24, Latvian representative in Moscow Jānis Peters met with the new US ambassador Robert Strauss and triumphantly showed him Yeltsin's recognition decree. According to Peters, Strauss refused to accord any value to the document and joked that it should be given to his wife, who "loved collecting such papers."[134]

At the same time, pressure from the Congress was rapidly rising. On August 22, sixteen members of Congress (eleven Democrats and five Republicans) wrote a letter to President Bush asking him to extend the official diplomatic recognition to the Baltic states, stating that "they deserve that recognition and the United States must lead the way to restoration of Baltic sovereignty."[135] The following day Senator Slade Gorton warned Bush that Congress was going to debate the issue and eventually make the attribution of MFN status to the USSR conditional on the Baltic independence recognition. "It would be better for all of us," Gorton concluded, if "that position is pre-empted by you and by the administration, rather than being forced by the Congress."[136]

The international community was also pushing the United States toward recognition. In his memoirs, Bush wrote that he had asked America's allies to wait before acting on the Baltic question,[137] but none of the main ones actually did wait. On August 26, 1991, the day George Bush met Canadian prime minister Brian Mulroney in Maine, Canada announced its wish to establish diplomatic relations with Estonia, Latvia, and Lithuania. During Bush and Mulroney's joint press conference, the US president was trying to explain the reasons for his hesitation regarding the Baltic situation. He alluded to the possible Lithuanian border problems and stated that he was waiting to see the results of the Soviet parliament meeting and the position of the EC.[138] On August 27 the EC issued a statement that greeted the Baltic countries on the restoration of their independence and affirmed EC members' wish to establish diplomatic relations with Estonia, Latvia, and Lithuania.

The same day the NSC staff prepared a letter from Bush to Gorbachev. In this message, which turned out to be the last one between the two presidents on the Baltic question, Bush urged Gorbachev to recognize the independence of the Baltic states as "quickly as possible" because "the USSR would be better off with them as neighbors than as unwilling members of the Union."[139] The US president argued that even though the United States was willing to grant recognition after the Soviet Union did, he would not be able to wait longer than two days.[140] Bush mentioned that he was open to discussing the Baltic question on the phone. The letter was handed to Gorbachev on August 28. The Soviet president did not call Bush but through diplomatic channels requested that he wait until the meeting of the new Union Council scheduled for September 2.[141]

On August 30, Bush called Landsbergis and told him that he was going to make an important announcement in two days that "will please" the Lithuanian side very much. However, he asked Landsbergis not to hold a press announcement about American plans to recognize the Baltic states. On September 2, Bush called Gorbunovs to let him know that in one hour the United States was going to formally recognize the Baltic states.[142] At 9:30 he conveyed the same message to Rüütel, who thanked Bush but insisted that, from his perspective, the USSR and Gorbachev were personally still opposed to Baltic independence, and he asked for his support.[143]

At 10 A.M. George Bush held a press conference at his summer home in Maine and announced that "The United States has always supported the independence of the Baltic states and is now prepared immediately to establish diplomatic relations with their governments."[144]

The same day, Latvian representative in Moscow Jānis Peters asked Mikhail Gorbachev to put the question of recognition to the ballot during the emergency session of the Congress of People's Deputies. The Soviet leader refused to do so. The motivation for his refusal was ambiguous. According to Peters, Gorbachev, on the one hand, was still evoking the need to respect the Soviet constitution and, on the other, was simply stating that the Congress of People's Deputies would never give a positive response to the question of Baltic independence.[145]

Paradoxically, even though thousands of Soviet troops were still stationed in the Baltic countries, Estonia, Latvia, and Lithuania did not place very high importance on Soviet recognition. Jānis Peters has even mentioned in his memoirs that for him, USSR recognition was necessary only to the extent that it could trigger US recognition, but not the other way around.[146] The Lithuanian leadership, which had considered the country independent since March 11, 1990, felt that international recognition guaranteed the irreversibility of their independence and thus saw

Soviet recognition as a mere formality. For the Latvian government, the Soviet decision was more important, as it was eager to demonstrate the finality of Latvian independence not only to the outside world but also to its ethnically diverse population. Thus, a group of Latvian lawyers was sent to Moscow to prepare the Soviet recognition text.

However, when the newly established Soviet State Council met to discuss the Baltic question on September 6, Lithuania did not send anybody and Latvia was represented only by Peters. The only high-ranking leader who flew to Moscow was Estonian prime minister Edgar Savisaar. Even he was in a somewhat light-hearted mood and jokingly told the Latvians before entering the meeting room, "So they too have decided to liberate us."[147]

The Soviet State Council's meeting went smoothly for the Balts; nobody in the room opposed the recognition. Bakatin, who had assumed the position of the head of the KGB, Nazarbayev, and Yeltsin supported it actively. Belarus and Ukraine wanted to be involved in the negations regarding the practical matters of the Baltic-Soviet separation but did not argue against it. Armenian leader Levon Ter-Petrosyan was the most ambiguous, pointing at "the right to self-determination of all republics" and that claiming that "the Baltics must not be contrasted with others."[148] Yet at the end, everybody agreed that the Council should proceed to recognize the Baltic states, leaving all practical questions, including the future of Russian minorities, Soviet troops, and property, to later negotiations. This more than anything else showed the weakening of the USSR. The need to follow the Soviet constitution and to carefully negotiate the "divorce" had suddenly disappeared, and the Estonian prime minister exited the room with an unconditional Soviet recognition in hand. "I thought that now one period of my life was over," he later wrote in his memoir. "Latvian ambassador Jānis Peters and our representative Jüri Kahn were waiting for me in the corridor. We stood and hugged each other there, at a corner of Kremlin's corridor."[149]

Later during the day, Gorbachev called Riga and talked to Gorbunovs. When a Latvian journalist asked if the Soviet president had congratulated him, Gorbunovs answered: "I did not receive any congratulation, but I did receive well wishes to myself and our nation!"[150]

Four days after obtaining Soviet recognition, Baltic officials returned to Kremlin as representatives of foreign states. On September 10, Estonia, Latvia, and Lithuania were accepted as full members of the CSCE, and thus their delegations attended a reception organized by Gorbachev in honor of CSCE ministers who had arrived in Moscow for the summit. It was Jānis Peters's turn to be touched by the historical change. "It was like a fairy tale," he remembered years later. "It suddenly seemed to me that half a century had passed between September 6 and September 10."[151] The unexpected feeling of victory was deepened by memories of the previous CSCE summit in Paris: "The person who along with the foreign ministers of Lithuania and Estonia, upon the request of the Soviet delegation, was thrown out of the conference hall of the same organization in Paris, now in the status of foreign minister of the Republic of Latvia was present at the Kremlin and clinked glasses with whoever he wished. Including those who threw him out, for today he was their guest."[152]

After attending the CSCE summit, James Baker traveled to the newly recognized Baltic states.[153] The mood in there was euphoric, and the atmosphere of the meetings generally positive. The only disagreement that arose was over the Russian minority. While seeing the Latvian position as "reasonable," Baker was less positive regarding the Estonian wish to see all Russians involved in the Soviet defense structures, internal security, and military-industrial sector leave Estonia. He was particularly concerned about those Lithuanian politicians who seemed "less tolerant toward Russians."[154] During the coming years the question of Russian minorities in the Baltics would become a central problem of Latvian and Estonian internal and external politics. Paradoxically in all three countries, the balance of power between the moderate and nationalist forces would change, leading to the adoption of very inclusive citizenship laws in Lithuania and very restrictive ones in Estonia and Latvia.

On September 11, 1991, George Bush invited leaders of the Baltic American community and the chargés d'affaires from the Baltic legations to the White House. Six days later, he met with the three Baltic acting presidents and their foreign ministers when they came to the United States to attend the ceremony for the admission of their countries to the United Nations.[155]

In less than a month, Estonia, Latvia, and Lithuanian had achieved full international recognition. Meanwhile, the future of other Soviet republics looked ambiguous. By late September all of them, except Russia, Belarus, and Kazakhstan, had proclaimed independence, but none of them had been recognized either by Gorbachev and Yeltsin or by the international community. After all, the Baltic countries had achieved what they had always wanted; their case had been considered as an exception in the Soviet context: they were allowed to leave the Union, while other Soviet republics were still expected to find some sort of modus vivendi.

Conclusion

Memoirs of the US decision makers about the end of the Cold War as well an important number of the scholarly accounts of these events are built around the narrative of American agency. Most academic and popular works on the Soviet collapse narrate these events focusing on Moscow and the RSFSR. And there is a good argument for focusing on superpower activities. Decisions and actions made in Moscow and Washington have to be studied, because those who stand at the top of international or domestic power structures have unmatched potential to shape historical processes. The Russian role in the Soviet collapse is a crucial topic not only because of Yeltsin's politics but also because of the dominant position that Russians had in the USSR. Yet, this volume has taken a different approach, studying the relations between those at the top of international and domestic power hierarchies with those situated at their margins. It shows how at the time of deep historical change the disruption of existing power structures causes uncertainty that limits the agency of the former and opens windows of opportunity for the latter. This approach avoids reproducing imperial as well as strictly national perspectives. It narrates the Estonian, Latvian, and Lithuanian push for independence as a regional endeavor embedded in the larger dynamics of Perestroika, the end of the Cold War, and the demise of the Soviet Union.

Uncertainty in most cases is caused not by lack of information but by the abundance of it. This indeed was the key problem for both Americans and Soviets in the late 1980s. Gorbachev's reforms produced a whirlpool of change that disrupted existing patterns, structures, and routines of the Soviet life. The ground upon which the existing Soviet society had been

Politics of Uncertainty. Una Bergmane, Oxford University Press. © Oxford University Press 2023.
DOI: 10.1093/oso/9780197578346.003.0007

built was not just trembling, it was falling apart. The unpredictability of the Soviet internal dynamics limited American willingness to engage with Soviet collapse more generally and with the Baltic question in particular. At the same time, the saturation of the domestic agenda limited Gorbachev's capacity to deal with the center-republic relations in general and the Baltic question in particular.

While the Soviet leadership had no plan of how to deal with them, by the spring of 1990 Tallinn, Riga, and Vilnius had both a clear goal—independence—and a relatively strong internal agreement of how to achieve it. Independence had to be restored, rather than proclaimed anew, and it had to be done using Soviet institutions instead of creating alternative ones. Historians outside the Baltic states have often overlooked the effort that it took for the Baltic societies to arrive at this consensus. As this book has emphasized, during the Perestroika years Baltic nations were not monolithic objects but vibrant and pluralistic societies. The fact that the large majority of people living in the Baltic countries rallied around the independence project in the 1990 elections and 1991 referendums was the result of an internal cohesion process that was accelerated by Moscow's failures to meaningfully respond to Baltic grievances. All Baltic demands—economic autonomy, new Union Treaty, political autonomy, the acknowledgment of the existence of secret protocols, and finally independence—were met only after Tallinn, Vilnius, and Riga had unceasingly pressured the central government or had already moved toward new more ambitious projects. The only Baltic initiative that was approved without hesitation was the creation of popular fronts. Yet there was a deep misperception about their supposed role. While Gorbachev saw them as allies, popular fronts perceived themselves as serving local, national interests first and foremost. Thus the popular fronts acted outside the previously established imperial pattern, rejecting the idea that Moscow had the final say in Baltic domestic affairs.

Beginning in the spring of 1990, Baltic governments sought international visibility and recognition through internationalization of the Baltic question, believing that only external pressures would push Soviet leadership toward accepting Estonian, Latvian, and Lithuanian statehood. American uncertainty driven by prudence was initially disappointing for Baltic activists, governments, and diasporas, especially because it was not consistently applied to all possible tracks of American foreign policy. When it came to German unification on American terms, the Bush administration did not hesitate to be actively involved or to pressure Gorbachev, despite Soviet warnings that German NATO membership could be disastrous for the stability of his power. In other words, the United States had its priorities: there were issues worth risking a general destabilization, such as

German unification, and there were issues, such as Baltic independence or Eastern European democratization, that were not. This doesn't mean that the United States did not support Eastern European and Baltic causes in principle or that it did not attempt to provide limited and cautious support. Rather, it means that the Bush administration was unwilling to undertake large-scale, bold actions as it did in the case of Germany unification.

The Bush administration was obviously not the only government that prioritized German unification over any other end of the Cold War issues and feared large-scale destabilization. So did Paris, London, and of course Bonn. These Western foreign policy priorities led to an unequal application of the self-determination principle that often characterizes international approaches to state recognition. German rights to self-determination were emphasized, Baltic rights to self-determination downplayed.

State recognition is never just a simple acknowledgment that a certain political entity has met criteria of statehood; it is a political decision that produces and reproduces hierarchies of international relations. Some claims made in the name of right of self-determination are judged more legitimate than others, and the criteria of these judgments are arbitrary. As international relations scholars have highlighted, states tend to impose (explicitly or implicitly) a wide set of normative, disciplining criteria upon claimants of statehood, making them embrace specific "rightful" identities.[1] However, the Baltic case shows that these criteria are rooted not only in normative expectations but also in geopolitical interests: Soviet consent was perceived as a major precondition to international recognition of Baltic independence.

These dynamics once again reproduced the hierarchal approach to national aspiration that often shape international relations. German claims for unity were perceived as legitimate, and the United States was ready to actively back them; Baltic claims for independence also were perceived as legitimate but the United States was not willing to actively back them; the independence claims of other Soviet republics were not perceived as legitimate and were not backed. The Baltics' geographical situation also played in their favor. Unlike, for example, Azerbaijan or Georgia, they were not just a periphery of the Soviet empire, they were the Western periphery of it. On the one hand, it enabled them to claim sameness with the West by affirming their Europeanness and thus improve their positions in the racialized hierarchies of national aspirations. On the other hand, the active interest that Nordic countries and Poland took in the Baltic situation increased their visibility on the international stage. Similar tendencies can be seen in Soviet internal dynamics. Dominated, and at the same time admired, by the "Russian elder brother," Baltic countries were placed at the top of Soviet ethnic hierarchies. This position in the Soviet collective imagination helped them to attract sympathy from liberal and democratic fractions of Soviet elites and gain visibility among the general reform supporting public.

When it came to the US position, the uncertainty of the situation ended up playing in Baltic favor, as a lack of grand strategy regarding the Soviet collapse left room for flexibility in American foreign policy. In other words, the US policy was cautious, but reactive to the events on the ground. The US position in the international system, pressures from the Baltic diaspora and Congress, the non-recognition policy, and fear that the Baltic-Soviet standoff could jeopardize German reunification pushed the United States toward deeper involvement in the Baltic situation.

The triangular relations between Baltic capitals, Moscow, and Washington were asymmetric and uneven. In most cases they consisted of one or all Baltic countries acting to push their independence project further, Moscow reacting to Baltic actions, and the United States reacting to Soviet reactions. While US interests in the Baltic situation, and their insistence on the non-use of force, did not bring independence to Estonia, Latvia, and Lithuania, they limited the possibility to use of force against the independence movements. The Perestroika years were a moment in Soviet history when external perceptions were of crucial importance for Soviet actors for both material and non-material reasons. There was, of course, the undeniable need for Western financial assistance, but at the same time there was also the non-material urge to seek Western recognition. The Perestroika project as such was built around the idea of reintegrating the international community and reclaiming a certain version of European identity. This pro-Western shift was driven by Gorbachev and his liberal advisors, fueled by the societal attraction to Western lifestyle and culture, and fully embraced by Russian democrats. Navigating the uncharted waters between the Stalinist past, which had become the defining other, and the Western/European community into which they wanted to integrate, these actors sought to project an image of conformity with Western normative expectations to the outside world. Thus international visibility had not only protective effects, but also helped Estonians, Latvians, and Lithuanians make allies among Russian democrats.

Since 1989, the Estonian, Latvian, and Lithuanian leaderships had looked for an international solution to their situation. However, in the spring of 1991 it occurred to them that the decisive support for their independence actually could come from inside the Soviet Union. The most important factor that contributed to Baltic independence was the Russian rejection of the Soviet state. It assured the support of Yeltsin, increased his popularity in the RSFSR, and helped the Latvian and Estonian governments obtain the support of their Russian minorities.

In other words, the stage of the Soviet final power struggle was the Soviet Union itself, and the agents of the Soviet demise were those who lived in the Soviet Union. The international community was the audience for this confusing play. Yet, instead of being just spectators, the United States and the European countries, or the so-called West, influenced the actors just by their mere presence. The outside regard for the Soviet internal dynamics was crucial. Actors involved in the Soviet power struggle acted and reacted to each other, always keeping in mind the presence of the external gaze upon them.

The years that followed the restoration of Baltic independence and the collapse of the USSR have often been seen as the era of lost opportunities: a time when the West, namely the United States, failed to integrate Russia into a more inclusive international order. This narrative is once again based upon the idea of unlimited American power: a presumed US capacity to shape the external course and internal dynamics of a country of the size of Russia. It also assumes that that the end of the Cold War was a clear-cut moment after which it was possible to make the world anew. That, however, was not the case. The tumultuous years that followed the Soviet collapse can be best understood as an era of what sociologist Pierre Bourdieu called hysteresis—a period in time when actors had not yet adapted to the new social context and operated using their previously learned practices. These dynamics can very well be seen in the Baltic-Russian relations after 1991. Despite the promising cooperation in the years between 1989 and 1991, the Perestroika era allies were not able to find a common language after the collapse of the USSR. This was due to two overlapping processes: Russia's attempts to secure post-imperial influence in the former Soviet Union, and Estonian and Latvian attempts to secure their core-nation status in Estonia and Latvia. Neither Russian imperialism nor Baltic nationalism seemed to fit Western ideas about the new post–Cold War world order, yet they made perfect sense for actors in the region, as their understanding of the world was shaped by their previous positions in the Soviet imperial power hierarchies. It turned out that Yeltsin had committed a similar mistake to the one that Gorbachev had made years earlier. While the Soviet leader had thought that support for Baltic reform ideas would secure their willingness to remain in the Union, the Russian president had believed that his support for Baltic independence would make them willing to maintain privileged relations with Moscow. Yet that was not the case: pro-Western orientation remained a strong point of consensus in Baltic countries, despite domestic upheavals in the 1990s. Baltic states were not interested in becoming members of the Commonwealth of Independent States and saw Russia's "near abroad" concept—used to designate Russia's special relations with former Soviet republics—as a postcolonial trap. The situation was worsened by Russia dragging on the withdrawal of Soviet troops from the Baltic countries and Latvia and Estonia adopting restrictive citizenship laws. The new legislation made citizenship automatic only for the pre-1940 citizens of independent Estonia and Latvia and their descendants, while Soviet era immigrants were bound to pass a citizenship exam that included national language tests.[2] The introduction of these measures came after a shift to the right in Estonian and Latvian politics in 1992 (Estonia) and 1993 (Latvia) parliamentary elections. In the Lithuanian case, the 1992 elections brought former pro-independence communists back to power, and the country that had experienced less immigration during the Soviet period granted citizenship to all its inhabitants. The rise of tensions in Baltic-Russian relations, however, did not mean a complete shift away from Russia in Baltic politics. In all three Baltic countries, important fractions of local business and political elites saw economic and cultural links with Russia as an asset and source of profit, and a similar perception was shared on the Russian side. Thus, trade relations remained highly active despite political rows. Furthermore, until the late 2000s, Lithuania, Latvia, and Estonia did little to limit their dependency from Russian gas.

In the early years after the restoration of independence, the Baltic countries saw their future as first and foremost European. This initial leaning toward Europeanism rather than trans-Atlanticism partly resulted from the pre-1991 dynamics. The "return to Europe" narrative had been a strong mobilizing element during the independence struggle, while the perceived lack of US support for Baltic independence had made many Baltic officials skeptical toward a possible US long-term commitment to the Baltic countries. At the same time, Tallinn, Riga, and Vilnius were driven toward the EU by the regional dynamics. The pre-1991 Nordic interest in the Estonian, Latvian, and Lithuanian future resulted in ever-deepening cooperation in the Baltic Sea Region. In 1990 and 1991, Baltic officials and activists, as well as the Americans, had articulated a vision of Baltic states as "three little Finlands," implying that Estonia, Latvia, and Lithuania would aspire toward some sort of neutral position in the post–Cold War Europe. Yet in the early 1990s, Finland as well as Sweden broke with their Cold War neutrality and joined the EU in 1995. By 1994, most of the Central and Eastern European countries were preparing EU membership applications. Having rejected the Russian CIS project, the Baltic countries followed Poland, Hungary, Romania, and Slovakia and handed their membership requests to Brussels in the fall and winter of 1995.

It took nine long years for the Baltic countries to actually join the EU. The process was complicated and demanding, as all potential member states had to implement serious domestic reforms and integrate the European Acquis Communautaire into their legislation. For Estonia and Latvia, one of the most important tasks was to meet Western, not just European but also American, demands in terms of ethnic minority protection. Feeling that their approach regarding Soviet-era migrants was not met with understanding not only in the East but also in the West, Estonia and Latvia invited OSCE to establish missions in Tallinn and Riga in order to monitor minority treatment in their countries, and the OSCE high commissioner Max van der Stoel put forward a series of recommendations to facilitate Russian speakers' integration and access to citizenship. Implementation of these recommendations became one of the key preconditions for Estonian and Latvian accession to both the EU and NATO. While Russian insistence upon these issues was perceived as post-imperial interference in Estonian and Latvian domestic affairs, Western demands on the matter were met and in 2001 the OSCE closed its mission in Tallinn and Riga. Thus, ironically, the situation of the Russian-speaking population of the Baltic states was improved as a result of Baltic attempts to finalize their exit from the Russian zone of influence.

Another important task that the West expected the Baltic countries to accomplish before they were allowed to join the EU or NATO was to acknowledge and to condemn the role of local collaborators in the Holocaust. This was not an easy task for several reasons. During the Soviet period the Holocaust commemoration was silenced and limited to small gatherings as the official narrative about the Second World War focused upon the heroic Russian/Soviet struggle, and thus the general public had limited understanding about the scope of the Nazi crimes or the nature of the local collaboration. Baltic national identities were deeply rooted in narratives of righteous victimhood and suffering, making it challenging to accept the idea of local collaboration with the Nazi regime. The most problematic issue was the legacy of Estonian and Latvian SS Legions, who had been part of Nazi combat forces but had not taken part in the Holocaust. After Baltic independence, former legionnaires and their families both in Estonia and Latvia, and in the diaspora, sought public recognition of what they saw as their heroic struggle against the USSR and/or their suffering caused by the illegal mobilization carried out by the Nazi regime. It took time and an intense dialogue with Western (both European and American) partners for various actors (on both political and societal levels) in Estonia and especially in Latvia to accept that any attempts to officialize the commemoration of forces that fought on the Nazi side was incompatible with their self-proclaimed adherence to European values. While coming to terms with the magnitude of the crimes committed on their soil by the Nazi regime and local collaborators, the Baltic countries just like their Central and Eastern European neighbors felt deeply frustrated by what they saw as Western European lack of knowledge about the Soviet repressions. After the Baltic accession to the EU, Baltic deputies at the European parliament deployed considerable efforts to officialize the commemoration of Soviet crimes at the European level. This Baltic experience of both learning new and promoting their own perspectives upon European history has been a crucial element of the European integration, leading to an emergence of a transnational European memory space in which a wide variety of groups negotiate their understandings of the past.

The Baltic road to NATO was as long as their quest for the EU membership, but much more uncertain and controversial. Scholars and pundits who criticize NATO enlargement as provocative and disrespectful toward Russian "legitimate" security interests see Baltic accession to NATO as particularly unwise and harmful to overall Russian-Western relations. From this perspective the fact that all former Eastern bloc countries and the three Baltic states have become members of the EU and NATO is considered not as an achievement, but analyzed only in relation to Russia, asking the eternal question of whether Russia was alienated by NATO and to a lesser extent by EU enlargements. When it comes to the EU, the international press often depicts the current illiberal tendencies in Poland and Hungary as some sort of collective failure of the "new member states," lumping Central, Eastern, and Baltic Europe into one group defined by its communist past and failure to be "European enough." Following this logic, the Baltic states should have embraced some form of uncertain neutrality for the sake of the greater good instead of angering Russia with their push for NATO membership. This idea bears a strong resemblance with the earlier belief from 1990 that Estonia, Latvia, and Lithuania should postpone their independence aspirations until a more important matter, the German reunification, was achieved. Meanwhile, Estonia, Latvia, and Lithuania have seen their NATO membership as a proactive move to secure their sovereignty and independence. By 1995, NATO's Article 5 had emerged as the only tangible instrument for guaranteeing the irreversibility of Baltic independence through a collective Western commitment to their defense. No other international organization, state, or group of states was willing or able to offer the same level of deterrence against the future threats from their increasingly unpredictable Eastern neighbor. While Baltic relations with Yeltsin's Russia were complicated but manageable, the uncertainty about what and who would follow Yeltsin's tenure was growing. At the same time, the Central and Eastern European push for NATO membership made the Baltic states fear that they would be left behind and fall back into the Russian zone of influence.

By this time the United States had started to gradually return to European affairs after trying to refocus on domestic issues in the early 1990s in the context of the ongoing war in Bosnia and Hercegovina. In 1994 the United States had helped the Baltic countries to negotiate withdrawal of Russian troops from their territories, thus improving its image among the Baltic political elites. The same year, Bill Clinton traveled to Riga, becoming the first American president to visit the Baltic states. Uncertain about the prospects of a possible NATO membership and upset about what they perceived as a lack of European commitment to their security, the Baltic states started to gradually shift toward the American superpower as their main ally in the post–Cold War world.

The Baltic diaspora once again played an important role in these dynamics in two ways. Baltic American organizations continued to use their networks in Washington to advocate for Baltic NATO membership, while a number of North American Estonians, Latvians, and Lithuanians played key roles in Baltic politics and diplomacy. In 1998, a former high-ranking civil servant in the US Environmental Protection Agency, Valdas Adamkus, was elected president of Lithuania. In 1999, Latvian Canadian scholar Vaira Vīķe-Freiberga became the first female president of Latvia. In 2006, the Estonian parliament chose Toomas Hendrik Ilves, an Estonian American born in Sweden who had served as Estonian ambassador in the United States and as Estonian foreign minister, to be the next president of the country. These and other high-ranking officials used their positions in domestic politics to keep the Baltic countries on their pro-Western track while also at the same time utilizing their own cultural capital and language skills to project an attractive image of the Baltic countries in the West.

The late 1990s was a complicated time for Baltic foreign policy. Russia strongly opposed Baltic NATO membership, and the international community seemed unwilling to defy this opposition. Various actors such Russia, France, and the United States were trying to find alternative solutions to the question of Baltic security. In 1997, Russia proposed unilateral guarantees that only increased Baltic anxiety. At the same time, France envisaged a special security regime for Baltic and Nordic neutrals, which none of the concerned viewed with enthusiasm. The United States proposed to sign a charter of cooperation with the Baltic countries, which they did without feeling reassured about their future prospects. At the same time, the Baltic states' own relations were at their lowest point since 1991. While their earlier cooperation and unity was driven by the common understanding that either all or none of the Baltic states would become independent, the NATO and the EU membership quests led to a feeling of competition among them. In the late 1990s it looked as though Estonia, which had been more successful in its economic reforms, could join the EU before Latvia and Lithuania, while Lithuania was perceived as more ready for NATO. At the same time, Estonia seemed to be shifting away from the "Baltic" label and claiming a Nordic identity. Meanwhile, Lithuania was increasingly embracing and exploring its Central European roots through celebration of its medieval statehood and the Polish-Lithuanian commonwealth.

The key breakthrough for the Baltic NATO membership occurred around 2000/2001. While the shock of September 11 definitely played a role in pushing the United States toward a more assertive support for the Baltic states, the George W. Bush administration had already started to shift toward this direction earlier for several reasons. The Baltic states had actually delivered the promised reforms; support for Estonian, Latvian, and Lithuanian membership in the Congress was growing; and the Russian resistance to the idea was weakening. The first years of Vladimir Putin's tenure were marked by a brief improvement in Russia's relations with the West, and it seemed that the new Russian president had accepted the Baltic final departure from the Russian zone of influence. In 2001 he told American journalists that when it came to a Baltic membership in NATO, Russia was not in a position "to tell people what to do."[3] In 2002 he claimed that Baltic membership would be "no tragedy" as long as the Alliance did not install new military infrastructure on the Baltic soil.[4]

In 2004 the three Baltic states achieved what no other former Soviet republic had been able to achieve: they joined both the North Atlantic Alliance and the European Union. Why was this push toward the West possible for the Baltic countries but not for the other countries that gained independence after Soviet collapse? The credit to a very large extent goes to the Baltic countries themselves, as they were willing and able to implement the necessary reforms, fight local corruption, and secure their democracies. At the same time, the Baltic success was also due to the fact that the possibility of joining EU and NATO served as a strong stimulus for Baltic societies and policymakers to address the issues like Russian speakers' rights and corruption. The West, even if reluctant at the beginning, was willing to consider and embrace Baltic membership. Meanwhile, Russia, initially hostile to the Baltic plans, came to accept the Baltic final exit from its zone of influence. The attitude of Putin is particularly interesting knowing that Georgian and Ukrainian attempts to approach the Western world have been one of the reasons behind Russian military aggression against these countries. These dynamics seem to once again repeat the Perestroika era attitude summed up by historian Serhii Plokhy: "What was good for the Baltics was considered bad for Ukraine."[5] The differences in the Russian and Western treatment of the Baltic countries and Ukraine can to some extent be explained by the size of Ukraine and the richness of its natural resources. It can also be argued that Putin accepted Baltic NATO membership in the very early years of his presidency, when his regime was still weak and the relations with the West relatively good. At the same time, both in the Western and Russian cases, the subjective perception of the Baltic states as an exception in the so-called post-Soviet space did play a role. This long-term idea rooted in the Soviet imaginaries about the "Western" and "European" Baltic republics and Western non-recognition policy was reinforced by Baltic successful democratic transitions and their push toward the West that started immediately after the restoration of independence. In other words, by 2001 Putin had made his peace with the loss of the Baltic countries not only because of their size, but also because they were not anymore perceived as belonging to the "Russian world" or the "near-abroad" in the same way it was imagined to be the case for Ukraine and Georgia. Just as various Soviet actors during Perestroika had believed that the Soviet Union could be preserved without the Baltic countries, Putin believed that Estonia, Latvia, and Lithuania were not crucial for the survival of the informal Russian empire in the post-Soviet space.

The Baltic accession to the EU and NATO was indeed no tragedy for Russia. Though the 1998–1999 economic crisis had weakened Baltic-Russian trade relations, Russia was still able to exercise considerable economic and by consequence political influence in the Baltics. The fading of that influence and the deterioration of Baltic Russian relations over the coming twenty years were first and foremost the consequence of Russian aggressions on Georgia and Ukraine. It was the Ukrainian and Belarusian gas disputes with Gazprom in the late 2000s as well as the Russian war in Georgia that pushed first Lithuanian and then also Estonian and Latvian political elites to limit their dependency on Russian gas. Until the 2014 Ukrainian crisis, the only boots-on-the-ground NATO presence in the Baltics was the Baltic air-policing mission, which various NATO member states assured in rotation. It was only in response to Russian annexation of Crimea and Russian aggression in Eastern Ukraine that NATO member states agreed in 2016 to deploy rotating battle groups to the Baltic states and Poland. Russian actions toward Ukraine have also deepened the Baltic sense of shared destiny. While the Baltic internal frictions of the late 1990s early 2000s had eased up after their accession to NATO and the EU, it was the shock of 2014 that turned a new page in Estonian, Latvian, and Lithuanian cooperation.

Today, more than thirty years after the restoration of independence, all three Baltic states see the Russian Federation as the key menace to their sovereignty and independence and perceive the United States as their key ally. Baltic trans-Atlanticism is mostly due to a shared understanding that no European state would be willing or capable to replace Washington as their main security provider. In the light of the Russian war in Ukraine, the Estonian, Latvian, and Lithuanian choices to seek NATO and EU membership and to do it early appear to have been an important contribution to securing their independence. The Finnish and Swedish 2022 decision to apply for membership in the North Atlantic Alliance reconfirms the Baltic feeling that neutrality at the Russian borders is not an option. At the same time, the key to the Baltic successful exit from the Russian zone of influence to some extent was the legacy of their twenty years of independence between the two world wars, as it made them a special case in the eyes of both Soviet/Russian and Western actors.

NOTES

INTRODUCTION

1. Memorandum of conversation between Bush and Gorbachev, June 1, 1990, 11:00–11:48, George Bush Presidential Library (here after GBPL), Bush Presidential Records, Scowcroft Collection, Special Separate USSR Notes Files, Gorbachev Files, OA/ID 91127–005.
2. Kārina Pētersone and Ilze Būmane, *Valstsvīrs Anatolijs Gorbunovs* (Riga: Zvaigzne ABC, 2020), 307–308.
3. Michael W. Doyle, *Empires* (Ithaca, NY, and London: Cornell University Press, 1986), 45.
4. Brian C. Rathbun, "Uncertain about Uncertainty: Understanding the Multiple Meanings of a Crucial Concept in International Relations Theory," *International Studies Quarterly* 51, no. 3 (2007): 533–557.
5. Timothy J. Naftali, *George H. W. Bush* (New York: Macmillan, 2007), 84–88.
6. See, for example, the collection of documents declassified by the National Security Archive *NATO Expansion: What Gorbachev Heard*. Acessed December 13, 2021, https://nsarchive.gwu.edu/briefing-book/russia-programs/2017-12-12/nato-expansion-what-gorbachev-heard-western-leaders-early.
7. Robert English, "The Sociology of New Thinking: Elites, Identity Change, and the End of the Cold War," *Journal of Cold War Studies* 7, no. 2 (2005): 43–80; Robert English, *Russia and the Idea of the West: Gorbachev, Intellectuals, and the End of the Cold War* (New York: Columbia University Press, 2000); Robert G. Herman, "Identity, Norms and National Security: The Soviet Foreign Policy Revolution and the End of the Cold War," in *The Culture of National Security*, ed. Peter Katzenstein (New York: Columbia University Press, 1996), 271–316; Iver B. Neumann, *Russia and the Idea of Europe: A Study in Identity and International Relations* (Milton Park: Routledge, 2017); Marie-Pierre Rey, "Europe Is Our Common Home: A Study of Gorbachev's Diplomatic Concept," *Cold War History* 4, no. 2 (2004): 33–65.
8. Mikhail Gorbachev, *Gody trudnykh resheniy. Izbrannoye. 1985–1992* (Moscow: Alfaprint, 1993), 53; Anatoly Chernyaev, ed., *Otvechaya na vyzov vremeni. Vneshnyaya politika perestroyki: dokumental'nyye svidetelstva* (Moscow: Ves Mir, 2010), 139, 146.
9. "Ostavka bol'she, chem zhizn'. Beseda Fedora Burlatskogo s Eduardom Shevardnadzem," *Literaturnaia gazeta*, April 10, 1991.
10. Aleksandr Yakovlev, *Muki prochteniya bytiya: perestroyka: nadezhdy i realnosti* (Moscow: Novosti, 1991), 181.

11. "Vremya trebuyet Novogo Myshleniya. Zapis besedy M. S. Gorbacheva s uchastnikami Issyk-Kulskogo foruma, " *Literaturnaia gazeta*, November 5, 1986, 1–2, East View; "Vystupleniye General'nogo sekretarya TsK KPSS M. S. Gorbacheva na 43-y sessii General'noy Assamblei OON (7 dekabrya 1988)," accessed March 3, 2018, https://news.un.org/ru/audio/2013/02/1002831; Address given by Mikhail Gorbachev to the Council of Europe, July 6, 1989, accessed on March, 5, 2020, http://www.cvce.eu/obj/address_given_by_ mikhail_gorbachev_to_the_council_of_europe_6_july_1989-en-4c021687- 98f9-4727-9e8b-836e0bc1f6fb.html. See also "XIX Vsesoyuznaya konferentsiya KPSS: Vneshnaya Politika i Diplomatiya," *Pravda*, July 26, 1988, 4.

12. Una Bergmane, Between empire and democracy: the complex legacy of Mikhail Gorbachev, UCL Europe Blog, September 6, 2022, https://ucleuropeblog.com/ 2022/09/06/between-empire-and-democracy-the-complex-legacy-of-mikhail- gorbachev/accessed November 5, 2022

13. James Addison Baker and Thomas M. DeFrank, *The Politics of Diplomacy: Revolution, War, and Peace, 1989–1992* (New York: Putnam, 1995), 63; George Bush and Brent Scowcroft, *A World Transformed* (New York: Knopf, 1998), 206; Norman A. Graebner, Richard Dean Burns, and Joseph M. Siracusa, *Reagan, Bush, Gorbachev: Revisiting the End of the Cold War* (Westport, CT: Praeger Security International, 2008), 132–134; Hal Brands, *Making the Unipolar Moment: U.S. Foreign Policy and the Rise of the Post–Cold War Order* (Ithaca, NY: Cornell University Press, 2016), 319; James Graham Wilson, *The Triumph of Improvisation: Gorbachev's Adaptability, Reagan's Engagement, and the End of the Cold War* (Ithaca, NY: Cornell University Press, 2014), 183; Serhii Plokhy, *The Last Empire: The Final Days of the Soviet Union* (New York: Simon & Schuster, 2015).

14. Peter J. Katzenstein, "Introduction," in *The Culture of National Security: Norms and Identity in World Politics*, ed. Peter J. Katzenstein (New York: Columbia University Press, 1996), 5.

15. Una Bergmane, "'Is This the End of Perestroika?': International Reactions to the Soviet Use of Force in the Baltic Republics in January 1991," *Journal of Cold War Studies* 22, no. 2 (2020): 26–57.

16. Robert R. Williams, *Hegel's Ethics of Recognition* (Berkeley: University of California Press, 1997), 2.

17. Christopher Daase, Caroline Fehl, et al., eds., *Recognition in International Relations: Rethinking a Political Concept in a Global Context* (Basingstoke: Palgrave Macmillan, 2015); Thomas Lindemann and Erik Ringmar, eds., *The International Politics of Recognition* (Boulder, CO: Paradigm Publishers, 2012).

18. Mark Leonard and Andrew T. Small, *Norwegian Public Diplomacy* (London: Foreign Policy Centre, 2005), 1.

19. Matthew Connelly, *A Diplomatic Revolution: Algeria's Fight for Independence and the Origins of the Post–Cold War Era* (New York: Oxford University Press, 2002).

20. In 1973 the GDP per capita in the whole Soviet Union was $6058, that of Estonia was $8656, closely followed by Latvia, Kazakhstan and Lithuania with respectively $7780, $7593, and $7589. By 1990 the difference between the Baltic countries and the rest of the Union had increased. Estonia still had $10,733, the highest GDP per capita in the USSR, Latvia was second with $9841 and Lithuania was third with $8591. They were followed by Russia with $7762 and Georgia with $7569. The Soviet average was $6871 and the lowest GDP per

capita in the USSR was in Tajikistan with $2995. Agnus Madison, *The World Economy: a Milleniume Perespective* (Paris: OECD, 2006, 185.

21. On the concept of ontological (in)security see Anthony Giddens, *Modernity and Self-Identity: Self and Society in the Late Modern Age* (Stanford, CA: Stanford University Press, 1991); Martin J. Bayly, "Imperial Ontological (in) Security: 'Buffer States,' International Relations and the Case of Anglo-Afghan Relations, 1808–1878," *European Journal of International Relations* 21, no. 4 (2015): 816–840; Riccardo Valente and Sergi Valera Pertegas, "Ontological Insecurity and Subjective Feelings of Unsafety: Analysing Socially Constructed Fears in Italy," *Social Science Research* 71 (2018): 160–170.

22. Kaarel Piirimäe, "Estonia 'Has Not Time': Existential Politics at the End of Empire," *Connexe: les espaces postcommunistes en question* 6 (2020): 21–50

23. See George Herbert Mead, *Mind, Self, and Society: The Definitive Edition* (Chicago: University of Chicago Press, 2015).

24. Erik Ringmar, "Introduction," in *The International Politics of Recognition* (Boulder, CO: Paradigm Publishers, 2012), 3–23.

25. Anne de Tinguy, "Effondrement ou suicide?," in *L'effondrement de l'Empire soviétique*, ed. Anne de Tinguy (Brussels: Bruylant, 1998); Vladislav Zubok, *Collapse: The Fall of the Soviet Union* (New Haven, CT: Yale University Press, 2021); Philip Hanson, *The Rise and Fall of the Soviet Economy: An Economic History of the USSR from 1945* (London; New York: Routledge, 2014); Mark R. Beissinger, *Nationalist Mobilization and the Collapse of the Soviet State* (Cambridge: Cambridge University Press, 2002); Rasma Karklins, *Ethnopolitics and Transition to Democracy: The Collapse of the USSR and Latvia* (Baltimore: Woodrow Wilson Center Press; Johns Hopkins University Press, 1994); David Pryce-Jones, *The War That Never Was: The Fall of the Soviet Empire, 1985–1991* (London: Phoenix, 2001); Astrid S. Tuminez, "Nationalism, Ethnic Pressures, and the Breakup of the Soviet Union," *Journal of Cold War Studies* 5, no. 4 (2003): 81–136; Ronald Grigor Suny, *The Revenge of the Past: Nationalism, Revolution, and the Collapse of the Soviet Union* (Stanford, CA: Stanford University Press, 1993); Edward W. Walker, *Dissolution: Sovereignty and the Breakup of the Soviet Union* (Lanham, MD: Rowman & Littlefield, 2003); Valerie Bunce, *Subversive Institutions: The Design and the Destruction of Socialism and the State* (Cambridge: Cambridge University Press, 1999); Stephen Kotkin, *Armageddon Averted: The Soviet Collapse, 1970–2000* (Oxford; New York: Oxford University Press, 2008).

26. James Mann, *The Rebellion of Ronald Reagan: A History of the End of the Cold War* (London: Penguin Books, 2010); Peter Schweizer, *Victory: The Reagan Administration's Secret Strategy That Hastened the Collapse of the Soviet Union* (New York: Atlantic Monthly Press, 1996).

27. English, "The Sociology of New Thinking"; Herman, "Identity, Norms and National Security"; Nina Tannenwald and William C. Wohlforth, "Introduction: The Role of Ideas and the End of the Cold War," *Journal of Cold War Studies* 7, no. 2 (2005): 3–12; Kaarel Piirimäe, "Gorbachev's New Thinking and How Its Interaction with Perestroika in the Republics Catalysed the Soviet Collapse," *Scandinavian Journal of History*, published online August 2020, https://doi.org/10.1080/03468755.2020.1784268; Nina Tannenwald, "Ideas and Explanation: Advancing the Theoretical Agenda," *Journal of Cold War Studies* 7, no. 2 (2005): 13–42.

28. Mark Kramer, "The Collapse of East European Communism and the Repercussions within the Soviet Union (Part 1)," *Journal of Cold War Studies* 5, no. 4 (2003): 178–256; Mark Kramer, "The Collapse of East European Communism and the Repercussions within the Soviet Union (Part 2)," *Journal of Cold War Studies* 6, no. 4 (2004): 3–64; Mark Kramer, "The Collapse of East European Communism and the Repercussions within the Soviet Union (Part 3)," *Journal of Cold War Studies* 7, no. 1 (2005): 3–96.

29. Plokhy, *The Last Empire*.

30. Kristina Spohr, "Between Political Rhetoric and Realpolitik Calculations: Western Diplomacy and the Baltic Independence Struggle in the Cold War Endgame," *Cold War History* 6, no. 1 (2006): 1–42.

31. Andres Kasekamp, *A History of the Baltic States* (Houndmills: Palgrave Macmillan, 2010), vii–ix.

32. Ibid., 131.

33. Ibid., 139.

34. In 1945 there were 94 percent of ethnic Estonians in Estonia, 80 percent of Latvians in Latvia, and 78 percent of Lithuanians in Lithuania. In 1989 these numbers were respectively 62 percent, 52 percent, and 80 percent (Ibid., 155).

35. Mikhail Gorbachev, *Sobraniye sochineniy*, Vols. 9–27 (Moscow: Ves' Mir, 2009–2014); *Soyuz mozhno bylo sokhranit. Belaya kniga. Dokumenty i fakty o politike M. S. Gorbacheva po reformirovaniyu i sokhraneniyu mnogonatsional'nogo gosudarstva*, ed. Anatoly Chernyaev et al. (Moscow: ACT, 2007); *V Politbyuro TsK KPSS . . .: Po zapisyam Anatoliya Chernyayeva, Vadima Medvedeva, Georgiya Shakhnazarova (1985–1991)*, ed. Anatoly Chernyaev et al. (Moscow: Al'pina Biznes Buks, 2006).

CHAPTER 1

1. Bush and Scowcroft, *A World Transformed*, 222–223.

2. Elena Zubkova, *Pribaltika i Kreml, 1940–1953* (Moscow: ROSSPEN, 2008), 338–339.

3. Magnus Ilmjärv, *Silent Submission: Formation of Foreign Policy of Estonia, Latvia and Lithuania: Period from Mid-1920s to Annexation in 1940*, Acta Universitatis Stockholmiensis 24 (Stockholm: Stockholm University Department of History, 2004), 410–413; Andrejs Plakans, *Concise History of the Baltic States* (Cambridge: Cambridge University Press, 2011), 293–294.

4. Quoted in the "Constitutional Court of the Republic on Latvia, Judgment in Case No. 2007-10-0102," Riga, November 29, 2007, article 24,2, accessed December 17, 2021, http://www.satv.tiesa.gov.lv/web/wp-content/uploads/2007/04/2007-10-0102_Spriedums_ENG.pdf.

5. Mikhail Meltyukhov, *Upushchennyy shans Stalina. Sovetskiy Soyuz i bor'ba za Evropu: 1939–1941* (Moscow: Veche, 2000), 199.

6. William J. H. Hough III, "The Annexation of the Baltic States and Its Effect on the Development of Law Prohibiting Forcible Seizure of Territory," *New York Law School Journal of International and Comparative Law* 6, no. 2 (1985): 379.

7. Matthieu Boisdron, ed., *Diplomate en Lettonie: Carnets de Jean de Beausse, premier secrétaire à l'ambassade de France à Riga (décembre 1938–septembre 1940)* (Paris: Mens Sana, 2011), 111.

8. "Lithuanian Minister (Zadeikis) to the Secretary of State, July 13, 1940," *FRUS* 1940 (General Volume I), Document 395, accessed December 13, 2021, https://history.state.gov/historicaldocuments/frus1940v01/d395.

9. "Press Release Issued by the Department of State on July 23, 1940," *FRUS* 1940 (General Volume I), Document 412, accessed December 13, 2021, https://history.state.gov/historicaldocuments/frus1940v01/d412.

10. Ibid.

11. Oona A. Hathaway and Scott J. Shapiro, *The Internationalists: How a Radical Plan to Outlaw War Remade the World* (New York: Simon & Schuster, 2017), Introduction.

12. The Secretary of State to the Ambassador in Japan (Forbes), January 7, 1932, accessed on January 5, 2021, https://courses.knox.edu/hist285schneid/stimsondoctrine.html.

13. Bertram D. Hulen, "US Lashes Soviet for Baltic Seizure," *New York Times*, July 24, 1940.

14. Sabine Dullin, "How to Wage Warfare without Going to War?" *Cahiers du monde russe* 52, no. 2 (2012): 226.

15. "Stalin Collects," *New York Times*, October 3, 1939.

16. Eero Medijainen, "The USA, Soviet Russia and the Baltic States. From Recognition to the Cold War," in *The Baltic Questions during the Cold War*, ed. John Hiden et al. (London: Routledge, 2008), 29–30; Su-Mi Lee, "Understanding the Yalta Axioms and Riga Axioms through the Belief Systems of the Advocacy Coalition Framework," *Foreign Policy Analysis* 11, no. 3 (2015): 301–307.

17. Kennan did not particularly enjoy his time in Riga. In May 1932 he wrote in his diary: "Chekhov's characters complain of boredom. Boredom that arises from the comprehension of the futility of all their own actions. I live here in Riga fully as futilely as they lived on their estates. From day to day my hair gets thinner, my sense of humor less and my nerves weaker." Seeley G. Mudd Manuscript Library, Princeton, NJ (hereafter MML), George F. Kennan Papers, Box 230, Folder 22.

18. Quoted in Harold Jackson, "George Kennan," *The Guardian*, March 18, 2005, accessed December 19, 2021, https://www.theguardian.com/news/2005/mar/18/guardianobituaries.usa.

19. See Henderson's memoirs: Loy W. Henderson and George W. Baer, *A Question of Trust: The Origins of U.S.-Soviet Diplomatic Relations: The Memoirs of Loy W. Henderson* (Stanford, CA: Hoover Institution Press, 1986).

20. "Memorandum by the Assistant Chief of the Division of European Affairs (Henderson)," *FRUS* 1940 (General Volume I), Document 398, accessed December 20, 2021, https://history.state.gov/historicaldocuments/frus1940v01/d398.

21. Harry Truman Presidential Library, Oral History Interview with Loy W. Henderson, Washington, DC, June 14, 1973, by Richard D. McKinzie, accessed December 20, 2021, http://www.trumanlibrary.org/oralhist/hendrson.htm#oh2.

22. Atlantic Charter, August 14, 1941, accessed December 20, 2021, accessed on May 2, 2014, http://avalon.law.yale.edu/wwii/atlantic.asp.

23. Kaarel Piirimäe, *Roosevelt, Churchill and the Baltic Question: Allied Relations during the Second World War* (New York: Palgrave Macmillan 2014), 53.

24. Serhii Plokhy, *Yalta: The Price of Peace* (New York: Viking, 2010), 130.

25. Piirimäe, *Roosevelt, Churchill and the Baltic Question*, 57–80.

26. "Roosevelt-Stalin Meeting, December 1, 1943," *FRUS* 1943, *The Conferences at Cairo and Tehran*, Document 378, accessed on November 30, 2021, https://history.state.gov/historicaldocuments/frus1943CairoTehran/d378.

27. Ibid.

28. The US Department of Commerce lists 193,606 Lithuanian-born inhabitants of the United States in 1939, 20,673 Latvian, and 3,500 Estonian. However, the numbers of Americans of Lithuanian descent was higher as between 1899 and 1914 250,000 Lithuanians arrived in the US. See Kasekamp, *A History of the Baltic States*, 88; and US Department of Commerce, Bureau of the Census, *Statistical Abstract of the United States 1939* (Washington, DC: US Government Printing Office, 1940), 27.

29. "Roosevelt-Stalin Meeting, December 1, 1943."

30. Ibid.

31. Ibid.

32. Protocol of Proceedings of Crimea Conference, Washington, March 24, 1945, accessed December 21, 2021, http://avalon.law.yale.edu/wwii/yalta.asp.

33. "Dean Acheson, Acting Secretary of State, to the US Delegation at the Council of Foreign Ministers, Paris, July 27, 1946," *FRUS* 1946, III, Document 14, accessed on November 30, 2021, https://history.state.gov/historicaldocuments/frus1946 v03/d14.

34. Bohlen memorandum, January 9, 1945, quoted in Kaarel Piirimäe, *Roosevelt, Churchill and the Baltic Question*, 144.

35. H-19a Advisory Committee, "Future Status of the Baltic States," March 10, 1944, quoted in Piirimäe, *Roosevelt, Churchill and the Baltic Question*, 143.

36. For example, in 1949 the budget of the Latvian legations was of $73,500. In accounts it had $4,350 million in currency and $3,450 million in gold. The 1949 budget of the Estonian consulate was $57,500 and it possessed $999,400 in currency reserves and $2,880 million in gold reserves. The Lithuanian budget for the same year was $110,000 but the reserves were much smaller, as it possessed only about $4,639 in currency and $2,806 million in gold. Jonathan L'Hommedieu, "Exiles and Constituents: Baltic Refugees and American Cold War Politics, 1948–1960" (PhD diss., Turku University, 2011), 76.

37. Pauli Heikkilä, "Baltic States: Estonia, Latvia and Lithuania," in *East Central European Migrations during the Cold War*, ed. Anna Mazurkiewicz (Berlin: De Gruyter Oldenbourg, 2019), 48.

38. "Statement by the President upon Signing the Displaced Persons Act," June 25, 1948, accessed on November 30, 2021, https://www.trumanlibrary.gov/library/public-papers/142/statement-president-upon-signing-displaced-persons-act.

39. Heikkilä, "Baltic States: Estonia, Latvia and Lithuania," 50.

40. In the Baltic provinces of Estland, Courland, and Livonia serfdom was abolished in respectively in 1816, 1817, and 1819; in Lithuania and the Latvian region of Latgale it was abolished in 1861.

41. Kasekamp, *A History of the Baltic States*, 88.

42. Ibid.

43. US Bureau of the Census 1990, Census of Population. Detailed Ancestry Groups for States, 1992, 6, acessed December 20, 2021, https://usa.ipums.org/usa/resources/voliii/pubdocs/1990/cp-s/cp-s-1-2.pdf.

44. Ieva Zaķe, "'The Secret Nazi Network' and Post–World War II Latvian Émigrés in the United States," draft article, 4, accessed December 21, 2021, https://www.academia.edu/3068146/_THE_SECRET_NAZI_NETWORK_POST_WORLD_WAR_II_LATVIAN_IMMIGRANTS_AND_THE_HUNT_FOR_NAZIS_IN_THE_UNITED_STATES.

45. US Bureau of the Census 1990, Census of Population Ancestry of the Population in the United States, 442, 459, 461, accessed December 20, 2021, https://www.census.gov/library/publications/1993/dec/cp-3-2.html.

46. Ibid., 340, 357, 359.

47. Rogers Brubaker, "The 'Diaspora' Diaspora," *Ethnic and Racial Studies* 28, no. 1 (2005): 5–7.

48. Vahur Made, "The Estonian Government-in-Exile. A Controversial Project of State Continuation," in *The Baltic Question during the Cold War*, ed. John Hiden et al. (London; New York: Routledge, 2008), 134–144.

49. Zaķe, "'The Secret Nazi Network' and Post–World War II Latvian Émigrés in the United States," 5.

50. Anthony Giddens, *Modernity and Self-Identity: Self and Society in the Late Modern Age* (Hoboken, NJ: John Wiley & Sons, 2013), 41–48, Google Play Books.

51. Roundtable discussion *Activists (BATUN) Revisit Baltic Scandinavian Cooperation to Restore Baltic Independence, 1983–1991*, presentations of Heino Ainso and Uldis Bluķis, Yale Conference on Baltic and Scandinavian Studies, New Haven, March 14, 2014.

52. Jonathan H. L'Hommedieu, "Baltic Exiles and the U.S. Congress: Investigations and Legacies of the House Select Committee, 1953–1955," *Journal of American Ethnic History* 31, no. 2 (Winter 2012): 42.

53. Ibid.

54. Ieva Zake and Graham Gormley, "Integration or Separation? Nationality Groups in the US and the Republican Party's Ethnic Politics, 1960s–1980s," *Nationalities Papers* 38, no. 4 (2010): 469–490.

55. Email from BATUN activist Uldis Bluķis to the author of this book from August 20, 2014.

56. Ibid.

57. Ibid.

58. Plakans, *Concise History of the Baltic States*, 307–308; Kasekamp, *A History of the Baltic States*, 137.

59. Richards Plavnieks, *Nazi Collaborators on Trial during the Cold War: Viktors Arājs and the Latvian Auxiliary Security Police* (Cham: Springer International Publishing, 2018), Chapter 6: "The United States: Perjury, The Public, and The Passport."

60. Zake, "'The Secret Nazi Network' and Post–World War II Latvian Emigres in the United States," 96.

61. Ieva Zake, "Multiple Fronts of the Cold War: Ethnic Anti-Communism of Latvian Émigrés," in *Anti-Communist Minorities in the US: Political Activism of Ethnic Refugees*, ed. Ieva Zake (New York: Palgrave Macmillan, 2009), 135.

62. John B. Genys, "The Joint Baltic American Committee and the European Security Conference," *Journal of Baltic Studies* 9, no. 3 (1978): 248.

63. Bill Anderson, "Ford Is Urged to Cut Baltic Ties," *Chicago Tribune*, March 15, 1975; Bill Anderson, "New Stress over the Baltic Lands," *Chicago Tribune*, March 19, 1975.

64. Sarah B. Snyder, "'Jerry, Don't Go': Domestic Opposition to the 1975 Helsinki Final Act," *Journal of American Studies* 44, no. 1 (2010): 67–81.

65. Michael Cotey Morgan, *The Final Act: The Helsinki Accords and the Transformation of the Cold War* (Princeton, NJ: Princeton University Press, 2018).

66. "Report by Baltic Leaders on Human Rights Activities in the Soviet Occupied Baltics," *Baltic Bulletin*, May 1984; "The Role of Human Rights in the Helsinki

Process, Ambassador John D. Scanlan's Address," *Baltic Bulletin*, May 1985; "World Federation of Free Latvians Asks Reagan for Representation at the May 1985 Human Rights Meeting in Ottawa," *Baltic Bulletin*, May 1985.

67. See, e.g., "Eighth Annual BAFL Human Rights Conference," *Baltic Bulletin*, June 1989.

68. Maria Koinova, "Four Types of Diaspora Mobilization: Albanian Diaspora Activism for Kosovo Independence in the US and the UK," *Foreign Policy Analysis* 9, no. 4 (2013): 441.

69. Memorandum of conversation between Bush, Baker, and Soviet foreign minister Bessmertnykh, January 28, 1991, GBPL, accessed on December 28, 2021, http://bush41library.tamu.edu/files/memcons-telcons/1991-01-28--Bessmertnykh.pdf.

70. Mikhail Gorbachev, *Perestroika: New Thinking for Our Country and the World* (New York: Harper & Row, 1988), 119.

71. Some scholars report the offical number of two victims (Beissinger, *Nationalist Mobilization*, 74, Zubok, Collapse, 49), while others list 186, a number that emerged during a later investigation but was never oficailly confirmed. (Shoshana Keller, *Russia and Central Asia: Coexistence, Conquest, Convergence* (Toronto: University of Toronto Press, 2019), 240).

72. See Kramer, "The Collapse of East European Communism Union," Part 1.

73. *Soyuz mozhno bylo sokhranit*, 13

74. On the Soviet bloc see Mark Kramer, "The Demise of the Soviet Bloc," in *The End and the Beginning: The Revolutions of 1989 and the Resurgence of History*, ed. Vladimir Tismaneanu and Bogdan Iacob (Budapest: Central European University Press, 2012), 198–202.

75. Anna Whittington, "Contested Privilege: Ethnic Russians and the Unmaking of the Soviet Union," article accepted by *Journal of Modern History*.

76. On Soviet perceptions of Central Asia and its populations see: Whittington, "Contested Privilege," Jeff Sahadeo, Voices from the Soviet Edge: Southern Migrants in Leningrad and Moscow (Ithaca, NY : Cornell University Press, 2019)

77. Zubkova, *Pribaltika i Kreml*, 4

78. Suny, *The Revenge of the Past*, 155; Walker, *Dissolution*, 30.

79. Walker, *Dissolution*, 31.

80. Anu Mai Kol, "Economy and Ethnicity in the Hands of the State: Economic Change and the National Question in Twentieth-Century Estonia," in *Economic Change and the National Question in Twentieth-Century Europe*, ed. Alice Teichova et al. (Cambridge; New York: Cambridge University Press, 2000), 362.

81. Kasekamp, *A History of the Baltic States*, 126.

82. Domestic Stresses in the USSR, an Intelligence Assessment, April 1, 1986, 23, CIA, FOIA Electronic Reading Room, accessed January 22, 2022, https://www.cia.gov/readingroom/document/cia-rdp87t00787r000200180006-0.

83. Kasekamp, *A History of the Baltic States*, 155.

84. Pascal Bonnard, *Le gouvernement de l'ethnicité en Europe post-soviétique. Minorités et pouvoir en Lettoni* (Paris: Dalloz, 2013), 190.

85. Jeremy Smith, *Red Nations: The Nationalities Experience in and after the USSR* (Cambridge: Cambridge University Press, 2013), 249.

86. *Narodnoye khozyaystvo SSSR v 1990 g. Statisticheskiy ezhegodnik* (Moscow: Finansy i statistika 1991), 77.

87. Domestic Stresses in the USSR, 23.

88. Hélène Carrère d'Encausse, *L'empire éclaté: la révolte des nations en U.R.S.S.* (Paris: Flammarion, 1978), 273.

89. Kasekamp, *A History of the Baltic States*, 155.

90. Zigmantas Kiaupa, *The History of Lithuania* (Vilnius: Baltos lankos, 2005), 308.

91. Kasekamp, *A History of the Baltic States*, 139.

92. Timothy Snyder, *The Reconstruction of Nations: Poland, Ukraine, Lithuania, Belarus, 1569–1999* (New Haven, CT: Yale University Press, 2003), 91.

93. Violeta Davoliūtė, *The Making and Breaking of Soviet Lithuania: Memory and Modernity in the Wake of War* (London; New York: Routledge, 2013), 2.

94. Carrère d'Encausse, *L'empire éclaté*, 59.

95. Davoliūtė, *The Making and Breaking of Soviet Lithuania*, 2; Snyder, *The Reconstruction of Nations*, 94

96. In 1959 the Lithuanian urbanization rate was already 39 percent, while that of Latvia and Estonia was the highest in the USSR at 56 percent. In 1970 Estonia and Latvia were still ahead of the Soviet average (56%), with 65 percent and 62 percent respectively, while Lithuania had reached 50 percent. Carrère d'Encausse, *L'empire éclaté*, 59.

97. Davoliūtė, *The Making and Breaking of Soviet Lithuania*, 2.

98. Ibid., 3.

99. Interview with Trimi Velliste, founder and chairman of Estonian Heritage Society, Tallinn, June 18, 2013.

100. Ainė Ramonaitė and Rytė Kukulskytė, "Etnokultūrinis Judėjimas Sovietmečiu: Nematoma Alternatyva Sistemai?" *Lietuvos Etnologija: Socialines Antropologijos Ir Etnologijos Studijos* 14, no. 23 (2014): 161–181.

101. Juhan Saharov, "From an Economic Term to a Political Concept. The Conceptual Innovation of 'Self-Management' in Soviet Estonia," *Contributions to the History of Concepts* 16, no. 1 (2021): 127.

102. Edijs Bošs, "Aligning with the Unipole: Security Policies of Estonia, Latvia, and Lithuania, 1988–1998" (PhD diss., University of Cambridge, 2011), 47.

103. Beissinger, *Nationalist Mobilization and the Collapse of the Soviet State*, 171.

104. Ainė Ramonaitė, "Explaining the Birth of *Sąjūdis*: The Networking Power of Alternative Society in Soviet Lithuania," paper prepared for the 10th Conference on Baltic Studies in Europe "Cultures, Crises, Consolidations in the Baltic World," Tallinn University, June 16–19, 2013, 2.

105. Mark Beissinger, "The Intersection of Ethnic Nationalism and People Power Tactics in the Baltic States, 1987–1991," in *Civil Resistance and Power Politics: The Experience of Non-violent Action from Gandhi to the Present*, ed. Adam Roberts and Timothy Garton Ash (Oxford: Oxford University Press, 2009), 235.

106. Zubok, *Collapse*, 52; Kotkin, *Armageddon Averted*, 72.

107. Abstracts of the presentation by A. N. Yakovlev at the Politburo of the Central Committee of the CPSU "O poyezdke v Latviyskuyu i Litovskuyu SSR 8–13 avgusta 1988 g.," 18.08.1988, accessed December 20, 2021, https://www.alexan deryakovlev.org/fond/issues-doc/1023735.

108. Mikhail Gorbachev, *Memoirs* (New York: Doubleday, 1996), 340.

109. *Soyuz mozhno bylo sokhranit*, 66, 71–72; *V Politbyuro TsK KPSS*, 481.

110. Anatol Lieven, *The Baltic Revolution: Estonia, Latvia, Lithuania, and the Path to Independence* (New Haven, CT: Yale University Press, 1993), 223.

111. Beissinger, *Nationalist Mobilization*, 392, 399–401.

112. For more on the origins of Baltic nonviolence approach see Beissinger, "The Intersection of Ethnic Nationalism," 231–247; Kramer, "The Collapse of East European Communism," part 1, 46–47.

113. Saulius Grybkauskas, "Anti-Soviet Protests and the Localism of the Baltic Republics Nomenklatura: Explaining the Interaction," *Journal of Baltic Studies* 49, no. 4 (2018): 447–462.

114. Daina Bleiere, "The Formation and Development of the Soviet Latvian *Nomenklatura*: Path Dependency, Cleavages, and Imposed Unanimity," in *Moscow and the Non-Russian Republics in the Soviet Union. Nomenklatura, Intelligentsia and Centre-Periphery Relations*, ed. Li Bennich-Björkman and Saulius Grybkauskas (Milton Park, Abingdon; New York: Routledge, 2022), Bookshelf, 65.

115. Kotkin, *Armageddon Averted*, 105.

116. Smith, *Red Nations*, 218; Zubkova, *Pribaltika i Kreml*, 341; Renal'd Simonyan, "Kak mozhno bylo sokhranit' Sovetskiy Soyuz (Baltiyskiy rakurs)," *Sotsiologicheskiye issledovaniya*, no. 8 (2021), acessed December 20, 2021, https://ras.jes.su/socis/s013216250014595-7-1.

117. More on the ethnic compostion of the Baltic communist parties: Saulius Grybkauskas, *Governing the Soviet Union's National Republics. The Second Secretaries of the Communist Party* (London; New York: Routledge, 2021), 166–167.

118. Bleiere, "The Formation and Development of the Soviet Latvian *Nomenklatura*," 64

119. Pētersone and Būmane, *Valstsvīrs Anatolijs Gorbunovs*, 140–142.

120. Lieven, *The Baltic Revolution*, 231.

121. William E. Pomeranz, *Law and the Russian State: Russia's Legal Evolution from Peter the Great to Vladimir Putin* (London: Bloomsbury, 2018), 109–110.

122. Zubok, *Collapse*, 53; "Ob izmeneniyakh i dopolneniyakh Konstitutsii," *Pravda*, October 22, 1988.

123. Vaino Väljas, "Taasiseseisvumisest," in *Eesti iseseisvus võideti Moskvas*, ed. Andres Adamson (Tallinn: Argo, 2016), 24; Sandra Kalniete, *Es lauzu, tu lauzi, mēs lauzām, viņi lauza* (Riga: Jumava, 2000), Pirmās uzvaras, e-book; Virgilijus Čepaitis, "Sąjūdžio politinės akcijos," in *Kelias į Nepriklausomybę: Lietuvos Sąjūdis 1988–1991*, ed. Bronius Genzelis and Angonita Rupšytė (Kaunas: Šviesa, 2010), 79.

124. Dainis Īvans, *Gadījuma Karakalps* (Rīga: Vieda, 1995), 183.

125. Virgilijus Čepaitis, *Su Sąjūdžiu už Lietuvą nuo 1988. 06. 03.–1990. 03. 11.* (Vilnius: Tvermė, 2007), 153–155; Kalniete, *Es lauzu*, 1988. gada 22. novembris.

126. *Vneocherednaya desyataya sessiya Verkhovnogo Soveta SSSR (odinnadtsatyy sozyv), 29 noyabrya–1 dekabrya 1988 g. Stenograficheskiy otchet* (Moscow: Izdaniye Verkhovnogo Soveta SSSR, 1988), 72–75.

127. Pētersone and Būmane, *Valstsvīrs Anatolijs Gorbunovs*, 226–227.

128. *V Politbyuro TsK KPSS*, 416.

129. Vitaly Vorotnikov, *A bylo eto tak. . . . Iz dnevnika chlena Politbyuro TsK KPSS* (Moscow: Kniga i biznes, 1995), 233; Zubok, *Collapse*, 53.

130. *V Politbyuro TsK KPSS*, 416; Zubok, *Collapse*, 53.

131. Anatoly Chernyaev, *Diary 1987–1988*, 59, acessed November 29, 2021, https://nsarchive2.gwu.edu/NSAEBB/NSAEBB250/.

132. Vadim Medvedev, *V komande Gorbacheva: vzglyad iznutri* (Moscow: Bylina, 1994), Vokrug XIX partkonferentsii i posle nee, accessed November 29, 2021, http://lib.ru/MEMUARY/GORBACHEV/medvedev.txt.

133. Chernyaev, *Diary 1987–1988*, 59; Čepaitis, *Su Sąjūdžiu už Lietuvą*, 155.

134. Chernyaev, *Diary 1987–1988*, 59.

135. Medvedev, *V komande Gorbacheva*, Vokrug XIX partkonferentsii.

136. Vorotnikov, *A bylo eto tak*, 234.

137. *V Politbyuro TsK KPSS*, 419.

138. Simonyan, "Kak mozhno bylo sokhranit."

139. Zubok, *Collapse*, 54.

140. *Soyuz mozhno bylo sokhranit*, 54.

141. Renald Simonyan, *Rossiya i strany Baltii* (Moscow: Academia, 2003), 60.

142. Kalniete, *Es lauzu*, 1988. gada 22. novembris.

CHAPTER 2

1. Jacques Lévesque, "The East European Revolutions of 1989," in *The Cambridge History of the Cold War*, ed. Melvyn P. Leffler and Odd Arne Westad, vol. 3: *Endings* (Cambridge: Cambridge University Press, 2010), 311.

2. Memorandum from Scowcroft to Bush (prepared by Rodman), June 20, 1989, GBPL, Bush Presidential Files, Scowcroft Collection, USSR Collapse Files, U.S.-Soviet Relations, OA/ID 91117-003.

3. In the Latvian case the decision to focus on full independence was directly influenced by the Latvian diaspora. In mid-May 1989 representatives of both Tautas Fronte and National Congress met with the leadership of the World Federation of Free Latvians. Negotiations that took place in "La Ville au Maire" near Tours in France, resulted in a tactical agreement to restore the independence of Latvia. Dainis Īvāns, *Latvijas Tautas Fronte Rietumos* (Rīga: Elpa, 2001), 195–200.

4. Kramer, "The Collapse of East European Communism and the Repercussions within the Soviet Union," Part 1), 206.

5. Ibid., 207.

6. See Michel Foucault, *Language, Counter-Memory, Practice: Selected Essays and Interviews* (Ithaca, NY: Cornell University Press, 1977); Duncan Bell, "Mythscapes: Memory, Mythology, and National Identity," *British Journal of Sociology* 54, no. 1 (March 2003): 66.

7. Philippe Perchoc, "European Memory beyond the State: Baltic, Russian and European Memory Interactions (1991–2009)," *Memory Studies* 12, no. 6 (2019): 679–680.

8. Una Bergmane, "Les pays baltes et le démantèlement de l'Union soviétique. La controverse au sujet du pacte germano-soviétique 1987-1989," *Matériaux pour l'histoire de notre temps* 3, no. 133–134 (2019): 78.

9. Serhy Yekelchyk, *Stalin's Empire of Memory: Russian-Ukrainian Relations in the Soviet Historical Imagination* (Toronto: University of Toronto Press, 2004), 4–5.

10. Suny, *The Revenge of the Past*, 156.

11. Vello Andreas Pettai, "Framing the Past as Future: The Power of Legal Restorationism in Estonia" (PhD diss., Columbia University, 2004), 206.

12. "MRP-AEG infobülletään nr 1, September 1987," *MRP-AEG infobülletään 1987–88* (Tallinn: Kirjastus SE&JS, 1998), 11–21.

13. Astra Mille, *Te Un Citadelē: Jānis Peters: Tumšsarkanā* (Rīga: Atēna, 2006), 220.

14. Graeme J. Gill, *Symbols and Legitimacy in Soviet Politics* (Cambridge; New York: Cambridge University Press, 2011), 5.

15. Jan Lipinsky, "Reception and Historiography of the MRP in (Soviet) Russia," in *The Baltic States at the End of the Cold War*, eds. Kaarel Piirimäe and Olaf Mertelsmann (Berlin: Peter Lang, 2018), 36–40

16. *V Politbyuro TsK KPSS*, 343.

17. Ibid., 343–344.

18. Anatoly Chernyaev, *Diary 1989*, 54, accessed November 29, 2021, https://nsarchi ve2.gwu.edu/NSAEBB/NSAEBB275/index.htm.

19. Raun, *Estonia and the Estonians*, 227; "PSRS tautas deputāti no Latvijas," *Padomju Jaunatne*, May 23, 1989; Richard J. Krickus, *Showdown: The Lithuanian Rebellion and the Breakup of the Soviet Empire* (Washington, DC: Brassey's, 1997), 64.

20. *Soyuz mozhno bylo sokhranit*, 464.

21. Vorotnikov, *A bylo eto tak*, 266; Chernyaev, *Diary 1989*, 21.

22. Chernyaev, *Diary 1989*, 21.

23. Vorotinkov, *A bylo eto tak*, 266.

24. *V Politbyuro TsK KPSS*, 482.

25. Vorotinkov, *A bylo eto tak*, 272.

26. *Pervy Syezd narodnykh deputatov SSSR 25 maya–9 iyunya 1989 g. Stenograficheskiy otchot* (Moscow: Izdaniye Verkhovnogo Soveta SSSR, 1989), 2:190.

27. Ibid., 464.

28. Ibid., 198–200.

29. Matthew Evangelista has argued that Gorbachev's successful political career could be explained by applying Riker's concept of heresthetic: the skill of framing and structuring the situation through language. Matthew Evangelista, "Norms, Heresthetics, and the End of the Cold War," *Journal of Cold War Studies* 3, no. 1 (2001): 13.

30. Ibid., 16.

31. Alexander Yakovlev, *Sumerki* (Moscow: Materik, 2003), 415, 419.

32. Valery Boldin, *Krushenie p'edestala: shtrikhi k portretu M. S. Gorbacheva* (Moscow: Respublika, 1995), 261–262.

33. Boris Khavkin, "Byl li u Sovetskogo Soyuza tretiy put'. Dokumenty 1939–1941 godov i preodoleniye proshlogo," *Nezavisimaya gazeta*, September 24, 2020, accessed November 15, 2021, https://nvo.ng.ru/history/2020-09-24/1_1110_p ath.html.

34. Interview with Andrei Grachev, deputy head of the CPSU Central Committee's International section (1989–1991), press secretary of Mikhail Gorbachev (1991), Paris, March 15, 2016.

35. Barbara A. Misztal, *Theories of Social Remembering* (Buckingham: Open University Press, 2003), 66.

36. *V Politbyuro TsK KPSS*, 500; Zubok, *Collapse*, 52.

37. Zubkova, *Pribaltika i Kreml*, 4.

38. English, *Russia and the Idea of the West*, 4–5.

39. Neuman, *Russia and the Idea of Europe*, 146–147.

40. Chernyaev, *Diary 1989*, 54; See also a report that seems (signature illegible) to be written by Georgy Shakhnazarov to Gorbachev on December 27, 1989 (Gorbachev Foundation, 2115).

41. Anatoly Chernyaev, *Diary 1990*, 30, accessed November 29, 2021, https://nsa rchive2.gwu.edu/NSAEBB/NSAEBB317/index.htm; *Diary 1991*, 6, accessed November 29, 2021, https://nsarchive2.gwu.edu/NSAEBB/NSAEBB345/ index.htm.

42. Memorandum of Conversation between US diplomat George Krol and Dainis Īvāns, deputy chairman of the Supreme Soviet of Latvia, Riga, March 29, 1991, LAMA, 1991_254_261.5.

43. Īvāns, *Gadījuma karakalps*, 232.

44. Plokhy, *The Last Empire*, 56–59

45. Nils R. Muižnieks, "The Influence of the Baltic Popular Movements on the Process of Soviet Disintegration," *Europe-Asia Studies* 47, no. 1 (1995): 3–25; Beissinger, *Nationalist Mobilization and the Collapse of the Soviet State*, 160–161.

46. Bošs, "Aligning with the Unipole: Security Policies of Estonia, Latvia, and Lithuania, 1988–1998," 79.

47. Anneli Reigas, "One Pen and the Truth: News from Moscow," in *Molotov-Ribbentrop Pact: Challenging Soviet History*, ed. Heiki Lindpere (Tallinn: The Foreign Policy Institute, 2009), 109.

48. *Второй съезд народных депутатов СССР 12–24 декабря, 1989 г: стенографический отчет*, 4:290.

49. Interview with Dainis Īvāns, chairman of *Tautas Fronte* (1988–1990), deputy speaker of the Supreme Soviet of Latvia (1990–1992), Riga, May 19, 2015.

50. "More than Two Million Join Human Chain in Soviet Baltics," *Reuters News*, August 23, 1989.

51. "Annexation Void Lithuania Say," *New York Times*, August 23, 1989; Esther B. Fein, "Baltic Citizens Link Hands to Demand Independence," *New York Times*, August 24, 1989. "Les Baltes manifestent pour leur indépendance," *Le Figaro*, August 24, 1989; "600 km lang protest," *Berlingske Tidende*, August 24, 1989; "Hunderttausende Balten begehren gegen die russische Vorherrschauft auf," *Frankfurter Zeitung*, August 24, 1989; "Mahtava ihmisketju Baltianmaiden lap," *Helsingin Sanomat*, August 24, 1989; "Lungn protest mot krigspakt," *Dagens Nyheter*, August 24, 1989; Sergio Sergi, "Il Baltico in rivolta. Erano un milione, mano nella mano," *L'Unità*, August 24, 1989.

52. Una Bergmane, *French and US Reactions Facing the Disintegration of the USSR: The Case of the Baltic States (1989–1991)* (PhD. diss., Sciences Po Paris 2016), 130–131; Niels von Redecker, *The Baltic Question and the British Press, 1989–1991* (Hamburg: Verlag Dr Kovač, 1998).

53. Michael Dobbs, "Baltic States Link in Protest 'So Our Children Can Be Free'," *Washington Post*, August 24, 1989, A1; Esther B. Fein, "Baltic Citizens Link Hands to Demand Independence," *New York Times*, August 24, 1989, A1; Andrew Katell, "Baltics Call Soviet Annexation a 'Crime,' Equate Hitler, Stalin," *Associated Press*, August 22, 1989.

54. Senator Helms (NC), "The Dark Legacy of Hitler and Stalin in the Baltic," Congressional Record, September 19, 1989, S20780.

55. Editorial, "Captive Nations," *Washington Post*, August 27, 1989.

56. Anthony Lewis, "Abroad and at Home. The Power of History," *New York Times*, August 27, 1989.

57. "Excerpts from Soviet Statement on Baltic Unrest," *New York Times*, August 27, 1989.

58. Bernard Cohen, "Moscou menace les Pays baltes," *Libération*, August 2, 1989.

59. Hervé Caumont, "L'URSS: langue de fer pour les Baltes," *Quotidien de Paris*, August 28, 1989.

60. David Remnick, "Gorbachev Shows His Tough Side; Nationalist Movements Are Learning His Tolerance Has Limits," *Washington Post*, August 30, 1989.

61. *Soyuz mozhno bylo sokhranit*, 87–88.

62. Esther B. Fein, "Gorbachev Said to Have Backed Attack on Baltic Movements," *New York Times*, August 30, 1989.

63. Chernyaev, *Diary 1989*, 29.

64. Andrus Park, *End of an Empire? A Conceptualization of the Soviet Disintegration Crisis 1985–1991* (Tartu: Tartu University Press, 2009), 109.

65. Spohr, "Between Political Rhetoric and Realpolitik Calculations," 5.
66. Ibid., 7.
67. *V Politbyuro TsK KPSS*, 508–509.
68. "O natsional'noi politike partii v sovremennykh usloviyakh: Doklad M. S. Gorbacheva, General'nogo sekretarya Tsentral'nogo Komiteta KPSS, na plenume Tsentral'nogo Komiteta KPSS 19 sentyabrya 1989 goda," *Pravda*, September 20, 1989.
69. Ibid.
70. Park, *End of an Empire?*, 114.
71. Vorotnikov, *A bylo eto tak*, 313.
72. Ibid., 311–313; *V Politbyuro TsK KPSS*, 527–531; *Soyuz mozhno bylo sokhranit*, 98–102.
73. Baker and DeFrank, *The Politics of Diplomacy*, 63.
74. Vladimir Lukin, "Novoye myshleniye—novyye prioritety," *Moskovskiye Novosti*, September 25, 1988 (quoted in Neumann, *Russia and the Idea of Europe*, 146–147).
75. "Minutes of the Meeting of the Politburo of the CPSU CC, 27–28 December 1988," *Cold War International History Project Bulletin*, no. 12/13 (2001): 24–25.
76. "Soviets Not the Evil Empire Anymore, Reagan Declares: Euphoric President Hails Pact," *Los Angeles Times*, December 11, 1987.
77. Third conversation between M. S. Gorbachev and FRG Chancellor Helmut Kohl, June 14, 1989, accessed January 20, 2020, https://digitalarchive.wilsoncenter.org/document/120811.
78. Bush and Scowcroft, *A World Transformed*, 46.
79. Memorandum from Rice to Scowcroft, February 7, 1989, GBPL, Scowcroft Collection, USSR Collapse Files, U.S-Soviet Relations, OA/ID 91117-001.
80. Ibid. See Blackwell's handwritten notes on the document.
81. Ibid. See president's handwritten notes on the Memorandum from Brent Scowcroft to the President, March 1, 1989.
82. Bush and Scowcroft, *A World Transformed*, 112–127; Baker and DeFrank, *The Politics of Diplomacy*, 45; Robert L. Hutchings, *American Diplomacy and the End of the Cold War: An Insider's Account of U.S. Policy in Europe, 1989–1992* (Baltimore: Johns Hopkins University Press, 1997), 10.
83. Gregory F. Domber, "Skepticism and Stability: Reevaluating U.S. Policy during Poland's Democratic Transformation in 1989," *Journal of Cold War Studies* 13, no. 3 (2011): 52–82; Konstantin Pleshakov, *There Is No Freedom without Bread!: 1989 and the Civil War That Brought Down Communism* (New York: Farrar, Straus & Giroux, 2009), 246; Mary Elise Sarotte, *1989: The Struggle to Create a Post–Cold War Europe* (Princeton, NJ: Princeton University Press, 2014), 21–24; Kristina Spohr, *Post Wall, Post Square: Rebuilding the World after 1989* (New Haven, CT: Yale University Press, 2019), 92.
84. Spohr, "Between Political Rhetoric and Realpolitik Calculations," 21.
85. "Mitterrand and Thatcher on German Unification, December 1989," in *The Cold War: A History in Documents and Eyewitness Accounts*, ed. Jussi M. Hanhimäki and Odd Arne Westad (Oxford: Oxford University Press, 2003), 609–612.
86. Gorbachev meeting with Genscher, December 5, 1989, accessed March 26, 2019, https://digitalarchive.wilsoncenter.org/document/120827.
87. Michael Cox, "The Uses and Abuses of History: The End of the Cold War and Soviet Collapse," *International Politics* 48, no. 4–5 (2011): 637.

88. Bush meeting with Baltic Americans, April 11, 1990, GBPL, Bush Presidential Records, NSC, Hutchings Files, Baltic States (2),OA/ID CF01029-007.

89. Bush meeting with Mitterrand, April 19, 1990, GBPL, accessed January 12, 2022, https://bush41library.tamu.edu/files/memcons-telcons/1990-04-19--Mitterrand%20[1].pdf.

90. Robert Jervis, *Perception and Misperception in International Politics* (Princeton, NJ: Princeton University Press, 2017), 217, 266.

91. Baker and DeFrank, *The Politics of Diplomacy*, 146–147.

92. James M. Lindsay, "Congress and Foreign Policy: Why the Hill Matters," *Political Science Quarterly* 107, no. 4 (1992): 609.

93. Senator Kasten, "Senate Concurrent Resolution 69," Congressional Record, September 14, 1989, S20563.

94. H.R. 2939, 101. Congress (1989–1990), September 20, 1989, accessed January 21, 2022, https://www.senate.gov/legislative/LIS/roll_call_lists/vote_menu_101_1.htm.

95. Letters from 120 Representatives to the President, October 16, 1989, National Security Archive (here after NSA), Box 4, Malta Summit, Letters from Concerned Citizens.

96. Michael Beschloss and Strobe Talbott, *At the Highest Levels. The Inside Story of the End of the Cold War* (New York: Open Road Media, 2016), 115, Google Play Books.

97. Baker and DeFrank, *The Politics of Diplomacy*, 169.

98. Beschloss and Talbott, 19.

99. Ibid., 20–21.

100. Ibid., 25.

101. Thomas W. Simons, US ambassador to Poland (1990–1993), Cambridge, US, May 29, 2012.

102. Hutchings, *American Diplomacy and the End of the Cold War*, 36, 373.

103. Thomas L. Friedman, "Baker, Outlining World View, Assesses Plan for Soviet Bloc," *New York Times*, March 28, 1989.

104. Sarotte, *1989*, 23; Wilson, *The Triumph of Improvisation*, 151.

105. Jack F. Matlock, *Autopsy on an Empire: The American Ambassador's Account of the Collapse of the Soviet Union* (New York: Random House, 1995), 269.

106. John B. Genys (Chairman of JBANC) to Bush, November 1, 1989, GBPL, Bush Presidential Records, Staff and Office Files, Schaefer Files, Baltic Americans, OA/ID07554-034, Case No. 090461.

107. The letter was signed by 7 Democrats and 10 Republicans. Letter from 16 US Senators to Bush, November 29, 1989, NSA, Box 4, Malta Summit, Letters from Concerned Citizens.

108. "Some have reported that the Soviets might retreat from their policy of liberalization in the Baltic States. We are concerned that this is one of the items on which the Soviets might ask our understanding." Letter from 32 Representatives, November 20, 1989, NSA, Box 4, Malta Summit, Letters from Concerned Citizens.

109. Baker to Bush, November 29, 1989, accessed November 29, 2021, http://www.gwu.edu/~nsarchiv/NSAEBB/NSAEBB298/index.htm.

110. See the analysis of Joshua R. Itzkowitz Shifrinson, "The Malta Summit and US–Soviet Relations: Testing the Waters Amidst Stormy Seas. New Insights from American Archives," CWIHP e-Dossier No. 40, accessed January 2, 2022, https://www.wilsoncenter.org/publication/the-malta-summit-and-us-soviet-relations-testing-the-waters-amidst-stormy-seas.

111. Beschloss and Talbott, *At the Highest Levels*, 147–148; Philip Zelikow and Condoleezza Rice, *Germany Unified and Europe Transformed. A Study in Statecraft* (Cambridge, MA: Harvard University Press, 1997), 129.
112. Timothy Naftali, *George H. W. Bush* (New York: Times Books, 2007), 109–110.
113. Soviet Transcript of the Malta Summit December 2–3, 1989, National Security Archive, accessed March 9, 2022, https://nsarchive2.gwu.edu/NSAEBB/NSAEBB 298/Document%2010.pdf.
114. Bush meeting with Gorbachev, second restricted bilateral session, Malta, December 3, 1989, GBPL, accessed January 23, 2022, https://bush41library. tamu.edu/archives/memcons-telcons.
115. Ibid.
116. Raymond L. Garthoff, *The Great Transition: American-Soviet Relations and the End of the Cold War* (Washington, DC: Brookings Institution, 1994), 407; Baker, *The Politics of Diplomacy*, 168–171; Spohr, *Post Wall, Post Square*, 199–200; Svetlana Savranskaya and Thomas Blanton, National Security Archive (NSA), "Bush and Gorbachev at Malta Previously Secret Documents from Soviet and U.S. Files on the 1989 Meeting, 20 Years Later," December 3, 2009, accessed January 12, 2022, http://www.gwu.edu/~nsarchiv/NSAEBB/NSAEBB298/index.htm.
117. Presentation by Sergey Radchenko at the LSE International History Department Cold War Research Cluster seminar, May 9, 2019.
118. Bush and Scowcroft, *A World Transformed*, 173.
119. Translation of a letter from Gorbachev to Bush, n.d., GBPL, NSC Files, Rice Files, Situation in Lithuania (1), OA/ID CF00719-001.
120. Shifrinson, "The Malta Summit and US-Soviet Relations."
121. Lévesque, "The East European Revolutions of 1989," 3:323–324.
122. Ibid.

CHAPTER 3

1. COREAU (European correspondence), Madrid to Paris, January 16, 1989, French Diplomatic Archives (Centre des Archives diplomatiques du ministère des Affaires étrangères, hereafter CAD), Europe (1986–1990), URSS 6592.
2. Richard Caplan, *Europe and the Recognition of New States in Yugoslavia* (Cambridge: Cambridge University Press, 2005), 55–60.
3. National Intelligence Council, "The Baltic Republics: Moscow Won't Force Them to Stay," January 29, 1990, accessed January 15, 2022, http://www.foia.cia.gov/ sites/default/files/document_conversions/89801/DOC_0001325096.pdf.
4. See Kristina Spohr, *Post Wall, Post Square*, Chapter 4.
5. Chernyaev, *Diary 1989*, 54; see also a report that seems (signature illegible) to be written by Georgy Shakhnazarov to Gorbachev on December 27, 1989 (Gorbachev Foundation, 2115); and Chernyaev to Gorbachev, Comments on the draft decisions of the plenum, January 21, 1990 (Gorbachev Foundation, 8190).
6. *Soyuz mozhno bylo sokhranit*, 121–122.
7. Interview with Andrei Grachev, deputy head of the CPSU Central Committee's International section (1989–1991), press secretary of Mikhail Gorbachev (1991), Paris, March 15, 2016.
8. *Soyuz mozhno bylo sokhranit*, 138–139.
9. Vorotnikov, *A bylo eto tak*, 358–359.
10. Gunārs Kusiņš, "1990. gada 4. maija deklarācija," *Nacionālā Enciklopēdija*, accessed June 21, 2022, https://enciklopedija.lv/skirklis/146164-1990%C2%A0g ada-4%C2%A0maija-deklar%C4%81cija; Marju Lauristin, "Supreme Soviet of

the ESSR / Supreme Council of the Republic of Estonia," accessed June 20, 2022, https://www.riigikogu.ee/en/introduction-and-history/history-riigikogu/supr eme-soviet-essr-supreme-council-republic-estonia/.

11. "Law on Secession from the USSR," *Seventeen Moments in Soviet History*, accessed June 20, 2022, https://soviethistory.msu.edu/1991-2/shevarnadze-resigns/shev arnadze-resigns-texts/law-on-secession-from-the-ussr/.

12. A document found in Chernyaev's papers in the Gorbachev Foundation Archive in 2012 gives an insight into the reasoning behind the law. The unsigned and undated *Memorandum of the Lithuanian Question* proposed to either dissuade the Lithuanians from their bid for independence by publishing a secession law project showing that the "price for independence would be too high," or to put the independence question to a vote at the Congress of People's Deputies who would then vote to reject it. Gorbachev Foundation, 18428, *Memorandum of the Lithuanian Question*, n.d.

13. Fredrik Doeser and Joakim Eidenfalk, "The Importance of Windows of Opportunity for Foreign Policy Change," *International Ara Studies Review* 16, no. 4 (2013): 393.

14. Sarotte, *1989*, 5.

15. Frédéric Bozo, *Mitterrand, la fin de la guerre froide et l'unification Allemande. De Yalta à Maastricht* (Paris: Jacob, 2005), 211.

16. Ibid., 216–217.

17. Ibid., 217–218.

18. André Liebich, "Les promesses faites à Gorbatchev: l'avenir des alliances au crépuscule de la guerre froide," *Relations internationales* 147, no. 3 (2011): 94–96; Joshua R. Itzkowitz Shifrinson, "Deal or No Deal? The End of the Cold War and the U.S. Offer to Limit NATO Expansion," *International Security* 40, no. 4 (2016): 41–42; Svetlana Savranskaya and Tom Blanton, *NATO Expansion: What Gorbachev Heard*, accessed January 20, 2022, https://nsarchive.gwu.edu/brief ing-book/russia-programs/2017-12-12/nato-expansion-what-gorbachev-heard-western-leaders-early#_edn7.

19. James F. Dobbins, State Department European Bureau, Memorandum to National Security Council: NATO Strategy Review Paper for October 29 Discussion, October 25, 1990, accessed January 10, 2022, https://nsarchive. gwu.edu/document/16141-document-27-james-f-dobbins-state-department. Regarding the alleged promise debate see also Mary Elise Sarotte, *Not One Inch: America, Russia, and the Making of Post–Cold War Stalemate* (New Haven, CT: Yale University Press, 2021).

20. Shifrinson, "Deal or No Deal?"38.

21. Spohr, *Germany and the Baltic Problem after the Cold War*, 20.

22. Bozo, *Mitterrand, La fin de la guerre froide*, 228–241.

23. Meeting between Kohl and Soviet Ambassador Kwizinski, Bonn, March 22, 1990. *Deutsche Einheit. Sonderedition aus den Akten des Bundeskanzleramtes 1989/90. Dokumente zur Deutschlandpolitik*, ed. Hanns Jürgen Küsters and Daniel Hofmann (Munich: R. Oldenbourg, 1998), 967.

24. Sarotte, *1989*, 158.

25. Bush meeting with Mitterrand, April 19, 1990, GBPL, accessed January 12, 2022, https://bush41library.tamu.edu/files/memcons-telcons/1990-04-19--Mitterr and%20[1].pdf.

26. Ibid.

27. Lawrence McQuillan, "US Refrains from Recognizing Lithuania," *Reuters News*, March 12, 1990.

28. Sarotte, *1989*, 185.

29. Statement by the foreign ministers of the Baltic States, October 2, 1990, Estonian State Archive, ERA 1608.2.477. See the same document in Lithuanian Diplomat Archives (Lietuvos užsienio reikalų ministerijos archyvas, hereafter LURMA): F.3, A.3, L.2.

30. Jonas Mekas, "No, My Friend, We Won't Go Slow," *New York Times*, March 29, 1990.

31. Kaarel Piirimäe, "Estonia 'Has Not Time': Existential Politics at the End of Empire,": 21–50.

32. Spohr, "Between Political Rhetoric and Realpolitik Calculations," 15.

33. Lennart Meri meeting with Curtis W. Kamman and Paul Goble, May 13, 1991, transcripts of meetings 1990–1992 (quoted in Piirimäe, "Estonia Has Not Time." Perceptions of the post–Cold War as a Window of Opportunity paper presented at the Conference "Post–Cold War. Change and Continuity in the Making of a New World Order at the Turn of the 1990s," October 27–28, 2016, University of Minnesota.)

34. Data from Dow Jones Factiva.

35. William Safire, "World to Vilnius: Suffer," *New York Times*, April 23, 1990; William Safire, "Essay: Baltic to Baghdad," *New York Times*, March 30, 1990; A. M. Rosenthal, "How to Desert a Friend," *New York Times*, April 15, 1990.

36. "Tiananmen in Vilnius?" *Wall Street Journal*, March 27, 1990; Editorial, "The Lithuanian Alternative," *Washington Post*, March 28, 1990.

37. Leslie H. Gelb, "Behind the Lithuania Crisis," *New York Times*, March 23, 1990.

38. John B. Oakes, "Lean On the Lithuanians," *New York Times*, April 21, 1990.

39. Editorial, "Lithuanian and Soviet Disunion," *St. Louis Post Dispatch*, March 23, 1990; Editorial, "For Now Mr. Bush Sets Right Tone," *St. Petersburg Times*, March 30, 1990.

40. Wilson, *The Triumph of Improvisation*, 184.

41. Bush and Scowcroft, *A World Transformed*, 241–42.

42. Scott Sutherland to David Demarest, "Lithuanian American Groups," April 6 , 1990, GBPL, Bush Presidential Records, Office of Public Liaison, James Schaefer Files, Lithuania (1), OA/ID 07554-028.

43. Walter V. Kazlauskas to Bush, n.d., GBPL, WHORM Subject Files, CO091, Case no. 203442.

44. Jonas Urbonas, chairman of the Lithuanian-American Federation, to Bush, March 31, 1990, GBPL, WHORM Subject Files, CO091, Case no. 133434.

45. David J. Shestokas to John Sununu, March 31, 1990, GBPL, WHORM Subject Files, CO091.

46. Lucija Mazeika (Californian Republican Heritage Groups) to Bush, May 14, 1990, GBPL, Bush Presidential Records, WHORM Subject Files, CO091, Case no. 142735.

47. North American Support groups of Tautas Fronte to Bush, April 7, 1990, GBPL, Bush Presidential Records, WHORM Subject Files, CO091.

48. WHORM Subject Files, CO091: Danguole Klimas (Lithuanian American Community) to Bush, March 19, 1990, Case No. 130969; Kazis Bobelis (President of the Supreme Committee for the Liberation of Lithuania to Bush) Case No. 9008260; Aldona Pintsch (Federation of Lithuanian Women's Club) to Bush,

March 21, 1990, Case No. 9008256; Eugene Ashely (Knights of Lithuania) to Bush, March 20, 1990, Case No: 9008270.

49. Estonian National Congress in Sweden to Bush, May 2, 1990, GBPL, WHORM Subject Files, CO048, Case No. 139606.

50. GBPL, WHORM Subject Files, CO091: Melvin Laszczynski to President Bush, May 10, 1990, Case No. 141963; David W. Tsai (President of Center for Taiwan International Relations), April 12, 1990, Case No. 133667; Ukrainian Congress Committee of America to President Bush, March 30, 1990, Case No. 141128; Alfred Hong, President, New York Republican State Committee Heritage Group Council to President Bush, April 4, 1990, Case No. 131059.

51. Ambassador Davies to President Bush, March 30, 1990, GBPL, WHORM Subject Files, CO091.

52. Robert T. Davis, "Recognize Lithuania," *Washington Post*, April 8, 1990.

53. GBPL, WHORM Subject Files, CO091: Peter Sørensen to President Bush, May 9, 1990, Case No. 141298; See also Representative Amory Houghton to President Bush, May 4, 1990; Perkins Bass to President Bush, April 20, 1990, Case No. 136701; Roy Gustaves (National Association of Retired Veteran Railway Employees) to President Bush, April 26, 1990, Case No. 137722; Henry Cornely to Congressman Bennett, April 20, 1990, Case No. 137900.

54. Memorandum of Conversation with Baltic American Leaders, April 11, 1990, GBPL, NSC Files, Hutchings Files, Baltics (2), OA/ID CF01411-017.

55. Ibid.

56. Senator Dole (D, KS), Congressional Record, March 21, 1990, S4872.

57. GBPL, The White House, Bush meeting with Mitterrand, April 19, 1990, Key Largo, Florida, accessed January 23, 2022, https://bush41library.tamu.edu/files/memcons-telcons/1990-04-19--Mitterrand%20[1].pdf.

58. Senator Armstrong (R, CO), Congressional Record, March 21, 1990, S 4868. See also Senator Helms (R, NC), Congressional Record, March 21, 1990, S 4865.

59. Senator Simon (D, IL), Congressional Record, March 21, 1990, S 4871.

60. "There is no moral equivalency. The Lithuanian people are right, and Mr. Gorbachev's Soviet Government is wrong." Representative Lieberman (D, CT), Congressional Record, April 3, 1990, H6380.

61. Senator (R, NC) Helms (and others), Amendment 1355, Congressional Record, March 21, 1990, S 4930; Representative Lantos (D, CA), Congressional Record, March 12, 1990, H4236.

62. Representative Miller (D, CA), Congressional Record, March 13, 1990, H4260-42621; Representative Kostmayer (D, PA), Congressional Record, April 3, 1990, H6343; Representative Broomfield (R, MI), Congressional Record, March 22, 1990, H4988; Senator Kyl (Republican, AZ), Congressional Record, April 19, 1990, S7412; Representative Torricelli (D, NJ), Congressional Record, March 21, 1990, H 4743.

63. Representative Durbin (D, IL); Representative Hoyer (D, MD); Congressional Record, June 6, 1990, H13190; Representative Russo (D, IL) Record, March 13, 1990, H4257–H4258; Senator Armstrong (R, CO) Congressional Record, March 21, 1990, H 4867–4868; Senator DeConcini (D, AZ), Congressional Record, April 25, 1990, S 8184–8185.

64. S. Con. Res. 108, Congressional Record, March 22, 1990, S 5115–5116.

65. Senator Helms, "The Right of Self-Determination of Lithuanian People," Congressional Record, March 22, 1990, S 5111.

66. S. Con. Res. 108, Congressional Record, March 22, 1990, S 5116.

67. The White House, Memorandum for Brent Scowcroft, Points to be made at the NSC meeting on Lithuania, April 23, 1990, GBPL, NSC Files, Rice Files, 1989–1991, Lithuania (2), OA/ID CF00071-002.

68. GBPL, NSC Files, Rice Files, 1989–1991, Baltics Other, The Situation in Lithuania, April 1990, OA/ID CF00720-004.

69. Memo from Teltschik to Kohl, March 29, 1990, in *Deutsche Einheit*, 987–988.

70. From Secretary of State to all Diplomatic Posts, "US Policy Statement Regarding Situation in Lithuania," March 24, 1990, GBPL, NSC, Rice Files, 1989–1991, Baltics, Cable Traffic 2, OA/ID CF00070-002.

71. Chernyaev, *Diary 1990*, 18.

72. GBPL, NSC Files, Hutchings Files, Baltic States (2), OA/ID CF01411-017: Memorandum for Brent Scowcroft from Robert Hutchings, "Next Steps on Lithuania," April 19, 1990; Telegram to Secretary of State from C. W. Kamman, "Options for Responding to Soviet Economic Sanctions against Lithuania," April 13, 1990. GBPL, Scowcroft Collection, USSR collapse files, U.S.-Soviet relations, Chronological Files, USSR collapse, Soviet relations Thru 1991 (April–May, 1990) (1), OA/ID 91118-002: Memorandum for Brent Scowcroft from Nicholas Rostow, "Lithuania and the International Court of Justice," April 24, 1990; Memorandum for Brent Scowcroft from Condoleezza Rice, "Letter to Landsbergis," April 26, 1990.

73. Memorandum of conversation between Baker and Gorbachev, May 18, 1990, GBPL, Scowcroft Collection, Special Separate USSR Notes Files, Gorbachev Files, Gorbachev (Dobrynin) Sensitive 1989–June 1990 (4), OA/ID 91126-004.

74. Baker to Bush, March 20, 1990, GBPL, NSC, Rice Files, 1989–1990, Baltics Other, OA/ID CF007720-004.

75. Francis X. Clines, "Upheaval in the East; Gorbachev Tells the Lithuanians to Turn In Arms," *New York Times*, March 22, 1990.

76. Baker and DeFrank, *The Politics of Diplomacy*, 239. Message from Baker to Shevardnadze, March 24, 1990, MML, James A. Baker III Papers (MC 197), Box 108, Folder 15.

77. From Secretary of State to all Diplomatic Posts, "US Policy Statement Regarding Situation in Lithuania," March 24, 1990, GBPL, NSC, Rice Files, 1989-1991, Baltics, Cable Traffic 2, OA/ID CF00720-002

78. "Swedish Army on Alert after Soviet Troop Movements in Lithuania," *Associated Press*, March 22, 1990.

79. Cable no. 128 from French Embassy in Copenhagen to French Foreign Ministry, March 26, 1990, CAD, Europe 1986–1990, 6592.

80. French Foreign Ministry, H. Reynaud, "Internal Situation in the USSR, Appendix: Reactions and Positions Regarding the Events in Lithuania," April 10, 1990, CAD Europe (1986–1990), 6793.

81. Bush and Scowcroft, *A World Transformed*, 218. See also Memo from Teltschik to Kohl, March 29, 1990, in *Deutsche Einheit*, 987–988.

82. Beschloss and Talbott, *At the Highest Levels*, 173–174, 179–180. See also Embassy in Moscow on Kennedy's meeting with Gorbachev, March 28, 1990, GBPL NSC, Rice Files, Baltics Other, OA/ID CF00720-004.

83. Bush and Scowcroft, *A World Transformed*, 226–227.

84. Matlock, *Autopsy on an Empire*, 345–346.

85. From American Embassy Moscow to Secretary of State, "Ambassador's Call on Yakovlev," March 30, 1990, GBPL, NSC Files 1989–1991, Baltic other, OA/ID CF00720-004.

86. Meeting between Baker and Shevardnadze, April 4, 1990, GBPL, Scowcroft Collection, Special Separate USSR Notes Files, Gorbachev Files, OA/ID 91126-004.

87. Ibid.

88. Meeting between Baker and Shevardnadze, April 5, 1990, GBPL, Scowcroft Collection, Special Separate USSR Notes Files, Gorbachev Files, OA/ID 91126-004.

89. Ibid.

90. Meeting between Baker and Shevardnadze, April 4, 1990.

91. Meeting between Baker and Shevardnadze, April 5, 1990.

92. Bozo, *Mitterrand, La fin de la guerre froide*, 241–247.

93. Sarotte, *1989*, 149.

94. French Foreign Ministry, Jacques Blot (director of the European Affairs Department), "Baltic Countries: The Conflict of Two Legitimacies," April 3, 1990, French National Archives (Archives Nationales, hereafter AN), 5 AG 4/CD 242, dossier 4.

95. Gorbachev, "Obrashenie prezidenta SSR k narody litovskogo SSR," *Pravda*, April 1, 1990.

96. *The Current Digest of the Soviet* Press, No. 14, Vol. 42, May 9, 1990, 12

97. Prezident SSSR M. Gorbachev, Predsedatel' Soveta Ministrov SSSR N. Ryzhkov, "Verkhovnyy Sovet Litovskoy SSR Sovet Ministrov Litovskoy SSR," *Pravda*, April 14, 1990.

98. Vytautas Landsbergis, *Lithuania, Independent Again: The Autobiography of Vytautas Landsbergis* (Cardiff: University of Wales Press, 2000), 189.

99. Letter from Mitterrand and Kohl to Landsbergis, April 26, 1990, AN, AG 54/CD 242, dossier 4.

100. "US Non-committal on Allies Lithuania Letter," *Reuters News*, April 28, 1990; David Hoffman and Ann Devory, "U.S. Quietly Encouraged Initiative," *Washington Post*, April 28, 1990.

101. Notes from phone call between Baker and Shevardnadze, April 18, 1990, MML, James A. Baker III Papers, Box 108, Folder 15.

102. Baker and DeFrank, *The Politics of Diplomacy*, 243.

103. Roland Dumas, *Le fil et la pelote: mémoires* (Paris: Plon, 1996), 396. Baker, *Politics of Diplomacy*, 240–244.

104. Meeting between Bush and Mitterrand, April 19, 1990, GBPL, accessed January 12, 2022, https://bush41library.tamu.edu/files/memcons-telcons/1990-04-19--Mitterrand%20[1].pdf.

105. Zelikow and Rice, *Germany Unified and Europe Transformed*, 257.

106. "URSS après la déclaration franco-allemande M. Dumas: 'Nous ne demandons pas aux Lituaniens de renoncer à leur indépendance,'" *Le Monde*, April 29, 1990.

107. "US Non-committal on Allies Lithuania Letter"; Hoffman and Devory, "U.S. Quietly Encouraged Initiative."

108. Memorandum from Scowcroft, "Points to Be Made at the NSC Meeting on Lithuania," April 23, 1990, GBPL, NSC Files, Rice Files, 1989–1991, Lithuania (2), ID/OA CF00719-002.

109. Ibid.

110. Peter Conradi, "Lithuania Waits for Moscow to Show Its Hand," *Reuters News*, April 16, 1990.

111. Memorandum from Brent Scowcroft, "Meeting with NSC Principals on Lithuania," April 23, 1990, GBPL, NSC Files, Rice Files, 1989–1991, Lithuania (2),OA/ID CF00719-002.

112. Lithuania: the US Response Talking Points, April 23, 1990; GBPL, NSC Files, Rice Files, 1989–1991, Situation in Lithuania 1990 (1), OA/ID CF00721-002.
113. Beschloss and Talbott, *At the Highest Levels*, 183–184; Bush and Scowcroft, *A World Transformed*, 224–225.
114. GBPL, NSC Files, Burns Files, Lithuania (2), CF01487-002: Memorandum from Robert Blackwill to Scowcroft, "Responding to Soviet Sanctions in Lithuania," April 25, 1999; Memorandum from Rice, Hutchings, Burns, Adrien Basora, Philip Zelikow to Scowcroft, through Robert Blackwill, "Package on US Response to Soviet Policy in Lithuania," n.d.
115. George H. W. Bush, *All the Best, George Bush: My Life in Letters and Other Writings* (New York: Simon & Schuster, 2013), 468, Google Play Books.
116. Ibid., 469
117. Letter from Gorbachev to Bush, April 30, 1990, GBPL, NSC Files, Rice Files, Baltics Cable Traffic (1), CF00720-001.
118. Bush and Scowcroft, *A World Transformed*, 226.
119. Bush's remarks and a question-and-answer session with the National Association of Agriculture Journalists, March 24, 1990, American Presidency Project, accessed January 12, 2022, https://www.presidency.ucsb.edu/docume nts/remarks-and-question-and-answer-session-with-the-national-association-agriculture; see Congressional Record April 25, 1990.
120. Senator D'Amato (D, NY), Congressional Record, May 1, 1990, S 8856.
121. Landsbergis, *Un peuple sort de prison*, 212–213.
122. Letter from Landsbergis to Mitterrand, May 2, 1990, CAD, Europe (1986–1990), 6682; *The Current Digest of the Russian Press*, No. 17, Vol. 42, May 30, 1990, 18.
123. Memorandum from Scowcroft, "Meeting with NSC Principals on Lithuania," May 6, 1990, GBPL, NSC Files, Rice Files, 1989–1991, Lithuania (2), OA/ID CF00071-002.
124. Statement by Press Secretary Fitzwater on the President's Meeting with Prime Minister Kazimiera Prunskienė of Lithuania, May 3, 1990, *The American Presidency Project*, accessed December 1, 2021, https://www.presidency.ucsb.edu/documents/statement-press-secretary-fitzwater-the-presidents-meeting-with-prime-minister-kazimiera.
125. Memo from Scowcroft, "Meeting with Prime Minister Kazimiera Prunskienė of Lithuania," May 2, 1990, Scowcroft Collection, USSR collapse files, U.S.-Soviet relations Chronological Files, OA/ID 91118-002.
126. Beschloss and Talbott, *At the Highest Levels*, 184–185.
127. Bush and Scowcroft, *A World Transformed*, 228–229; Joseph Kazickas, *Odyssey of Hope: The Story of a Lithuanian Immigrant's Escape from Communism to Freedom in America and the Return to His Beloved Homeland* (Vilnius: Tyto Alba, 2006), 307.
128. Meeting between Mitterrand and Prunskienė, May 10, 1990, AN, 5AG4/CDM 48, dossier 11.
129. Joseph Kazickas, *Odyssey of Hope*, 312–313.
130. Meeting between Kohl and Prunskienė, May 11, 1990, in *Deutsche Einheit*, 1103–1104.
131. Meeting between Kohl and Hurd, May 15, 1990, in *Deutsche Einheit*, 1119.
132. Meeting between Mitterrand and Prunskienė, May 10, 1990.
133. Meeting between Kohl and Shevardnadze, May 4, 1990, in *Deutsche Einheit*, 1085.
134. French Ministry of Foreign Affairs, memo: The West Facing Events in Lithuania, May 9, 1990, CAD, Europe (1986–1990), 6674.

135. Meeting between Mitterrand and Prunskienė, May 10, 1990.
136. Meeting between Kohl and Prunskienė, May 11, 1990, in *Deutsche Einheit*, 1104.
137. French Foreign Ministry, "Internal Situation in the USSR (Latest Elements)," May 23, 1990, CAD, Europe (1986–1990), 6682.
138. Sarotte, *1989*, 142.
139. Pētersone and Būmane, *Valtsvīrs Anatolijs Gorbunovs*, 397–398.
140. Letter from Gorbunovs to Gorbachev, May 4, 1990, Latvian State Archives (Latvijas Valsts arhīvs, hereafter LVA), f.270, a.8, l.8.
141. *The Current Digest of the Russian Press*, No. 18, Vol. 42, June 6, 1990, 13.
142. Declaration by President Gorbachev as Read on Vremya, May 14, 1990, GBPL, NSC Files, Rademaker Files, Baltic States (5), OA/ID CF01029-011. *The Current Digest of the Russian Press*, No. 20, Vol. 42, June 20, 1990, 4, 5.
143. Latvian Representative in Vilnius to Foreign Minister Jurkans, December 27, 1990 LVA, F 270, a. 8, l. 41.
144. Edijs Bošs, "Aligning with the Unipole: Security Policies of Estonia, Latvia, and Lithuania, 1988–1998" (PhD diss., University of Cambridge, 2011), 77.
145. Anatol Lieven, *The Baltic Revolution: Estonia, Latvia, Lithuania and the Path to Independence* (New Haven, CT: Yale University Press, 1993), 241.
146. Eduards Bruno Deksnis and Tālavs Jundzis, *The Parliamentary Route to the Restoration of Latvian Statehood 1989–1993* (Riga: Apgāds Mantojums, 2010), 90.
147. Interview with Dainis Īvāns, chairman of *Tautas Fronte* (1988–1990), deputy speaker of the Supreme Soviet of Latvia (1990–1992), Riga, May 19, 2015.
148. Park, *End of an Empire?*, 133.
149. From Embassy in Moscow to secretary of state, Baltic leader letter to President Bush, May 16, 1990, GBPL, NSC Files, Burns Files, Subject File, Lithuania 2, OA/ID CF01487-002.
150. French Foreign Ministry, memo: internal situation in the USSR (latest elements), May 23, 1990, CAD, Europe (1986-1990), 6682.
151. Ibid.
152. Edgar Savisaar, *Peaminister: Eesti lähiajalugu 1990–1992* (Tartu: Kleio, 2004), 186–187.
153. Chernyaev, *Diary 1990*, 32.
154. CIA National Intelligence Daily, June 13, 1990, CIA, FOIA Electronic Reading Room, accessed January 22, 2022, http://www.foia.cia.gov/sites/default/files/document_conversions/89801/DOC_0005301368.pdf.
155. Baker and Gorbachev, May 18, 1990, GBPL, Scowcroft Collection, Special Separate USSR Notes Files, Gorbachev Files, Memorandum of Conversation, OA/ID 91126-004.
156. Haslonher, Theme Paper: The Baltics, May 21, 1990, US Department of State, Virtual Reading Room, accessed June 21, 2021, https://foia.state.gov/.
157. Meeting between Baker and Prunskienė, Spaso House, Moscow, May 15, 1990, MML, James A. Baker III Papers (MC 197), Box 109, Folder 1.
158. Senator Dole (R, KS) Congressional Record, May 15, 1990, S 10323.
159. European correspondence, cable from Dublin to Paris, May 25, 1990, CAD, Europe (1986–1990), 6682.
160. Memorandum for the president from James Baker, May 4, 1990, GBPL, Scowcroft Collection, Special Separate USSR Notes Files, Gorbachev Files, OA/ID 91127-002; Beschloss and Talbott, *At the Highest Levels*, 186–187.

161. Spohr, *Germany and the Baltic Problem after the Cold War*, 22–23. Also see Meeting between Kohl and Shevardnadze, May 4, 1990, *Deutsche Einheit*, 1079–1085.

162. Baker and Gorbachev, May 18, 1990, GBPL.

163. Memorandum of the conservation, aid to the Soviet Union, May 29, 1990, GBPL, Scowcroft Collection, USSR collapse files, U.S.-Soviet relations Chronological Files, OA/ID 91118-003.

164. Memorandum of telephone conversation between Bush and Kohl, The White House, May 30, 1990, accessed December 2, 2021, https://bush41library.tamu. edu/archives/memcons-telcons.

165. Bush and Scowcroft, *A World Transformed*, 284–285.

166. Memorandum of conversation, Bush and Gorbachev, June 1, 1990, 11:00–11:48, GBPL, Scowcroft Collection, Special Separate USSR Files, Gorbachev Files, OA/ ID 911207-005.

167. Ibid.

168. Bush and Scowcroft, *A World Transformed*, 284–285.

169. "Amendment proposed by Mr. Durbin," Congressional Record, June 6, 1990, H 13189.

170. H. Amdt. 476 to H.R. 4653, accessed May 6, 2022, https://www.congress.gov/ amendment/101st-congress/house-amendment/476/.

171. *V Politbyuro TsK KPSS*, 599.

172. Landsbergis, *Lithuania, Independent Again*, 201.

173. Pētersone and Būmane, *Valstsvīrs Anatolijs Gorbunovs*, 397–398.

174. The Current Digest of the Soviet Press, No. 24, Vol. 42, July 18, 1990, 26.

175. Ibid.

176. Memorandum from Rodman, subject: FYI, June 26, 1990, GBPL, NSC Files, Rademaker Files, Baltic States (5) OA/ID CF01029-011.

CHAPTER 4

1. Savisaar, *Peaminister*, 395.

2. Statement of the Council of the Baltic States on the Coming Political Resolution of the German Question and the Further Development of the Helsinki Process, Vilnius, September 5, 1990, AN, 5 AG 4/CD 242, dossier 1. See the same document in LURMA: F3, A3, L2.

3. S. Res. 334, Reaffirming United States Policy Regarding the Independence of the Baltic States, October 10, 1990, accessed December 3, 2021, https://trackb ill.com/bill/us-congress-senate-resolution-334-an-original-resolution-reaf firming-united-states-policy-regarding-the-independence-of-the-baltic-states/ 223742/.

4. Lennart Meri, "Allocution d'ouverture de M. Lennart Meri, ministre estonien des affaires étrangères," in *France-Estonie: regards mutuels, actes du colloque franco-estonien Tallinn, Tartu, 16–20 juin 1991* (Paris: Association France-Estonie, 1997), 9.

5. Joseph Kazickas, *Odyssey of Hope*, 312–313.

6. Letter from the American Latvian Association (Martins Zvaners) to Baltic activists July 18, 1990; personal Archives of Ojārs Kalniņš.

7. American Latvian Association, letter to Valdis Pavlovskis from Ojārs Kalniņš, July 18, 1990; Personal Archives of Ojārs Kalniņš.

8. Memorandum of Conversation, Godmanis and Bush, July 30, 1990, GBPL, NSC Files, Burns and Hewet Files, Latvia, OA/ID CF01498-026.

9. Savisaar, *Peaminister*, 354

10. Memo from Brent Scowcroft, subject: Meeting with Prime Minister Edgar Savisaar and Foreign Minister Lennart Meri, October 12, 1990, GBPL, NSC Files, Rademaker Files, Baltic States, OA/ID CF010209-009.

11. Memorandum of Conversation, Godmanis and Bush, July 30, 1990.

12. Savisaar, *Peaminister*, 359.

13. Ibid.

14. Statement by the foreign ministers of the Baltic States, October 2, 1990.

15. George Bush, Address before a Joint Session of the Congress on the Persian Gulf Crisis and the Federal Budget Deficit, accessed December 12, 2021, https://bush41library.tamu.edu/archives/public-papers/2217.

16. Statement by the Foreign Ministers of the Baltic States, October 2, 1990.

17. Ibid.

18. See Juha-Matti Ritvanen, "The Change in Finnish Baltic Policy as a Turning Point in Finnish-Soviet Relations. Finland, Baltic Independence and the End of the Soviet Union 1988–1991," *Scandinavian Journal of History* 47, no. 3 (2022): 280–299.

19. Mikkel Runge Olesen, "The Beginnings of Danish Foreign Policy Activism: Supporting Baltic Independence 1990–1991," *Scandinavian Journal of History*, 2022, published online ahead of print, https://doi.org/10.1080/03468 755.2022.2034664.

20. See Mart Kuldkepp, "Baltic Liberation First-hand: Sweden's Pro-Baltic Foreign Policy Shift and Swedish Diplomatic Reporting in 1989–1991," *Scandinavian Journal of History* 47, no. 3 (2022): 325–346.

21. Olesen, "The Beginnings of Danish Foreign Policy Activism," 11

22. Snyder, *The Reconstruction of Nations*, 239–255.

23. Spohr, "Between Political Rhetoric and Realpolitik Calculations," 23; Spohr, *Germany and the Baltic Problem after the Cold War*, 27.

24. Speech by Sten Andersson, minister of foreign affairs of Sweden at the CSCE meetings in New York on October 1, 1990, National Archives of Estonia (here after Rahvusarhiiv), ERA.1608.2.477.

25. Statement by Krzysztof Skubiszewski, CSCE meetings in New York, October 1, 1990, Rahvusarhiiv, ERA.1608.2.477.

26. CSCE meeting in New York, October 1, 1990, statements by Uffe Ellmann-Jensen (Denmark) and Kjell Magne Bondevik (Norway), Rahvusarhiiv, ERA.1608.2.47.

27. Statement by Jon Baldvin Hanibalsson, October 1, 1990, Rahvusarhiiv, ERA.1608.2.47.

28. Spohr, *Germany and the Baltic Problem after the Cold War*, 26.

29. Bush and Scowcroft, *A World Transformed*, 367.

30. Donald Rigel and 21 Members of Congress to the President of the USA, September 22, 1990, LAMA, 1990_70_261.3.

31. Legal affairs department to European affairs department, June 14, 1990, AN, 5AG4/CDM 7, dossier 3.

32. Interview with Pierre Morel, French Ambassador to the Conference on Disarmament in Geneva (1986–1991); Diplomatic Advisor to Francois Mitterrand (1991–1992).

33. Ibid.

34. Alan Elsner, "Baker Soothes Baltic Ministers Sidelined at Summit," *Reuters News*, November 18, 1990.

35. Ibid.

36. Stephen Handelman, "East Meets West This Week to Draft Plans for a New Europe," *Toronto Star*, November 18, 1990.

37. Aina Nagobads-Ābols, *Parīze, Madride, Lisabona un atpakaļ Rīgā* (Rīga: Zinātne, 2000), 57.

38. Savisaar, *Peaminister*, 375–376; "Baltic Foreign Ministers Excluded from Summit," *Associated Press*, November 19, 1990; Colin McIntyre, "Baltic Republics Kicked out of CSCE Summit," *Reuters News*, November 19, 1990; Serge Schmemann, "Summit in Europe: Reporter's Notebook," *New York Times*, November 20, 1990; Annika Savill, "The CSCE Summit—Inside File—Thaw Leaves Baltics Out in the Cold," *The Independent*, November 21, 1990; Françoise Thom, "Le honteux lâchage des Baltes," *Quotidien de Paris*, November 11, 1990; "Veto soviétique pour les baltes," *Le Monde*, November 21, 1990; "Les trois Républiques baltes auraient souhaité une sortie 'plus scandaleuse,'" *Le Monde*, November 22, 1990; Claude Sarraute, "Ces ne sont pas les Koweitens les Baltes!" *Le Monde*, November 22, 1990.

39. CSCE Summit in Paris November 1990, statements by prime ministers: Gro Harlem Brundtland (Norway), Mażowiecki (Poland), Poul Schlüter (Denmark), LAMA, 1990_94_404.7 and LURMA F3,A3,L3.

40. Savill, "The CSCE Summit—Inside File—Thaw Leaves Baltics Out in the Cold."

41. Statement by Ingvar Carlson, prime minister of Sweden, at the CSCE Summit in Paris, November 21, 1990, LAMA, 1990_94_404.7 and LURMA, F3,A3,L3

42. "Baltic Foreign Ministers Excluded from Summit," *Associated Press*, November 19, 1990

43. Mauno Koivisto, *Kaksi kautta. 2, Historian tekijät* (Helsinki: Kirjayhtymä, 1995), 385.

44. Interview with Janis Jurkans, Latvian foreign minister (1991–1992), Riga, March 2, 2010; interview with Algirdas Saudargas, Lithuanian foreign minister (1990–1992), Brussels, March 24, 2010.

45. Landsbergis, *Lithuania, Independent Again*, 301.

46. Nagobads-Ābols, *Parīze, Madride, Lisabona*, 58

47. Estonian American National Council, Mari-Ann Rikken to JBANC, re: Paris Summit, November 19, 1990, Rahvusarhiiv, ERA.1608.2.478.

48. Interview with Pierre Morel, French Ambassador to the Conference on Disarmament in Geneva (1986–1991); Diplomatic Advisor to François Mitterrand (1991–1992).

49. French Foreign Ministry, René Roudaut, memo, reactions of Landsbergis, November 22, 1990, AN, 5 AG 4/CD 242, dossier 4.

50. Savisaar, *Peaminister*, 396, 399; *Soyuz mozhno bylo sokhranit*, 164

51. Kotkin, *Armageddon Averted*, 90–91.

52. Archie Brown, *The Gorbachev Factor* (Oxford: Oxford University Press, 1997), 269–271.

53. Cable no. 213 from French Ambassador in the USSR Jean-Marie Mérillon to French Foreign Ministry, Lituanie-les conséquences intérieures de la crise (2/2), n.d., CAD, Europe (1991–1995), 7667.

54. Memorandum of conversation between Krol and Īvāns, March 29, 1991.

55. Ibid.

56. Plokhy, *The Last Empire*, 59–60.

57. Savisaar, *Peaminister*, 421.

58. Ainius Lasas, "Bloody Sunday: What Did Gorbachev Know about the January 1991 Events in Vilnius and Riga?" *Journal of Baltic Studies* 38, no. 2 (June 2007): 183.

59. Ibid.

60. Kramer, "The Collapse of East European Communism and the Repercussions within the Soviet Union," Part 2, 46.

61. "Latvijas Tautas frontes valdes paziņojums visiem Latvijas neatkarības atbalstītājiem," *Latvijas Jaunatne*, December 13, 1990.

62. Memorandum of conversation between Krol and Krastinš, December 17, 1990; Latvian Diplomatic Archives (Latvijas Ārlietu ministrijas arhīvs, hereafter LAMA), 1990_66_4261.4.

63. Selective Martial Law in the USSR: Distinguishing the Variants, November 26, 1990, GBPL, Scowcroft collection, USSR Collapse, US-Soviet relations chronological files, OA/ID 91119-002.

64. Memorandum from Condoleezza Rice to Robert Gates, Senior Small Group Meeting on Soviet Contingencies, December 18, 1990, OA/ID 91119-002.

65. The Soviet Republics: The Independence Claims, Legal Issues and U.S Policy, n.d., OA/ID 91119-002.

66. Soviet Crisis Contingencies, n.d., OA/ID 91119-002.

67. Senior Soviet Group, December 19, 1990, OA/ID 91119-002.

68. Memorandum from Brent Scowcroft to the President, Responding to the Toughening Line in Moscow, December 21, 1990, OA/ID 91119-002.

69. George Bush, "Remarks on the Waiver of the Jackson-Vanik Amendment and on Economic Assistance to the Soviet Union," December 12, 1990, American Presidency Project, accessed January 12, 2022, https://www.presidency.ucsb.edu/documents/remarks-the-waiver-the-jackson-vanik-amendment-and-economic-assistance-the-soviet-union.

70. CRS Report for Congress, U.S. Assistance to the Former Soviet Union 1991–2001: A History of Administration and Congressional Action, January 15, 2002, accessed January 16, 2022, https://wikileaks.org/wiki/CRS:_U.S._Assistance_to_the_former_Soviet_Union_1991-2001:_A_History_of_Administration_and_Congressional_Action,_January_15,_2002.

71. Beschloss and Talbott, *At the Highest Levels*, 264.

72. Telephone Conversation, Bush and Gorbachev, January 1, 1991, GBPL, accessed May 12, 2021, http://bush41library.tamu.edu/files/memcons-telcons/1991-01-01--Gorbachev.pdf.

73. Statement by the Council of the Baltic States, January 8, 1991, AN, AG 4/CD 242, dossier 4.

74. Lieven, *The Baltic Revolution*, 245.

75. Gorbachev, *Memoirs*, 577.

76. GBPL, Dan Quayle Vice President Records, Subject Files, Highlights Baltics, OA/ID 27037-018: American Embassy in Moscow to Secretary of State, subject: Imposition of Presidential Rule in Lithuania, January 10, 1990; Memorandum for the Vice President from Carnes Lord, subject: Crackdown looming in the Baltics and Caucasus, January 11, 1991.

77. Telephone Conversation, Bush and Gorbachev, January 11, 1991, GBPL, accessed August 12, 2017, https://bush41library.tamu.edu/archives/memcons-telcons; Memorandum for the Vice President from Carnes Lord, subject: Crackdown Looming in the Baltics and Caucasus, January 11, 1991, OA/ID 27037-018.

78. Exchange with reporters on the telephone conversation with Gorbachev, January 11, 1991, accessed February 11, 2022, https://www.presidency.ucsb.edu/ documents/exchange-with-reporters-the-telephone-conversation-with-soviet-president-mikhail-gorbachev. See also Spohr, *Post Wall, Post Square,* 369–370.

79. *Soyuz mozhno bylo sokhranit,* 197–199; Pētersone and Būmane, *Valstsvīrs Anatolijs Gorbunovs,* 326; Savisaar, *Peaminister,* 441–442; *V Politbyuro TsK KPSS,* 641–643; Gorbachev, *Memoirs* (London: Doubleday, 1997), 577–578.

80. Riga OMON unit was initially subordinated to the Latvian Interior Ministry, but after Latvia declared transition period toward independence, it refused the orders of the new leadership and in the fall of 1990 was attached to Soviet Interior Ministry.

81. *V Politbyuro TsK KPSS,* 480.

82. *Soyuz mozhno bylo sokhranit,* 187.

83. Ibid.

84. For a good summary of the debate see Lasas, "Bloody Sunday."

85. When it comes to the shooting in Riga on January 20, he denies any involvement of central authorities and claims that they were instigated by "the radically minded local separatists." Gorbachev, *Memoirs,* 576–581.

86. Zubok, *Collapse,* 132.

87. Aivars Kļavis and Guntars Laganovskis, "Patiesība par leģendu," *Latvijas Vēstnesis,* January 1, 2004, accessed January 12, 2022, https://www.vestne sis.lv/ta/id/83250. Interview with commander of the Riga OMON Cheslav Mlynnik: "Ya—soldat, a ne myasnik," *Rosbalt,* November 12, 2016, accessed January 12, 2022, https://www.rosbalt.ru/world/2016/11/12/1566341.html.

88. See the 2021 ruling of Lithuanian Court of Appeal on January 1991 events: Lietuvos Apeliacinis teismas, Baudžiamoji byla Nr. 1A-34-1020/2021, 2021 m. kovo 31 d., available at: https://www.apeliacinis.lt/naujienos/sausio-13-osios-ivykiu-bylos-nagrinejimas/1008?fbclid=IwAR3RRIA16qmvddsixV7SPth01 XY9-BW_kQGLtUPJfqAWDTH5sWsQq-ap7hA.

89. *Soyuz mozhno bylo sokhranit,* 195.

90. *Baudžiamoji byla Nr. 1A-34-1020/202120,* 20.

91. Gorbachev, *Memoirs,* 577.

92. Vladimir Kryuchkov, *Lichnoye delo* (Moscow: Olimp, 1996), 2:31.

93. Gorbachev, *Sobraniye sochineniy,* 24:35–36; Taylor, "The Soviet Military and the Disintegration of the USSR," *Journal of Cold War Studies* 1, no. 1 (2003): 40–43.

94. Savisaar, *Peaminister,* 447–448.

95. Savisaar, *Peaminister,* 429, 433–434; Alexander Yakovlev, *Perestroyka. 1985– 1991* (Moscow: Mezhdunarodnyy fond Demokratiya, 2008), 602–604; Anatoly Chernyaev, *Diary 1991,* 5–17, accessed January 12, 1991, https://nsarchive2.gwu. edu/NSAEBB/NSAEBB345/index.htm.

96. Chernyaev, *Diary 1991,* 7.

97. Ibid., 8.

98. Alexander Yakovlev, *Sumerki* (Moscow: Materik, 2005), 499.

99. Interview with Andrei Grachev, deputy head of the CPSU Central Committee's International section (1989–1991), press secretary of Mikhail Gorbachev (1991), Paris, March 15, 2016.

100. Chernyaev, *Diary 1991,* 10. Gorbachev Foundation, 8780, Letter from Chernyaev to Gorbachev, n.d.,

101. *The Current Digest of the Russian Press,* No. 3, Vol. 43, February 20, 1991, 9–10.

102. *The Current Digest of the Russian Press,* No. 2, Vol. 43, February 13, 1991, 10.

103. Ibid., 9–10.
104. *The Current Digest of the Russian Press*, No. 3, Vol. 43, February 20, 1991, 11–19.
105. The original Russian version was published as "Golos intelligentsia," *Argumenty i fakty*, January 17, 1991. English translation in "An Appeal for Democracy in the Baltic Republics," *New York Review of Books*, March 28, 1991.
106. Collection of telegrams received by the Kremlin in January/February 1991, Fond 89, Yale University, Sterling Library, 89-28-32.
107. *The Current Digest of the Russian Press*, No. 2, Vol. 43, February 13, 1991, 9.
108. Walker, *Dissolution*, 113.
109. The impact that the political orientation of these various news outlets had on coverage of the Baltic crisis varied slightly from country to country, but generally the differences between the center-right and center-left press were minor. For the most part, the press was limited to the choice of stronger or milder rhetorical tools. For example, in France and Germany the center-left newspapers (e.g., *Le Monde* and *Süddeutsche Zeitung*) argued that Perestroika might have come to an end, whereas the Catholic *La Croix* and conservative *Frankfurter Allgemeine Zeitung* talked about the return of Stalinism. See Noël Copin, "Toujours le stalinisme," *La Croix*, January 15, 1991; "Zurück zum Stalinismus," *Frankfurter Allgemeine Zeitung*, January 15, 1991; Daniel Vernet, "Coup de grâce pour la perestroïka," *Le Monde*, January 15, 1991; and "Litauen: 'Wir können nicht glauben, dass dies auf Befehl Gorbatschows geschieht': Ein blutiger Akt im baltischen Drama," *Süddeutsche Zeitung*, January 14, 1991.
110. Vernet, "Coup de grâce pour la perestroïka"; Peter Gumbel, "Besieged Baltics: Lithuania Crackdown Signals a Bloody End to Era of Perestroika," *Wall Street Journal*, January 14, 1991.
111. A. M. Rosenthal, "The New World Order Dies," *New York Times*, January 15, 1991; "Skammens tystnad: Perestrojkan dog med blodbadet i Vilnius," *Aftonbladet*, January 14, 1991.
112. Editorial, "No New Iron Curtain," *The Times*, January 15, 1991.
113. "Zurück zum Stalinismus"; "Moskova palaa keskiaikaan," *Helsingin Sanomat*, January 14, 1991
114. Jürgen Martschukat and Silvan Niedermeier, *Violence and Visibility in Modern History* (New York: Palgrave Macmillan, 2013), 3.
115. Olli Kivinen, "Kuka yrittää sammuttaa liekin?," *Helsingin Sanomat*, January 14, 1991; and "Zurück zum Stalinismus."
116. Czesław Miłosz, "Lituanie le grand mensonge," *Le Monde*, January 23, 1991.
117. Martschukat and Niedermeier, *Violence and Visibility in Modern History*, 3.
118. Walker, *Dissolution*, 77; Donald Rayfield, *Edge of Empires: A History of Georgia* (London: Reaktion Books, 2012), 378.
119. Charles King, *The Ghost of Freedom: A History of the Caucasus* (New York: Oxford University Press, 2008), 207; Zubkova, *Pribaltika i Kreml*, 4.
120. *V Politbyuro TsK KPSS*, 642.
121. Beschloss and Talbott, *At the Highest Levels*, 177.
122. Kramer, "The Collapse of East European Communism and the Repercussions within the Soviet Union," Part 2, 46-48.
123. CAD, Europe (1991–1995), 7667: Cable no. 50 from French Embassy in Prague to French Foreign Ministry, January 14, 1991, Cable no. 16 from French Embassy in Oslo to French Foreign Ministry, January 14, 1990.
124. "Marssijat vaativat Koivisto eroa Helsingissä," *Helsingin Sanomat*, January 14, 1991.

125. "Støt Litauen. Mød op. Protest mod overfaldet på Litauen," *Politiken*, January 14, 1991.

126. "Skriv till Gorbatjov," *Expressen*, January 14, 1991.

127. "Sorgflor på flaggorna. Montagsdemonstration for Baltikum samlade 5000," *Dagens Nyheter*, January 14, 1991.

128. Interview with Dainis Īvāns, chairman of Tautas Fronte (1988–1990), deputy speaker of the Supreme Soviet of Latvia (1990–1992), Riga, May 19, 2015.

129. "Das offizielle Warschau tut sich schwer mit einer Stellungnahme," *Frankfurter Allgemeine Zeitung*, January 15, 1991.

130. Snyder, *The Reconstruction of Nations*, 253.

131. Ibid., 254.

132. Cable from French Embassy in Stockholm to French Foreign Ministry, January 24, 1991, CAD, Europe (1991–1995), 7667.

133. French Foreign Ministry, "Situation in Lithuania: International Reactions," January 14, 1991, CAD, Europe (1991–1995), 7667.

134. "Prague Urges Allies to Quit Warsaw Pact as a Protest," *Wall Street Journal Europe*, January 14, 1991.

135. Cable no. 75 from French embassy in London to the French Foreign Ministry, January 14, 1991, CAD Europe (1991–1995), URSS 7667.

136. Alan Riding, "Soviet Crackdown; Europeans Warn Soviet about Aid," *New York Times*, January 14, 1991.

137. See publications of extracts from Kohl-Gorbachev conversations published by *Der Spiegel* in 2011: Christian Neef, "Secret Papers Reveal Truth behind Soviet Collapse," *Der Spiegel*, August 11, 2011, accessed January 10, 2022, https://www.spiegel.de/international/europe/the-gorbachev-files-secret-papers-reveal-truth-behind-soviet-collapse-a-779277.html.

138. "Kohl Struggles to Salvage Policy to Support Gorbachev," *The Guardian*, January 15, 1991.

139. Joint declaration by French and German Ministers of Foreign Affairs, January 13, 1991, AN, 5AG 4/CD 242, dossier 4.

140. Yuri Dubinin, *Moscou-Paris dans un tourbillon diplomatique: Témoignage d'ambassadeur* (Paris: Imaginaria, 2002), 368.

141. Letter from François Mitterrand to Mikhail Gorbachev, January 17, 1991, Private Archive.

142. Memorandum for Brent Scowcroft from Condoleezza Rice, Responding to Moscow, January 21, 1991, GBPL, NSC Files, Rice Files, Soviet Union/USSR, Subject Files, Baltics, OA/ID CF00718-009.

143. Cable from French embassy in Washington no. 91 to French Foreign Ministry, January 13, 1991, CAD, Europe (1991–1995), 7667.

144. James Addison Baker and Thomas M. DeFrank, *The Politics of Diplomacy: Revolution, War, and Peace, 1989–1992* (New York: Putnam, 1995), 380.

145. Don Oberdorfer, "Moscow Warned on Baltic Repression," *Washington Post*, January 18, 1991.

146. Memorandum of telephone conversation between Bush and Gorbachev, January 18, 1991, GBPL accessed January 21, 2022, https://bush41library.tamu.edu/archives/memcons-telcons.

147. Ibid.

148. Memorandum for Brent Scowcroft from Condoleezza Rice, Responding to Moscow, January 21, 1991.

149. "A Peace Laureate's Putsch," *Wall Street Journal*, January 14, 1991.

150. "Attack in Lithuania Threatens Democracy," *USA Today*, January 14, 1991.
151. Editorial, "Gorbymania R.I.P.," *Los Angeles Daily News*, January 15, 1991.
152. William Safire, "Gorbachev's 'Bloody Sunday," *New York Times*, January 17, 1991.
153. Mary McGrory, "When Diplomacy Slept," *Washington Post*, January 20, 1991.
154. 102nd Congress (1991–1992): H.R.533, H.Con.Res.35; H.Res.41; H.J.Res.80; H.Res.36; H.R.559; S.Res.16.; H.Con.Res.50, S.J.Res.42.
155. 102nd Congress (1991–1992): S.Res.14, H.Con.R.40.
156. Memorandum of Conversation, Bush, Baker, and Bessmertnykh, January 28, 1991, GBPL, accessed December 28, 2021, http://bush41library.tamu.edu/files/memcons-telcons/1991-01-28--Bessmertnykh.pdf.
157. Memorandum from Burns to Scowcroft, Your Meeting with Representatives of Major Baltic-American Organizations: January 22, 1991, GBPL, NSC Files, Hutching Files, Baltic States 1, OA/ID CF01411-016.
158. Interview with Mari-Ann Kelam, leading Estonian diaspora activist, Tallinn, June 18, 2013.
159. Ibid.
160. Letter from Bush to Gorbachev, January 23, 1990, MML, James A. Baker III Papers, Box 109, Folder 9. Scowcroft to Bush, Letter to President Gorbachev concerning Baltic situation, n.d., GBPL, NSC Files, Burns Files, Subject Files, GB-Gorbachev Correspondence (3), OF/ID 01487-005.
161. Letter from Bush to Gorbachev, January 23, 1990, MML, James A. Baker III Papers, Box 109, Folder 9.
162. "Canada Suspends Credit to Soviet Union," *Toronto Star*, January 22, 1991.
163. Alan Riding, "Baltic Assaults Lead Europeans to Hold Off Aid," *New York Times*, January 23, 1991.
164. Taylor, "The Soviet Military and the Disintegration of the USSR," 40–42; Savisaar, *Peaminister*, 485–486.
165. See the front pages of the January 14, 1991, editions of *Aftenposten*, *Dagens Nyheter*, *Frankfurter Allgemeine Zeitung*, *Helsingin Sanomat*, *Le Figaro*, *Politiken*, *Rzeczpospolita*, the *Guardian*, the *Times*, the *New York Times*, the *Wall Street Journal*, the *Washington Post*, and *Süddeutsche Zeitung*.
166. Matt Roush, "TV Commentary: On the Air, Doom, Gloom and Optimism," *USA Today*, January 14, 1991.
167. Note in the papers of Latvian prime minister Ivars Godmanis, n.d., LVA, F.270, A.8, L.11.
168. Chernyaev, *Diary 1991*, 10.
169. Cable from French embassy in Moscow to French Foreign Ministry, January 13, 1991, CAD, Europe (1991–1995), 7667.
170. Ibid.; Matlock, *Autopsy on an Empire*, 455.
171. *The Current Digest of the Russian Press*, No. 4, Vol. 43, February 27, 1991, 11–12.
172. French Foreign Ministry, René Roudaut, memo, Soviet explications on the armed intervention in Vilnius, January 21, 1991, January 21, 1991, CAD, Europe (1991-1995), sier7667.
173. Matlock, *Autopsy on an Empire*, 471.
174. Beschloss and Talbott, *At the Highest Levels*, 275.
175. Ibid., 285.
176. Memorandum of Conversation, Bush, Baker and Bessmertnykh, January 28, 1991, GBPL, accessed December 28, 2021, http://bush41library.tamu.edu/files/memcons-telcons/1991-01-28--Bessmertnykh.pdf.
177. Ibid.

178. Ibid.
179. "Troops Leaving Baltics, Soviets Say; Convoys on the Move, but Lithuanians Skeptical on Withdrawal," *Washington Post*, January 31, 1991.
180. An unofficial translation of Gorbachev's letter to Mitterrand, February 5, 1991, AN, 5AG 4/CD 242, dossier 4.
181. Ibid.
182. Ibid.
183. Koivisto, *Historian tekijät*, 402, 403.
184. Respectively the former, the current, and the future chairmen of the EC Council of Ministers
185. Chernyaev, *Diary 1991*, 27.
186. Andreï Gratchev, *Gorbatchev, le pari perdu?: De la perestroïka à la fin de la guerre froide* (Paris: Armand Colin, 2011), 232.

CHAPTER 5

1. Cable from Latvian Legation in Washington to the Foreign Ministry in Riga, August 2, 1991, LDA, 1991_265_261.
2. Landsbergis, *Lithuania, Independent Again*, 301–302.
3. Walker, *Dissolution*, 143.
4. Ibid., 119.
5. See various US assessments of the Soviet future in GBPL, USSR Collapse, US-Soviet Relations, Chronological Files, Chronological Files, OA/ID 91119-002: The Soviet Republics: Independence Claims, Legal Issues and U.S. policy, n.d.; Selective Martial Law in the USSR: Distinguishing the Variants, November 26, 1990; Soviet Crisis Contingencies, n.d.; Memorandum from Brent Scowcroft to the President, Responding to Toughening Line in Moscow, December 21, 1990; Memorandum to the President from Brent Scowcroft, Coping with Soviet Union's Internal Turmoil [February 1991].
GBPL, Brent Scowcroft Collection, USSR Collapse Files, US-Soviet Relations, Chronological Files, OA/ID 91118-007: From the embassy in Moscow to the secretary of state, Looking into the Abyss: The Possible Collapse of the Soviet Union and What We Should Do about It, July 27, 1990; Memorandum for the president, from Brent Scowcroft, Turmoil in the Soviet Union and US Policy, August 18, 1990.
Central Intelligence Agency, Office of Soviet Analysis, The Soviet Cauldron, April 1991, accessed January 12, 2022, https://www.cia.gov/library/center-for-the-study-of-intelligence/csi-publications/books-and-monographs/at-cold-wars-end-us-intelligence-on-the-soviet-union-and-eastern-europe-1989-1991/art-1.html. NSC electronic briefing book, The Gorbachev File, CIA Memorandum, The Gorbachev Succession, April 1991, accessed January 12, 2022, https://nsarchive.gwu.edu/document/21550-document-13
6. Memorandum to the president from Brent Scowcroft, Coping with Soviet Union's Internal Turmoil [February 1991].
7. Ibid.
8. From the embassy in Moscow to the secretary of state, Looking into the Abyss.
9. Memorandum for the president, from Brent Scowcroft, Turmoil in the Soviet Union and US policy.
10. Memorandum for Brent Scowcroft from Condoleezza Rice, Responding to Moscow, January 21, 1991.
11. Beschloss and Talbott, *At the Highest Levels*, 315–317.

12. Memorandum to the president from Brent Scowcroft, Coping with Soviet Union's internal turmoil.
13. Memorandum of Conversation between Bush and Yeltsin, June 20, 1991, accessed January 17, 2020, http://bush41library.tamu.edu/files/memcons-telcons/1991-06-20--Yeltsin.pdf.
14. Ibid.
15. Ibid.; Memorandum of Telephone Conversation between Bush and Gorbachev, June 21, 1991, 10:00–10:38, GBPL, accessed January 24, 1991, https://bush41library.tamu.edu/files/memcons-telcons/1991-06-21-Gorbachev.pdf.
16. Memorandum to the president from Brent Scowcroft, Coping with Soviet Union's Internal Turmoil.
17. Ukrainian Congress Committee of America to Bush, March 18, 1991, GBPL, NSC Files, Burns and Hewett Files, Russia Subject Files, U.S. Relations with Russia, Policy on the Debate over the Union, OA/ID CF01536-013.
18. Joint Stament by the Foreign Ministers of Iceland and Estonia, January 21, 1991, Rahvusarhiiv, ERA 1608.2.68.
19. Gudni Jóhannesson, "The Might of the Weak? Icelandic Support for Baltic Independence, 1990–1991," draft paper posted online on author's personal website, accessed January 22, 2022, http://gudnith.is/.
20. *The Current Digest of the Russian Press*, No. 7, Vol. 43, March 20, 1991, 24.
21. James P. Nichol, *Diplomacy in the Former Soviet Republics* (London: Praeger, 1995), 116.
22. *The Current Digest of the Russian Press*, No. 12, Vol. 43, April 24, 1991, 14.
23. Foreign Minister in Sweden, Germany and Switzerland, February 2, 1991, Rahvusarhiiv, ERA 1608.2.68.
24. Nagobads-Ābols, *Parīze, Madride, Lisabona Un Atpakaļ Rīgā*, 80.
25. LVA, F.290, A. 11, L. 560: Rapport on Meeting between Polish Delegation and the Deputy Speaker of the Parliament Andrejs Krastins, January 21, 1991; Rapport on Meeting between Deputy Speaker of the Parliament Andrejs Krastins and Delegation of Swedish Deputies, January 23, 1991; Gorbunovs Meeting with the Delegation from the Dutch Parliament, April 10, 1991, LVA, F.290, A. 11, L. 560.
26. Gorbunovs Meeting Members of Helsinki Commission, February 12, 1991; Gorbunovs Meeting with the Delegation of the US Lawmakers, April 3, 1991, LVA, F.290, A. 11, L. 560
27. 102 Congress (1991–1992): S.670, S.Res.83, H.J.Res.179, S.J.Res.89, H.R.1879, H.Res.142, S.Res.119, H.Res.41, S.J.Res.42, S.670.
28. Points to Be Made for Meeting with President Landsbergis, Prime Minister Savisaar and Prime Minister Godmanis, n.d, GBPL, NSC files, Burns and Hewett Files, Subject Files, President's Meeting with Landsbergis, OA/ID CF01422-021.
29. Nichol, *Diplomacy in the Former Soviet Republics*, 115.
30. Ibid., 125.
31. The Representative of Latvian Government in Moscow Jānis Peters to Godmanis, April 19, 1991, LVA, F. 270, A. 8, L. 15.
32. David C. Gombert to Bob Gates, March 12, 1991, GBPL, NSC Files, Burns and Hewett Files, Latvia, OA/ID CF01430-018.
33. Gorbachev, *Memoirs*, 609.
34. Beschloss and Talbott, *At the Highest Levels*, 309.
35. Quoted in Zubok, *Collapse*, 142.
36. CRS Report for Congress, U.S. Assistance to the Former Soviet Union 1991–2001: A History of Administration and Congressional Action, January 15, 2002,

accessed January 16, 2022, https://wikileaks.org/wiki/CRS:_U.S._Assistance_
to_the_former_Soviet_Union_1991-2001:_A_History_of_Administration_and_
Congressional_Action,_January_15,_2002.

37. *The Current Digest of the Russian Press*, No. 7, Vol. 43, March 20, 1991, 24–25.

38. From Legation of Latvia in Washington to Jurkāns, April 26, 1991, LAMA, 1991_
256_261.7.

39. Ibid.

40. Savisaar, *Peaminister*, 538.

41. "Statement by the Leaders of the Baltic States on the Independence of Estonia,
Latvia and Lithuania, May 8, 1991," in *Together: Council of the Baltic States 1990–
1992 Documents* (Vilnius: Lithuanian Institute of International Political and
Economic Relations, 1996), 57–58.

42. On the Estonian case see Kaarel Piirimäe, "Gorbachev's 'Last Trench
Line': Estonian Diplomacy towards the East and the Soviet Crackdown in the
Baltic State in January 1991," in *The Baltic States at the End of the Cold War*
(Berlin: Peter Lang, 2018), 294–315.

43. Zubok, *Collapse*, 152.

44. Secretary Baker and the Latvian Govrenment, July 20, 1990, Personal Archives
of Ojārs Kalniņš.

45. Spohr, *Germany and the Baltic Problem after the Cold War*, 28; CIA National
Intelligence Daily, July 28, 1990, Wilson Center Digital Archive, accessed
January 22, 2022, https://digitalarchive.wilsoncenter.org/document/209642.

46. Andra Jauce, "Par lielo politiku un ikdienu," *Latvijas Jaunatne*, January 15, 1991.

47. Zubok, *Collapse*, 146.

48. Landsbergis, *Lithuania, Independent Again*, 294.

49. Darius Mereckis and Morvenas Morkvėnas, "The 1991 Treaty as a Basis for
Lithuanian-Russian Relations," *Lithuanian Foreign Policy Review* 1 (1998): 3,
accessed January 21, 2022, http://lfpr.lt/wp-content/uploads/2015/07/LFPR-1-
Mereckis_Morkvenas.pdf.

50. A Possible Way Out for Lithuania, March 28, 1990, GBPL, NSC Files, Rice Files,
1989–1991, Baltic Cable Traffic, OA/ID CF00720-002.

51. Memo from the American Latvian Association in the United States to
Condoleezza Rice, March 30, 1990, GBPL, NSC Files, Rice Files, Subject Files,
Baltics Other, OA/ID CF00720-004.

52. Cable from French Embassy in Prague no. 160 to French Foreign Ministry,
January 15, 1991, CAD, Europe (1991–1995), 7667.

53. Cable from French Embassy in Copenhagen no. 64 to French Foreign Ministry,
January 12, 1991, CAD, Europe (1991–1995), 7667.

54. The day after the referendum its leading newspaper *Gazeta* wrote: "It is upon us
to convince Lithuanians that we are not looking for the reestablishment of the
domination . . . nor change our borders, nor look for special privileges in their
country . . . it is upon us to calm Lithuania sensibilities." Cable from French
Embassy in Warsaw no. 277 to French Foreign Ministry, February 12, 1991, CAD,
Europe (1991–1995), 7667.

55. Press Guidance on Referenda in Latvia and Estonia, n.d., GBPL, NSC Files, Burns
and Hewett Files, Russia Subject Files: Latvia, CF 01498-026.

56. Memorandum of conversation between Mitterrand and Gorbunovs, May 16,
1991, AN, 5 AG 4/CD 314, dossier 13.

57. Pierre Morel, memo for the president, May 16, 1991, AN 5AG4/CD 314,
dossier 14.

58. Amomn Cheskin, *Russian Speakers in Post-Soviet Latvia* (Edinburgh: Edinburg University Press, 2016), 52.
59. Mara Lazda, "Reconsidering Nationalism: The Baltic Case of Latvia in 1989," *International Journal of Politics, Culture, and Society* 22, no. 4 (2009): 517–536.
60. Beissinger, *Nationalist Mobilization and the Collapse of the Soviet State*, 387.
61. Ibid., 420
62. "Soobshcheniye Tsentral'noy komissii referenduma SSSR. Ob itogakh referenduma SSSR, sostoyavshegosya 17 marta 1991 goda," *Pravda*, March 27, 1991.
63. Estonian Ministry of Foreign Affairs, Press Release in Response to Remarks Made by Mikhail Gorbachev, April 20, 1991, Rahvusarhiiv, ERA.1608.2.68.
64. Das Kaman Reports on Baltic Visits, May 17, 1991, GBPL, NSC files, Burns and Hewett Files, Russia Subject Files, Independence Negations, OA/ID CF01433-006.
65. From Latvian Legation in Washington to Jurkāns, April 26, 1991, LAMA, 1991_256_261.7.
66. Latvian-US relation in March 1991, n.d., LAMA, 1991.252.261.2.
67. Memorandum from Scowcroft to Bush, meeting with President Arnold Rüütel of Estonia, GBPL, NSC Files Rademaker Files, Subject Files, Baltic States (1), March 29, 1991, OA/ID CF01029-007.
68. Das Kaman Reports on Baltic Visits, May 17, 1991.
69. CIA Report, Status of Talks between Moscow and the Baltic Republics, May 3, 1991, GBPL, NSC Files, Burns and Hewett Files, Russia Subject Files, Policy on Debate over the Union, OA/ID CF01536-013.
70. Baltic Working Group, Situation report, No. 144, June 13, 1991, GBPL, NSC Files, Burns and Hewett Files, Russia Subject Files, Political Situation, Union-Republic Issues, OA/ID CF01433-005.
71. Ibid.
72. Daina Bleiere, "Sarunas ar Kremli par Latvijas neatkarības atzīšanu-vai tās bija iespējamas?," in *1990. Gada 4. Maija Latvijas Neatkarības Deklarācija: starptautiskie un iekšpolitiskie aspekti*, ed. Inesis Feldmanis and Jānis Taurēns (Riga: LU Akadēmiskais apgāds, 2011), 94–98.
73. Memorandum Hewett to Scowcroft, Your Meeting with President Arnold Rüütel, July 25, 1991, GBPL, NSC files, Burns and Hewett Files, Russia Subject Files, OA/ID CF01422-012.
74. Lars Peter Fredén, *Baltijas brīvības ceļš un Zviedrijas diplomātija: 1989–1991* (Riga: Atēna, 2007), 179.
75. English translation of the appeal sent from Latvian Foreign Ministry to Latvian Legation in Washington, July 15, 1991, LAMA, 1991_256_261.7.
76. CIA Report, Status of Talks between Moscow and the Baltic Republics, May 3, 1991.
77. Interview with the commander of Riga OMON who has been tried in absentia by Lithuanian courts, accessed January 15, 2022, https://www.rosbalt.ru/world/2016/11/12/1566341.html.
78. Cable from French embassy in Moscow to French Foreign Ministry, June 4, 1991, CAD, Europe (1991–1995), 7667.
79. Memorandum from Hewett to Scowcroft, July 22, 1991.
80. Telegram from Jack Matlock to Jim Baker, Danger in the Baltics, June 5, GBPL, NSC files, Burns and Hewett files, Russia Subject Files, Independence Negotiations (1), OA/ID CF1433-005.

81. Beschloss and Talbott, *At the Highest Levels*, Chapter 18.
82. Bozo, *Mitterrand, la fin de la guerre froide*, 365.
83. Bush and Scowcroft, *A World Transformed*, 508.
84. Memorandum of conversation, Bush and Gorbachev, London, July 17, 1991, GBPL, accessed January 25, 2022, http://bush41library.tamu.edu/files/memc ons-telcons/1991-06-17--Gorbachev.pdf.
85. Anatoly Chernyaev, *Diary 1991*, 91.
86. Memorandum of conversation, Bush and Gorbachev, London, July 17, 1991.
87. Bush and Scowcroft, *A World Transformed*, 509.
88. Memorandum from Hewett to Scowcroft, July 25, 1991, GBPL, NSC files, Burns and Hewett Files, Subject Files, Moscow summit, OA/ID CF01422-010.
89. Ibid.
90. Letter from Lennart Meri to Jim Baker, July 2, 1991, Rahvusarhiiv, ERA 1608.2.69.
91. Letter from Vytautas Landsbergis to George Bush, July 3, 1991, LAMA, 1991_ 265_261.
92. Draft Letter from the Latvian Government to George Bush, n.d., LAMA, 1991_ 265_261.
93. Draft Letter from Latvian Prime Minister Godmanis to the Estonian and Lithuanian Prime Ministers, July 10, 1991, LAMA, 1991_265_261.
94. Letter from Jaak Leiman, Ivars Godmanis and Gediminas Vagnorius to George Bush, July 11, 1991, LAMA 1991_265_261.
95. Memorandum from Hewett to Scowcroft, July 25, 1991.
96. From Latvian Permanent Representative in Moscow to Godmanis, July 30, 1991, LAMA, 1991_265_261.
97. Telefax from Latvian Legation in Washington to Latvian Foreign Ministry, August 13, 1991, LAMA, 1991_265_261.
98. Plokhy, *The Last Empire*, 77–78.
99. George Bush, Remarks to the Supreme Soviet of the Republic of the Ukraine in Kiev, Soviet Union, August 1, 1991, American Presidency Project, accessed December 12, 2021, https://www.presidency.ucsb.edu/documents/remarks-the-supreme-soviet-the-republic-the-ukraine-kiev-soviet-union.
100. Plokhy, *The Last Empire*, 80–81.
101. Ibid.
102. Letter from Brent Scowcroft to Congressman Cox, n.d., GBPL, NSC Files, Burns and Hewett Files, Russia Subject Files, OA/ID CF01433-007.
103. George Bush, Remarks at the Arrival Ceremony in Moscow, July 30, 1991, American Presidency Project, accessed December 12, 2021, https://www.preside ncy.ucsb.edu/documents/remarks-the-arrival-ceremony-moscow.
104. George Bush, Remarks at the Moscow State Institute for International Relations, July 30, 1991, American Presidency Project, accessed December 12, 2021, https://www.presidency.ucsb.edu/documents/remarks-the-moscow-state-instit ute-for-international-relations.
105. From Latvian Legation in Washington to Jurkāns, July 31, 1991, LAMA, 1991_ 256_261.7.
106. Plokhy, *The Last Empire*, 70.
107. Three to three meeting with Gorbachev, July 31, Novo-Ogarevo, USSR, GBPL, accessed January 22, 2022, http://bush41library.tamu.edu/files/memcons-telc ons/1991-07-31--Gorbachev%20%5B1%5D.pdf.
108. Beissinger, *Nationalist Mobilization and the Collapse of the Soviet State*, 426.

109. Telcon. between Mitterrand and Bush, August 19, 1991, accessed January 21, 2022, https://bush41library.tamu.edu/files/memcons-telcons/1991-08-19--Mitterrand.pdf.

110. Bush and Scowcroft, *A World Transformed*, 520.

111. George Bush, Remarks and an Exchange with Reporters in Kennebunkport, Maine, on the Attempted Coup in the Soviet Union, August 19, 1991, American Presidency Project, accessed January 12, 2022, https://www.presidency.ucsb.edu/documents/remarks-and-exchange-with-reporters-kennebunkport-maine-the-attempted-coup-the-soviet.

112. Plokhy, *The Last Empire*, 111–112.

113. At the same time, a letter was received also from the organizers of the coup; see Letter from Gennady Yanayev to President Bush, Unofficial translation, August 20, 1991. GBPL, NSC files, Burns and Hewett Files, Chron. Files, August 1991 (1), OA/ID CF01407-007.

114. George Bush, Statement on the Attempted Coup in the Soviet Union, August 19, 1991, accessed December 12, 2021, https://www.presidency.ucsb.edu/documents/statement-the-attempted-coup-the-soviet-union.

115. Telcon., Bush with Lubbers, GBPL, accessed December 28, 2021, https://bush41library.tamu.edu/archives/memcons-telcons.

116. Bush and Scowcroft, *A World Transformed*, 524.

117. Telephone Interview with George Albert Krol, political officer, Consulate General Leningrad/St. Petersburg, Russia/USSR (1990–1992).

118. See more on this in Taylor, "The Soviet Military and the Disintegration of the USSR"; for a slightly different account, see Zubok, *Collapse*, 210–211.

119. Chernyaev, *Diary 1991*, 114

120. Telcon., Yeltsin and Bush, USSR, August 20, 1991, GBPL, NSC files, Burns and Hewett Files, Chron. Files, August 1991 (1), OA/ID CF01407-007.

121. Gordon M. Hahn, *Russia's Revolution from Above, 1985–2000: Reform, Transition, and Revolution in the Fall of the Soviet Communist Regime* (New Brunswick, NJ: Transaction Publishers, 2002), 449.

122. Ibid., 428.

123. Archie Brown, *The Gorbachev Factor*, 300; Plokhy, *The Last Empire*, 135.

124. Interview with Jānis Peters, representative of Latvian Government in Moscow (1990–1992), Latvian ambassador to the Russian Federation (1992–1997), Riga, May 15, 2015.

125. Zubok, *Collpase*, 251.

126. Blūma Pētersone, *Valstsvīrs Anatolijs Gorbunovs*, 431–436; Fredén, *Baltijas brīvības ceļš un Zviedrijas diplomātija*, 204; "Krievijas Padomju Federatīvās Sociālistiskās Republikas prezidenta 24.08.1991 dekrēts par Latvijas Republikas atzīšanu," in *Dokumenti par Latvijas valsts starptautisko atzīšanu, neatkaribas atjaunošanu un diplomatiskajiem sakariem: 1918–1998*, ed. Alberts Sarkanis (Riga: Nordik, 1999), 227.

127. Dokumenti par Latvijas valsts starptautisko atzīšanu, 222.

128. Ibid., 226; Uffe Ellemann-Jensen has later argued that Danish decision was not triggered by Yeltsin's move, but by the news that Estonian was taking over to control of its borders. (Lars Gronbjerg, "The Baltic Independence Struggle and Danish Diplomacy 1988–1991," in *The Baltic States at the End of the Cold War*, 260.

129. Bernard Lecomte, *Le bunker: vingt ans de relations franco-soviétiques* (Paris: Editions J.-C. Lattès, 1994), 236.

130. Fredén, *Baltijas brīvības ceļš un Zviedrijas diplomātija*, 193–195.
131. Kristina Spohr has explained Geischner's support for recognition by his strong attachment to the Helsinki process. Spohr, *Germany and the Baltic Problem after the Cold War*, 31.
132. Lecomte, *Le bunker*, 236.
133. Interview with Roland Dumas, French foreign minister (1988–1993), Paris, March 16, 2010.
134. Interview with Jānis Peters, representative of Latvian Government in Moscow (1990–1992), Latvian ambassador to the Russian Federation (1992–1997), Riga, May 15, 2015.
135. "Senators Urge Recognition of Baltics," *Ukrainian Weekly*, September 1, 1991, accessed January 3, 1991, https://docslib.org/doc/13009013/the-ukrainian-weekly-1991-no-35.
136. Letter from Senator Slade Gorton to President Bush, August 23, 1991, GBPL, NSC Files, Burns and Hewett Files, USSR Chron. Files, August 1991 (1), OA/ID CF01407-007.
137. Bush and Scowcroft, *A World Transformed*, 574.
138. George Bush, The President's News Conference with Prime Minister Mulroney of Canada in Kennebunkport, Maine, August 26, 1991, American Presidency Project, accessed January 14, 2022, https://www.presidency.ucsb.edu/documents/the-presidents-news-conference-with-prime-minister-mulroney-canada-kennebunkport-maine.
139. Memorandum from Scowcroft to the president, subject: Message to President Gorbachev on the Baltics, n.d., GBPL, NSC Files, Burns and Hewett Files, Chron. Files, August 1991, OA/ID CF01407-007.
140. Ibid.
141. Bush and Scowcroft, *A World Transformed*, 538.
142. Telcon., Bush and Gorbunovs, September 2, 1991, GBPL, accessed January 25, 2022, http://bush41library.tamu.edu/files/memcons-telcons/1991-09-02--Gorbunovs.pdf.
143. Telcon., Bush and Rüütel, September 2, 1991, GBPL, accessed January 25, 2022, http://bush41library.tamu.edu/files/memcons-telcons/1991-09-02--Ruutel.pdf.
144. Ann Devroy, "Bush after Delay Grants Baltic States Formal Recognition," *Washington Post*, September 3, 1991.
145. Interview with Jānis Peters, representative of the Latvian government in Moscow (1990–1992), Latvian ambassador to the Russian Federation (1992–1997), Riga, May 15, 2015.
146. Jānis Peters, "Estonian Economists, Latvian Lawyers and Lithuanian Communists—Knuts Skujenieks," in *The Baltic Way to Freedom: Non-Violent Struggle of the Baltic States in a Global Context*, ed. Jānis Škapars (Riga: Zelta grauds, 2005), 318.
147. Ibid., 320.
148. Savisaar, *Peaminister*, 721–723
149. Ibid., 723
150. Andra Jauce, "Apsveikumu es nesaņēmu, bet laba vēlējumus sev un tautai—gan," *Latvijas Jaunatne*, January 7, 1991.
151. Peters, "Estonian Economists, Latvian Lawyers and Lithuanian Communists," 321.
152. Ibid.
153. Baker and DeFrank, *The Politics of Diplomacy*, 537.

154. Ibid., 537–538.
155. GBPL, NSC Files, Burn Hewett Files, POTUS Meeting with Baltics, OA/ID
CF01422-032: Memorandum of Conversation, September 17, 1991; Meeting with
Chargé d'Affaires of the Baltic States and Remarks to Baltic-American Leaders,
September 11, 1991.

CONCLUSION

1. Maija Spanu, "The Hierarchical Society: The Politics of Self-Determination and
the Constitution of New States after 1991," *European Journal of International
Relations* 26, no. 2 (2020): 372–396.
2. On ethnic relations and citizenship policies in Estonia and Latvia see: Amomn
Cheskin, *Russian Speakers in Post-Soviet Latvia,* Deniss Hanovs, "Can postcolonial
theory help explain Latvian politics of integration? Reflections on contemporary
Latvia as a postcolonial society," *Journal of Baltic Studies* 47, no. 1 (2016): 133-
153, Kristina Kallas, *Revisiting the triadic nexus: An analysis of the ethnopolitical
interplay between Estonia, Russia and Estonian Russians*, Tartu: University of
Tartu Press, 2016; Diana T. Kudaibergenova, *Toward Nationalizing Regimes
Conceptualizing Power and Identity in the Post-Soviet Realm,* Pittsburgh: University
of Pittsburgh Press, 2020.
3. National Public Radio's interview and listener call-in with Russian president
Vladimir Putin, broadcast November 15, 2001, https://legacy.npr.org/news/speci
als/putin/nprinterview.html.
4. Marcus Warren, "Putin Lets NATO 'Recruit' in Baltic," *The Telegraph*, June
25, 2002.
5. Plokhy, *The Last Empire*, 198.

BIBLIOGRAPHY

UNPUBLISHED PRIMARY SOURCES

George Bush Presidential Library
- Records on the Baltics states (FOIA Request 2000-1197-F)
- Records on Estonia, Latvia and Lithuania (FOIA request 2012-0360-F)
- Brent Scowcroft Collection

The State Archives of Estonia (Rahvusarhiiv)
- Consulate General of Estonia in New York (ERA.1608)

Latvian State Archives (LVA)
- Papers of Prime Minister Ivars Godmanis (F. 270, A. 8, L. 15)
- Foreign Affairs Committee of Supreme Soviet Latvia, meetings of chairman of the Supreme Soviet Anatolijs Gorbunovs (F. 290, A. 11, L. 560)

Diplomatic Archives of Latvia (LAMA)
- Various boxes of unprocessed documents.

Lithuanian Diplomatic Archives (LURMA)
- Documents of the CSCE meeting in New York (90.10-22) (F.3, A.3, L.2)
- Documents of the Accession of the Republic of Lithuania to the CSCE Position of Lithuania 28.09.1990–17.12.1991 (F.3, A.3, L.3)

GORBACHEV FOUNDATION

Sterling Library, Yale University, Slavic, East European & Central Asian Collection
- Fond 89: Archives of the Soviet Communist Party and Soviet State .

Mudd Manuscript Library, Princeton University
- James A. Baker III Papers
- George F. Kennan Papers

National Security Archives
- Collection "The End of the Cold War"
- Box 2: Geneva Summit 1, Reykjavík Summit

- Box 3: Domestic Stresses on the Soviet System, CIA Intelligence Assessment, November 1985; Rising Political Instability under Gorbachev: Understanding the Problem and Prospects for Resolution. CIA Intelligence Assessment, April 1989
- Box 4: Malta Summit, Washington Summit

French National Archives
- Série AG papiers des chefs de l'Etat Sous série: 5 AG 4 François Mitterrand 1981–1995
  - o CD 242, dossier 1
  - o CD 242, dossier 4
  - o CD 314, dossier 13

French Diplomatic Archives
- Direction d'Europe (1986–1990): URSS 6592, URSS 6682
- Direction d'Europe (1991–1995): URSS 7667

PRIVATE ARCHIVES OF AMBASSADOR OJĀRS KALNIŅŠ

Interviews
Aina Nagobads-Ābols, Latvian representative in France (1990–1991) and Latvian ambassador to France (1991–1997), Paris, February 26, 2010.

Janis Jurkāns, foreign minister of Latvia (1990–1992), Riga, March 2, 2010.

Algirdas Saudargas, foreign minister of Lithuania (1990–1992), Brussels, March 24, 2010.

Kārina Pētersone, diplomatic advisor to the Chairman of the Supreme Council of Latvia (1990–1993), Riga, March 2, 2010.

Malle Talvet-Mustonen, Estonian representative in France (1991), Tallinn, March 5, 2010.

Roland Dumas, French foreign minister (1988–1993), Paris, March 16, 2010.

Richard Bačkis, Lithuanian representative in France (1990–1991) and Lithuanian ambassador to France (1994–1998), Paris, March 17, 2010.

Ruth Lausma-Luik, chargée d'affaires at the Estonian Institute, Brussels, March 27, 2010.

Philippe de Suremain, deputy director of the European Affairs Department of the French Foreign Ministry (1989–1991), Paris, March 11, 2010.

Algirdas Saudargas, foreign minister of Lithuania (1990–1992), Brussels, March 24, 2010.

René Roudaut, deputy director of European Affairs Department of the French Foreign Ministry (1990–1992), Budapest, April 15, 2010.

Thomas W. Simons, US ambassador to Poland (1990–1993), Cambridge, MA, May 29, 2012.

Hubert Védrine, diplomatic advisor of François Mitterrand (1988–1991), secretary-general of the presidency (1991–1995), Paris, December 5, 2013.

Nicholas Burns, NSC senior director of Soviet affairs (1990–1991), Boston, March 12, 2013.

Paul A. Goble, special advisor for Soviet nationality and Baltic affairs at the US Department of State (1990–1991), April 17, 2013 (telephone interview).

Jack Matlock, US ambassador to the USSR (1987–1991), Princeton, April 17, 2013.

George Albert Krol, foreign service officer, Consulate Generàl Leningrad/St. Petersburg, Russia/USSR (1990–1992), April 22, 2013 (telephone interview).

Jaak Treiman, Estonian honorary consul in Los Angeles, April 24, 2013 (telephone interview).

Brent Scowcroft, US national security advisor (1989–1993), May 30, 2013 (telephone interview).

Trivimi Velliste, founder and chairman of Estonian Heritage Society, Tallinn, June 18, 2013.

Mari-Ann Kelam, leading Estonian diaspora activist, Tallinn, June 18, 2013.

Clyde Kull, advisor to Estonian minister of foreign affairs (1990–1991), Brussels, April 2, 2014

Pierre Morel, French ambassador to the Conference on Disarmament in Geneva (1986–1991); diplomatic advisor to François Mitterrand (1991–1992).

Ojārs Kalniņš, public affairs liaison officer, Latvian Legation in Washington (1990–1991); public relations director of the American Latvian Association (1990–1985), Riga, July 21, 2014.

Jānis Peters, representative of Latvian Government in Moscow 1990–1992, Latvian ambassador to the Russian Federation (1992–1997), Riga, May 15, 2015.

Dainis Īvāns, chairman of Tautas Fronte (1988–1990), deputy speaker of the Supreme Soviet of Latvia (1990–1992), Riga, May 19, 2015.

Andrei Grachev, deputy head of the CPSU Central Committee's International section (1989–1991), press secretary of Mikhail Gorbachev (1991), Paris, March 15, 2016.

PUBLISHED PRIMARY SOURCES

"Minutes of the Meeting of the Politburo of the CPSU CC, 27–28 December 1988." *Cold War International History Project Bulletin*, no. 12/13 (2001), 24–25.

Boisdron, Matthieu, ed. *Diplomate en Lettonie: Carnets de Jean de Beausse, premier secrétaire à l'ambassade de France à Riga (décembre 1938–septembre 1940)*. Paris: Mens Sana, 2011.

Bush, George H. W. *All the Best, George Bush: My Life in Letters and Other Writings*. London: Simon & Schuster, 2001.

Chernyaev, Anatoly, ed. *Otvechaya na vyzov vremeni. Vneshnyaya politika perestroyki: dokumental'nyye svidetelstva*. Moscow: Ves Mir, 2010.

Chernyaev, Anatoly, and Vladlen Loginov, eds. *Soyuz mozhno bylo sokhranit. Belaya kniga. Dokumenty i fakty o politike M. S. Gorbacheva po reformirovaniyu i sokhraneniyu mnogonatsional'nogo gosudarstva*. Moscow: ACT, 2007.

Chernyaev, Anatoly, Georgy Shakhnazarov, and Vadim Medvedev, eds. *V Politbyuro TsK KPSS . . .: Po zapisyam Anatoliya Chernyayeva, Vadima Medvedeva, Georgiya Shakhnazarova (1985–1991)*. Moscow: Al'pina Biznes Buks, 2006.

Constitutional Court of the Republic on Latvia, Judgment in Case No. 2007-10-0102 on the Law "On Authorization to the Cabinet of Ministers to Sign the Draft Agreement between the Republic of Latvia and the Russian Federation on the State Border between Latvia and Russia Initialed on August 7, 1997." Riga, November 29, 2007.

Etzold, Thomas H., and John Lewis Gaddis, eds. *Containment: Documents on American Policy and Strategy, 1945–1950*. New York: Columbia University Press, 1978.

Gorbachev, Mikhail. *Sobraniye sochineniy*. Vols. 9–27. Moscow: Ves' Mir, 2009–2014.

Gosudarstvennyĭ komitet SSSR po statistike. *Demograficheskiĭ Ezhegodnik SSSR*. Moscow: Finansy i statistika, 1990.

Hanhimäki, Jussi M., and Odd Arne Westad, eds. *The Cold War: A History in Documents and Eyewitness Accounts*. Oxford; New York: Oxford University Press, 2003.

Hofmann, Daniel, and Hanns Jürgen Küsters, eds. *Deutsche Einheit. Sonderedition aus den Akten des Bundeskanzleramtes 1989/90. Dokumente zur Deutschlandpolitik*. Munich: R. Oldenbourg, 1998.

Lietuvos Apeliacinis teismas, Baudžiamoji byla Nr. 1A-34-1020/2021, 2021 m. kovo 31d. https://www.apeliacinis.lt/naujienos/sausio-13-osios-ivykiu-bylos-nagri nejimas/1008?fbclid=IwAR3RRIA16qmvddsixV7SPth01XY9-BW_kQGLtUPJfq AWDTH5sWsQq-ap7hA.

Lindpere, Heiki, ed. *Molotov-Ribbentrop Pact: Challenging Soviet History*. Tallinn: Estonian Foreign Policy Institute, 2009.

MRP-AEG infobülletään 1987–88. Tallinn: Kirjastus SE&JS, 1998.

Narodnoye khozyaystvo SSSR v 1990 g. Statisticheskiy ezhegodnik. Moscow: Finansy i statistika, 1991

Pervy Syezd narodnykh deputatov SSSR 25 maya–9 iyunya 1989 g. Stenograficheskiy otchot. Vol 2. Moscow: Izdaniye Verkhovnogo Soveta SSSR, 1989.

Sarkanis, Alberts, ed. *Dokumenti par Latvijas valsts starptautisko atzīšanu, neatkarības atjaunošanu un diplomātiskajiem sakariem: 1918–1998*. Riga: Nordik, 1999.

Together: Council of the Baltic States 1990–1992 Documents. Vilnius: Lithuanian Institute of International Political and Economic Relations, 1996.

United States Department of State. *Foreign Relations of the United States Diplomatic Papers, 1940*. General Volume I. Washington, DC: U.S. Government Printing Office, 1940.

United States Department of State. *Foreign Relations of the United States Diplomatic Papers, The Conferences at Cairo and Tehran, 1943*. Washington, DC: U.S. Government Printing Office, 1943

United States Department of State. *Foreign Relations of the United States, 1946. Paris Peace Conference: Proceedings*. Volume III. Washington, DC: U.S. Government Printing Office, 1946.

Vneocherednaya desyataya sessiya Verkhovnogo Soveta SSSR (odinnadtsatyy sozyv), 29 noyabrya–1 dekabrya 1988 g. Stenograficheskiy otchet. Moscow: Izdaniye Verkhovnogo Soveta SSSR, 1988.

PRIMARY SOURCES PUBLISHED ONLINE

American Presidency project. http://www.presidency.ucsb.edu/index.php.

Arkhiv Aleksandra N. Yakovleva. https://www.alexanderyakovlev.org/.

Diary of Gorbachev's diplomatic aide Anatoly Chernyaev. http://nsarchive.gwu.edu/ NSAEBB/NSAEBB192/.

Freedom of Information Act Electronic Reading Room of the Central Intelligence Agency. http://www.foia.cia.gov/.

George H. W. Bush Presidential Library. Memcons and Telcons. https://bush41library. tamu.edu/archives/memcons-telcons.

Harry Truman Presidential Library. Oral History Interviews. https://www.trumanlibr ary.gov/library/oral-histories/oralhis.

Harry Truman Presidential Library. Public Papers. https://www.trumanlibrary.gov/ library/public-papers.

National Security Archive. Svetlana Savranskaya and Tom Blanton, *NATO Expansion: What Gorbachev Heard*. https://nsarchive.gwu.edu/briefing-book/ russia-programs/2017-12-12/nato-expansion-what-gorbachev-heard-western-leaders-early#_edn7.

US Bureau of the Census 1990. *Census of Population Ancestry of the Population in the United States*, 1993. https://www.census.gov/library/publications/1993/dec/cp-3-2.html.

US Bureau of the Census 1990. *Census of Population. Detailed Ancestry Groups for States*, 1992. https://usa.ipums.org/usa/resources/voliii/pubdocs/1990/cp-s/cp-s-1-2.pdf.

Virtual Reading Rome of the US State Department. https://foia.state.gov/Search/Search.aspx.

Yale Law School. Lillian Goldman Law Library. *The Avalon Project. Documents in Law, History and Diplomacy*. https://avalon.law.yale.edu/default.asp.

PUBLISHED SECONDARY SOURCES

Baker, James Addison, and Thomas M. DeFrank. *The Politics of Diplomacy: Revolution, War, and Peace, 1989–1992*. New York: Putnam, 1995.

Bayly, Martin J. "Imperial Ontological (in)Security: 'Buffer States.' International Relations and the Case of Anglo-Afghan Relations, 1808–1878." *European Journal of International Relations* 21, no. 4 (2015): 816–840.

Beissinger, Mark. "The Intersection of Ethnic Nationalism and People Power Tactics in the Baltic States, 1987–1991." In *Civil Resistance and Power Politics: The Experience of Non-violent Action from Gandhi to the Present*, edited by Adam Roberts and Timothy Garton Ash, 231–246. Oxford: Oxford University Press, 2009.

Beissinger, Mark R. *Nationalist Mobilization and the Collapse of the Soviet State*. Cambridge: Cambridge University Press, 2002.

Bell, Duncan. "Mythscapes: Memory, Mythology, and National Identity." *British Journal of Sociology* 54, no. 1 (March 2003): 63–81.

Beschloss, Michael, and Strobe Talbott. *At the Highest Levels: The Inside Story of the End of the Cold War*. New York: Open Road Media, 2016.

Bleiere, Daina. "Sarunas ar Kremli par Latvijas neatkarības atzīšanu–vai tās bija iespējamas?" In *1990. Gada 4. Maija Latvijas Neatkarības Deklarācija: starptautiskie un iekšpolitiskie aspekti*, edited by Inesis Feldmanis and Jānis Taurēns. Riga: LU Akadēmiskais apgāds, 2011, 89–111.

Boldin, Valery. *Krushenie p'edestala: shtrikhi k portretu M. S. Gorbacheva*. Moscow: Respublika, 1995.

Bonnard, Pascal. *Le gouvernement de l'ethnicité en Europe post-soviétique. Minorités et pouvoir en Lettonie*. Paris: Dalloz, 2013.

Bozo, Frédéric. *Mitterrand, la fin de la guerre froide et l'unification Allemande. De Yalta à Maastricht*. Paris: Jacob, 2005.

Brown, Archie. *The Gorbachev Factor*. Oxford: Oxford University Press, 1997.

Brubaker, Rogers. "The 'Diaspora' Diaspora." *Ethnic and Racial Studies* 28, no. 1 (2005): 1–19.

Bunce, Valerie. *Subversive Institutions: The Design and the Destruction of Socialism and the State*. Cambridge: Cambridge University Press, 1999.

Caplan, Richard. *Europe and the Recognition of New States in Yugoslavia*. Cambridge: Cambridge University Press, 2005.

Čepaitis, Virgilijus. "Sąjūdžio politinės akcijos." In *Kelias į Nepriklausomybę: Lietuvos Sąjūdis 1988–1991*, edited by Bronius Genzelis and Angonita Rupšytė. Kaunas: Šviesa, 2010, 73–93.

Čepaitis, Virgilijus. *Su Sąjūdžiu už Lietuvą nuo 1988. 06. 03.–1990. 03. 11*. Vilnius: Tvermė, 2007.

Connelly, Matthew. *A Diplomatic Revolution: Algeria's Fight for Independence and the Origins of the Post–Cold War Era*. New York: Oxford University Press, 2002.

Daase, Christopher, Caroline Fehl, et al., eds. *Recognition in International Relations: Rethinking a Political Concept in a Global Context*. Basingstoke, Hampshire: Palgrave Macmillan, 2015.

Davoliūtė, Violeta. *The Making and Breaking of Soviet Lithuania: Memory and Modernity in the Wake of War*. London: Routledge, 2013.

Deksnis, Eduards Bruno, and Tālavs Jundzis. *The Parliamentary Route to the Restoration of Latvian Statehood 1989–1993*. Riga: Apgāds Mantojums, 2010.

Doeser, Fredrik, and Joakim Eidenfalk. "The Importance of Windows of Opportunity for Foreign Policy Change." *International Area Studies Review* 16, no. 4 (2013): 390–406.

Domber, Gregory F. "Skepticism and Stability: Reevaluating U.S. Policy during Poland's Democratic Transformation in 1989." *Journal of Cold War Studies* 13, no. 3 (2011): 52–82.

Doyle, Michael W. *Empires*. Ithaca, NY: Cornell University Press, 1986.

Dubinin, Yuri. *Moscou-Paris dans un tourbillon diplomatique: Témoignage d'ambassadeur*. Paris: Imaginaria, 2002.

Dullin, Sabine. "How to Wage Warfare without Going to War?" *Cahiers du monde russe* 52, no. 2 (2012): 221–243.

Dumas, Roland. *Le fil et la pelote: mémoires*. Paris: Plon, 1996.

Encausse, Hélène Carrère de. *L'empire éclaté: la révolte des nations en U.R.S.S.* Paris: Flammarion, 1978.

English, Robert. *Russia and the Idea of the West: Gorbachev, Intellectuals, and the End of the Cold War*. New York: Columbia University Press, 2000. ProQuest EBook Central.

English, Robert. "The Sociology of New Thinking: Elites, Identity Change, and the End of the Cold War." *Journal of Cold War Studies* 7, no. 2 (2005): 43–80.

Engel, Jeffrey. *When the World Seemed New: George H. W. Bush and the End of the Cold War*. Boston: Houghton Mifflin Harcourt Publishing Company, 2017.

Evangelista, Matthew. "Norms, Heresthetics, and the End of the Cold War." *Journal of Cold War Studies* 3, no. 1 (2001): 5–35.

Foucault, Michel. *Language, Counter-Memory, Practice: Selected Essays and Interviews*. Ithaca, NY: Cornell University Press, 1977.

France-Estonie: Regards mutuels, actes du colloque franco-estonien Tallinn, Tartu, 16–20 juin 1991. Paris: Association France-Estonie, 1997.

Fredēns, Lars. *Baltijas brīvības ceļš un Zviedrijas diplomātija: 1989–1991*. Riga: Atēna, 2007.

Garthoff, Raymond L. *The Great Transition: American-Soviet Relations and the End of the Cold War*. Washington, DC: Brookings Institution, 1994.

Genys, John B. "The Joint Baltic American Committee and the European Security Conference." *Journal of Baltic Studies* 9, no. 3 (1978): 245–258.

Giddens, Anthony. *Modernity and Self-Identity: Self and Society in the Late Modern Age*. Hoboken, NJ: John Wiley & Sons, 2013.

Gill, Graeme J. *Symbols and Legitimacy in Soviet Politics*. Cambridge: Cambridge University Press, 2011.

Gorbachev, Mikhail. *Gody trudnykh resheniy. Izbrannoye. 1985–1992*. Moscow: Alfaprint, 1993.

Gorbachev, Mikhail. *Memoirs*. London: Doubleday, 1997.

Gorbachev, Mikhail. *Perestroika: New Thinking for Our Country and the World.* New York: Harper & Row, 1988.

Gratchev, Andreï. *Gorbatchev, le pari perdu?: De la perestroïka à la fin de la guerre froide,* Paris: Armand Colin, 2011.

Grybkauskas, Saulius. *Governing the Soviet Union's National Republics. The Second Secretaries of the Communist Party.* London: Routledge, 2021.

Gudni, Jóhannesson. "The Might of the Weak? Icelandic Support for Baltic Independence, 1990–1991." Draft paper posted online on author's personal website, accessed on January 22, 2022, http://gudnith.is/.

Gueslin, Julien. "Paris sur Baltique 1918–1949." *Regard sur l'Est,* July 1, 2003, https://regard-est.com/paris-sur-la-baltique-1918-1940.

Hahn, Gordon M. *Russia's Revolution from Above, 1985–2000: Reform, Transition, and Revolution in the Fall of the Soviet Communist Regime.* New Brunswick, NJ: Transaction Publishers, 2002.

Hanovs, Deniss. "Can postcolonial theory help explain Latvian politics of integration? Reflections on contemporary Latvia as a postcolonial society," *Journal of Baltic Studies* 47, no. 1 (2016): 133-153

Hanson, Philip. *The Rise and Fall of the Soviet Economy: An Economic History of the USSR from 1945.* London; New York: Routledge, 2014.

Hathaway, Oona A., and Scott J. Shapiro. *The Internationalists: How a Radical Plan to Outlaw War Remade the World.* New York: Simon & Schuster, 2017.

Heikkilä, Pauli. "Baltic States: Estonia, Latvia and Lithuania." In *East Central European Migrations during the Cold War,* edited by Anna Mazurkiewicz, 45–67. Berlin: De Gruyter Oldenbourg, 2019.

Henderson, Loy W., and George W. Baer. *A Question of Trust: The Origins of U.S.-Soviet Diplomatic Relations: The Memoirs of Loy W. Henderson.* Stanford, CA: Hoover Institution Press, 1986.

Herman, Robert G. "Identity, Norms and National Security: The Soviet Foreign Policy Revolution and the End of the Cold War." In *The Culture of National Security,* edited by Peter Katzenstein, 271–316. New York: Columbia University Press, 1996.

Hough, William J. H., III. "The Annexation of the Baltic States and Its Effect on the Development of Law Prohibiting Forcible Seizure of Territory." *New York Law School Journal of International and Comparative Law* 6, no. 2 (1985): 301–533.

Hutchings, Robert L. *American Diplomacy and the End of the Cold War. An Insider's Account of U.S. Policy in Europe, 1989–1992.* Baltimore; London: Johns Hopkins University Press, 1997.

Īvāns, Dainis. *Gadījuma Karakalps.* Riga: Vieda, 1995.

Īvāns, Dainis. *Latvijas Tautas Fronte Rietumos.* Riga: Elpa, 2001.

Jervis, Robert. *Perception and Misperception in International Politics.* Princeton, NJ: Princeton University Press, 2017.

Kazickas, Joseph. *Odyssey of Hope: The Story of a Lithuanian Immigrant's Escape from Communism to Freedom in America and the Return to His Beloved Homeland.* Vilnius: Tyto Alba, 2006.

Kallas, Kristina. *Revisiting the triadic nexus: An analysis of the ethnopolitical interplay between Estonia, Russia and Estonian Russians.* Tartu: University of Tartu Press, 2016.

Kalniete, Sandra. *Es lauzu, tu lauzi, mēs lauzām, viņi lūza.* Riga: Jumava, 2000.

Karklins, Rasma. *Ethnopolitics and Transition to Democracy: The Collapse of the USSR and Latvia*. Baltimore: Woodrow Wilson Center Press; Johns Hopkins University Press, 1994.

Kasekamp, Andres. *A History of the Baltic States*. Houndmills, Basingstoke; New York: Palgrave Macmillan, 2010.

Katzenstein, Peter J. "Introduction." In *The Culture of National Security: Norms and Identity in World Politics*, edited by Peter J. Katzenstein. New York: Columbia University Press, 1996, 1–7.

Keller, Shoshana. *Russia and Central Asia: Coexistence, Conquest, Convergence*. Toronto: University of Toronto Press, 2019.

Kennan, George F. "Communism in Russian History." *Foreign Affairs* 69, no. 4 (1990): 169–186.

Kiaupa, Zigmantas. *The History of Lithuania*. Vilnius: Baltos lankos, 2005.

King, Charles. *The Ghost of Freedom: A History of the Caucasus*. New York: Oxford University Press, 2008.

Koinova, Maria. "Four Types of Diaspora Mobilization: Albanian Diaspora Activism for Kosovo Independence in the US and the UK." *Foreign Policy Analysis* 9, no. 4 (2013): 433–453.

Koivisto, Mauno. *Kaksi kautta. 2, Historian tekijät*. Helsinki: Kirjayhtymä,1995.

Kol, Anu Mai. "Economy and Ethnicity in the Hands of the State: Economic Change and the National Question in Twentieth-Century Estonia." In *Economic Change and the National Question in Twentieth-Century Europe*, edited by Alice Teichova et al., 357–381. Cambridge: Cambridge University Press, 2000.

Kotkin, Stephen. *Armageddon Averted: The Soviet Collapse, 1970–2000*. New York: Oxford University Press, 2008.

Kramer, Mark. "The Collapse of East European Communism and the Repercussions within the Soviet Union (Part 1)." *Journal of Cold War Studies* 5, no. 4 (2003): 178–256.

Kramer, Mark. "The Collapse of East European Communism and the Repercussions within the Soviet Union (Part 2)." *Journal of Cold War Studies* 6, no. 4 (2004): 3–64.

Kramer, Mark. "The Collapse of East European Communism and the Repercussions within the Soviet Union (Part 3)." *Journal of Cold War Studies* 7, no. 1 (2005): 3–96.

Kramer, Mark. "The Demise of the Soviet Bloc." In *The End and the Beginning: The Revolutions of 1989 and the Resurgence of History*, edited by Vladimir Tismaneanu and Bogdan Iacob, 171–256. Budapest: Central European University Press, 2012.

Krickus, Richard J. *Showdown: The Lithuanian Rebellion and the Breakup of the Soviet Empire*. Washington, DC: Brassey's, 1997.

Kryuchkov, Vladimir. *Lichnoye delo*. Vol. 2. Moscow: Olimp, 1996.

Kudaibergenova, Diana T. *Toward Nationalizing Regimes Conceptualizing Power and Identity in the Post-Soviet Realm.*Pittsburgh: University of Pittsburgh Press, 2020.

Kuldkepp, Mart. "Baltic Liberation First-hand: Sweden's Pro-Baltic Foreign Policy Shift and Swedish Diplomatic Reporting in 1989–1991." *Scandinavian Journal of History* 47, no. 3 (2022): 325–346.

Landsbergis, Vytautas. *Lithuania, Independent Again: The Autobiography of Vytautas Landsbergis*. Cardiff: University of Wales Press, 2000.

Landsbergis, Vytautas. *Un peuple sort de prison*. Vilnius: Baltijos kopija, 2007.

Lasas, Ainius. "Bloody Sunday: What Did Gorbachev Know about the January 1991 Events in Vilnius and Riga?" *Journal of Baltic Studies* 38, no. 2 (June 2007): 179–194.

Lazda, Māra."Reconsidering Nationalism: The Baltic Case of Latvia in 1989." *International Journal of Politics, Culture, and Society* 22, no. 4 (2009): 517–536.

Lecomte, Bernard. *Le bunker: vingt ans de relations franco-soviétiques*. Paris: Editions J.-C. Lattès, 1994.

Leonard, Mark, and Andrew T. Small. *Norwegian Public Diplomacy*. London: Foreign Policy Centre, 2005.

Lévesque, Jacques. "The East European Revolutions of 1989." In *The Cambridge History of the Cold War*, edited by Melvyn P. Leffler and Odd Arne Westad. Vol. 3: *Endings*, 311–332. Cambridge: Cambridge University Press, 2010.

L'Hommedieu, Jonathan H. "Baltic Exiles and the U.S. Congress: Investigations and Legacies of the House Select Committee, 1953–1955." *Journal of American Ethnic History* 31, no. 2 (2012): 41–67.

Liebich, André. "Les promesses faites à Gorbatchev: l'avenir des alliances au crépuscule de la guerre froide." *Relations* internationales 147, no. 3 (2011): 85–96.

Lieven, Anatol. *The Baltic Revolution: Estonia, Latvia, Lithuania and the Path to Independence*. New Haven, CT: Yale University Press, 1993.

Lindemann, Thomas, and Erik Ringmar, eds. *The International Politics of Recognition*. Boulder, CO: Paradigm Publishers, 2012. T&F eBooks.

Lindsay, James M. "Congress and Foreign Policy: Why the Hill Matters." *Political Science Quarterly* 107, no. 4 (1992): 607–628.

Made, Vahur. "The Estonian Government-in-Exile. A Controversial Project of State Continuation." In *The Baltic Question during the Cold War*, edited by John Hiden et al., 134–144. London; New York: Routledge, 2008.

Madison, Agnus. *The World Economy: a Milleniume Perespective*. Paris: OECD, 2006F.

Mann, James. *The Rebellion of Ronald Reagan: A History of the End of the Cold War*. London: Penguin Books, 2010.

Matlock, Jack F. *Autopsy of an Empire. The American Ambassador's Account of the Collapse of the Soviet Union*. New York: Random House, 1995.

Mead, George Herbert. *Mind, Self, and Society. The Definitive Edition*. Chicago: University of Chicago Press, 2015.

Medijainen, Eero. "The USA, Soviet Russia and the Baltic States. From Recognition to the Cold War." In *The Baltic Questions during the Cold War*, edited by John Hiden et al. London; New York: Routledge, 2008, 21–33.

Medvedev, Vadim. *V komande Gorbacheva: vzglyad iznutri*. Moscow: Bylina, 1994. http://lib.ru/MEMUARY/GORBACHEV/medvedev.txt.

Meltyukhov, Mikhail. *Upushchennyy shans Stalina. Sovetskiy Soyuz i bor'ba za Evropu: 1939–1941*. Moscow: Veche, 2000.

Mereckis, Darius, and Morkvėnas, Rimantas. "The 1991 Treaty as a Basis for Lithuanian-Russian Relations." *Lithuanian Foreign Policy Review* 1 (1998): 1–9. http://lfpr.lt/wp-content/uploads/2015/07/LFPR-1-Mereckis_Morkvenas.pdf.

Mille, Astra. *Te un citadel. Jānis Peters: tumšsarkanā*. Riga: Atēna, 2006.

Misztal, Barbara A. *Theories of Social Remembering*. Buckingham: Open University Press, 2003.

Morgan, Michael Cotey. *The Final Act: The Helsinki Accords and the Transformation of the Cold War*. Princeton, NJ: Princeton University Press, 2018.

Muižnieks, Nils R. "The Influence of the Baltic Popular Movements on the Process of Soviet Disintegration." *Europe-Asia Studies* 47, no. 1 (1995): 3–25.

Naftali, Timothy J. *George H. W. Bush*. New York: Macmillan, 2007.

Nagobads-Ābols, Aina. *Parīze, Madride, Lisabona un atpakaļ Rīgā*. Riga: Zinātne, 2000.

Neumann, Iver B. *Russia and the Idea of Europe: A Study in Identity and International Relations*. Milton Park, Abingdon: Routledge, 2017.

Nichol, James P. *Diplomacy in the Former Soviet Republics*. London: Praeger, 1995.

Olesen, Mikkel Runge. "The Beginnings of Danish Foreign Policy Activism: Supporting Baltic Independence 1990–1991." *Scandinavian Journal of History*, 2022. Published online ahead of print, https://doi.org/10.1080/03468755.2022.2034664.

Park, Andrus. *End of an Empire? A Conceptualization of the Soviet Disintegration Crisis 1985–1991*. Tartu: Tartu University Press, 2009.

Perchoc, Philippe. "European Memory beyond the State: Baltic, Russian and European Memory Interactions (1991–2009)." *Memory Studies* 12, no. 6 (2019): 677–698.

Peters, Jānis. "'Estonian Economists, Latvian Lawyers and Lithuanian Communists'—Knuts Skujenieks." In *The Baltic Way to Freedom: Non-Violent Struggle of the Baltic States in a Global Context*, edited by Jānis Škapars. Riga: Zelta grauds, 2005, 310–321 .

Pētersone, Kārina, and Ilze Būmane. *Valstsvīrs Anatolijs Gorbunovs*. Riga: Zvaigzne ABC, 2020.

Piirimäe, Kaarel. "Estonia 'Has Not Time': Existential Politics at the End of Empire." *Connexe: les espaces postcommunistes en question* 6 (2020): 21–50.

Piirimäe, Kaarel. "Gorbachev's New Thinking and How Its Interaction with Perestroika in the Republics Catalyzed the Soviet Collapse." *Scandinavian Journal of History*. 47, no. 3 (2020): 300–324.

Piirimäe, Kaarel. *Roosevelt, Churchill and the Baltic Question: Allied Relations during the Second World War*. New York: Palgrave Macmillan, 2014.

Plakans, Andrejs. *Concise History of the Baltic States*. Cambridge: Cambridge University Press, 2011.

Plavnieks, Richards. *Nazi Collaborators on Trial during the Cold War: Viktors Arājs and the Latvian Auxiliary Security Police*. Cham: Springer International Publishing, 2018.

Pleshakov, Constantine. *There Is No Freedom without Bread!: 1989 and the Civil War That Brought Down Communism*. New York: Farrar, Straus & Giroux, 2009.

Plokhy, Serhii. *Yalta: The Price of Peace*. New York: Viking, 2010.

Plokhy, Serhii. *The Last Empire: The Final Days of the Soviet Union*. New York: Simon & Schuster, 2015.

Pomeranz, William E. *Law and the Russian State: Russia's Legal Evolution from Peter the Great to Vladimir Putin*. London: Bloomsbury, 2018.

Pryce-Jones, David. *The War That Never Was: The Fall of the Soviet Empire, 1985–1991*. London: Phoenix, 2001.

Ramonaitė, Ainė, and Rytė Kukulskytė. "Etnokultūrinis Judėjimas Sovietmečiu: Nematoma Alternatyva Sistemai?" *Lietuvos Etnologija: Socialines Antropologijos Ir Etnologijos Studijos* 14, no. 23 (2014): 161–181.

Rathbun, Brian C. "Uncertain about Uncertainty: Understanding the Multiple Meanings of a Crucial Concept in International Relations Theory." *International Studies Quarterly* 51, no. 3 (2007): 533–557.

Rayfield, Donald. *Edge of Empires: A History of Georgia*. London: Reaktion Books, 2012.

Redecker, Niels von. *The Baltic Question and the British Press, 1989–1991.*
  Hamburg: Verlag Dr. Kovač, 1998.

Rey, Marie-Pierre. "Europe Is Our Common Home: A Study of Gorbachev's Diplomatic
  Concept." *Cold War History* 4, no. 2 (2004): 33–65.

Ritvanen, Juha-Matti. "The Change in Finnish Baltic Policy as a Turning Point
  in Finnish-Soviet Relations. Finland, Baltic Independence and the End
  of the Soviet Union 1988–1991." *Scandinavian Journal of History* 47, no. 3
  (2022): 280–299.

Sahadeo, Jeff. *Voices from the Soviet Edge: Southern Migrants in Leningrad and Moscow.*
  Ithaca, NY : Cornell University Press, 2019.

Saharov, Juhan. "An Economic Innovation as an Icebreaker: The Contractual Work
  Experiment in Soviet Estonia in 1985." In *The Baltic States and the End of the
  Cold War*, edited by Kaarel Piirimäe and Olaf Mertelsmann. Berlin: Peter Lang,
  2018, 65–84.

Saharov, Juhan. "From an Economic Term to a Political Concept. The Conceptual
  Innovation of 'Self-Management' in Soviet Estonia." *Contributions to the History
  of Concepts* 16, no. 1 (2021): 116–140.

Sarotte, Mary Elise. *1989: The Struggle to Create a Post–Cold War Europe.* Princeton,
  NJ: Princeton University Press, 2014.

Sarotte, Mary Elise. *Not One Inch: America, Russia, and the Making of Post–Cold War
  Stalemate.* New Haven, CT: Yale University Press, 2021.

Savisaar, Edgar. *Peaminister: Eesti lähiajalugu 1990–1992.* Tartu: Kleio, 2004.

Schweizer, Peter. *Victory: The Reagan Administration's Secret Strategy That Hastened the
  Collapse of the Soviet Union.* New York: Atlantic Monthly Press, 1996.

Shifrinson, Joshua R. "Deal or No Deal? The End of the Cold War and the U.S. Offer to
  Limit NATO Expansion." *International Security* 40, no. 4 (2016): 7–44.

Simonyan, Renald. *Rossiya i strany Baltii.* Moscow: Academia, 2003.

Smith, Jeremy. *Red Nations: The Nationalities Experience in and after the USSR.*
  Cambridge: Cambridge University Press, 2013.

Snyder, Sarah B. "'Jerry, Don't Go': Domestic Opposition to the 1975 Helsinki Final
  Act." *Journal of American Studies* 44, no. 1 (2010): 67–81.

Snyder, Timothy. *The Reconstruction of Nations: Poland, Ukraine, Lithuania, Belarus,
  1569–1999.* New Haven, CT: Yale University Press, 2003.

Spanu, Maija. "The Hierarchical Society: The Politics of Self-Determination and
  the Constitution of New States after 1991." *European Journal of International
  Relations* 26, no. 2 (2020): 372–396.

Spohr, Kristina. "Between Political Rhetoric and Realpolitik Calculations: Western
  Diplomacy and the Baltic Independence Struggle in the Cold War Endgame."
  Cold War History 6, no. 1 (2006): 1–42.

Spohr, Kristina, *Post Wall, Post Square: Rebuilding the World after 1989.* New Haven,
  CT: Yale University Press, 2019.

Suny, Ronald Grigor. *The Revenge of the Past: Nationalism, Revolution, and the Collapse
  of the Soviet Union.* Stanford, CA: Stanford University Press, 1993. ACLS
  Humanities eBook.

Tannenwald, Nina. "Ideas and Explanation: Advancing the Theoretical Agenda."
  Journal of Cold War Studies 7, no. 2 (2005): 13–42.

Tannenwald, Nina, and William C. Wohlforth. "Introduction: The Role of Ideas and
  the End of the Cold War." *Journal of Cold War Studies* 7, no. 2 (2005): 3–12.

Taylor, Brian D. "The Soviet Military and the Disintegration of the USSR." *Journal of
  Cold War Studies* 1, no. 1 (2003): 17–66.

Tinguy, Anne de. "Effondrement ou suicide?" In *L'effondrement de l'Empire soviétique*, edited by Anne de Tinguy, 69–88. Brussels: Bruylant, 1998.

Tuminez, Astrid S. "Nationalism, Ethnic Pressures, and the Breakup of the Soviet Union." *Journal of Cold War Studies* 5, no. 4 (2003): 81–136.

Valente, Riccardo, and Sergi Valera Pertegas. "Ontological Insecurity and Subjective Feelings of Unsafety: Analyzing Socially Constructed Fears in Italy." *Social Science Research* 71 (2018): 160–170.

Väljas, Vaino. "Taasiseseisvumisest." In *Eesti iseseisvus võideti Moskvas*, edited by Andres Adamson. Tallinn: Argo, 2016, 15–33.

Vorotnikov, Vitaly. *A bylo eto tak. . . . Iz dnevnika chlena Politbyuro TsK KPSS.* Moscow: Sovet veteranov knigoizdaniya, SI-MAR, 1995.

Walker, Edward W. *Dissolution: Sovereignty and the Breakup of the Soviet Union.* Lanham, MD: Rowman & Littlefield, 2003.

Williams, Robert R. *Hegel's Ethics of Recognition.* Berkeley: University of California Press, 1997.

Yakovlev, Alexander. *Muki prochteniya bytiya: perestroyka: nadezhdy i realnosti.* Moscow: Novosti, 1991.

Yakovlev, Alexander. *Perestroyka. 1985–1991.* Moscow: Mezhdunarodnyy fond Demokratiya, 2008.

Yakovlev, Alexander. *Sumerki.* Moscow: Materik, 2005.

Yekelchyk, Serhy. *Stalin's Empire of Memory: Russian-Ukrainian Relations in the Soviet Historical Imagination.* Toronto: University of Toronto Press, 2004.

Zake, Ieva. "Multiple Fronts of the Cold War: Ethnic Anti-Communism of Latvian Émigrés." In *Anti-Communist Minorities in the US: Political Activism of Ethnic Refugees*, edited by Ieva Zake. New York: Palgrave Macmillan, 2009, 127–150.

Zake, Ieva. "'The Secret Nazi Network' and Post–World War II Latvian Émigrés in the United States." Draft article. https://www.academia.edu/3068146/ _THE_SECRET_NAZI_NETWORK_POST_WORLD_WAR_II_LATVIAN_ IMMIGRANTS_AND_THE_HUNT_FOR_NAZIS_IN_THE_UNITED_STATES.

Zake, Ieva, and Graham Gormley. "Integration or Separation? Nationality Groups in the US and the Republican Party's Ethnic Politics, 1960s–1980s." *Nationalities Papers* 38, no. 4 (2010): 469–490.

Zelikow, Philip, and Condoleezza Rice. *Germany Unified and Europe Transformed. A Study in Statecraft.* Cambridge, MA: Harvard University Press: 1997.

Zubkova, Elena. *Pribaltika i Kreml. 1940–1953.* Moscow: ROSSPEN, 2008.

Zubok, Vladislav. *Collapse: The Fall of the Soviet Union.* New Haven, CT: Yale University Press, 2021.

NEWSPAPERS

"600 km Long Protest." *Berlingske Tidene*, August 24, 1989.

"Annexation Void Lithuania Say." *New York Times*, August 23, 1989.

"An Appeal for Democracy in the Baltic Republics." *New York Review of Books*, March 28, 1991.

"Attack in Lithuania Threatens Democracy." *USA Today*, January 14, 1991.

"Les Baltes manifestent pour leur indépendance." *Le Figaro*, August 24, 1989.

"Baltic Foreign Ministers Excluded from Summit." *Associated Press*, November 19, 1990.

"Canada Suspends Credit to Soviet Union." *Toronto Star*, January 22, 1991.

"Eighth Annual BAFL Human Rights Conference." *Baltic Bulletin*, June 1989.

"Excerpts from Soviet Statement on Baltic Unrest." *New York Times*, August 27, 1989.

"Hunderttausende Balten begehren gegen die russische Vorherrschauft auf."
    Frankfurter Zeitung, August 24, 1989.
"Kohl Struggles to Salvage Policy to Support Gorbachev." *The Guardian*, January
    15, 1991.
"Latvijas Tautas frontes valdes paziņojums visiem Latvijas neatkarības
    atbalstītājiem." *Latvijas Jaunatne*, December 13, 1990.
"Litauen: 'Wir können nicht glauben, dass dies auf Befehl Gorbatschows
    geschieht': Ein blutiger Akt im baltischen Drama." *Süddeutsche Zeitung*,
    January 14, 1991.
"Lungn protest mot krigspakt." *Dagens Nyheter*, August 24, 1989.
"Mahtava ihmisketju Baltianmaiden lap." *Helsingin Sanomat*, August 24, 1989.
"Marssijat vaativat Koivisto eroa Helsingissä." *Helsingin Sanomat*, January 14, 1991.
"More than Two Million Join Human Chain in Soviet Baltics." *Reuters News*, August
    23, 1989.
"Moskova palaa keskiaikaan." *Helsingin Sanomat*, January 14, 1991.
"O natsional'noi politike partii v sovremennykh usloviyakh: Doklad M. S. Gorbacheva,
    General'nogo sekretarya Tsentral'nogo Komiteta KPSS, na plenume
    Tsentral'nogo Komiteta KPSS 19 sentyabrya 1989 goda." *Pravda*, September
    20, 1989.
"Ob izmeneniyakh i dopolneniyakh Konstitutsii." *Pravda*, October 22, 1988.
"Das offizielle Warschau tut sich schwer mit einer Stellungnahme." *Frankfurter
    Allgemeine Zeitung*, January 15, 1991.
"Ostavka bol'she, chem zhizn'. Beseda Fedora Burlatskogo s Eduardom
    Shevardnadzem." *Literaturnaia Gazeta*, April 10, 1991.
"A Peace Laureate's Putsch." *Wall Street Journal*, January 14, 1991.
"Prague Urges Allies to Quit Warsaw Pact as a Protest." *Wall Street Journal Europe*,
    January 14, 1991.
"PSRS tautas deputāti no Latvijas." *Padomju Jaunatne*, May 23, 1989.
"Report by Baltic Leaders on Human Rights Activities in the Soviet Occupied Baltics."
    Baltic Bulletin, May 1984.
"The Role of Human Rights in the Helsinki Process, Ambassador John D. Scanlan's
    Address." *Baltic Bulletin*, May 1985.
"Senators Urge Recognition of Baltics." *Ukrainian Weekly*, September 1, 1991.
"Skammens tystnad: Perestrojkan dog med blodbadet i Vilnius." *Aftonbladet*, January
    14, 1991.
"Skriv till Gorbatjov." *Expressen*, January 14, 1991.
"Sorgflor på flaggorna. Montagsdemonstration for Baltikum samlade 5000." *Dagens
    Nyheter*, January 15, 1991.
"Soviets Not the Evil Empire Anymore, Reagan Declares: Euphoric President Hails
    Pact." *Los Angeles Times*, December 11, 1987.
"Stalin Collects." *New York Times*, October 3, 1939.
"Støt Litauen. Mød op. Protest mod overfaldet på Litauen." *Politiken*, January
    14, 1991.
"Tiananmen in Vilnius?" *Wall Street Journal*, March 27, 1990.
"Les trois Républiques baltes auraient souhaité une sortie 'plus scandaleuse.'" *Le
    Monde*, November 22, 1990.
"Troops Leaving Baltics, Soviets Say; Convoys on the Move, but Lithuanians Skeptical
    on Withdrawal," *Washington Post*, January 31, 1991.
"URSS après la déclaration franco-allemande M. Dumas: 'Nous ne demandons pas aux
    Lituaniens de renoncer à leur indépendance.'" *Le Monde*, April 29, 1990.

"US Non-committal on Allies Lithuania Letter." *Reuters News*, April 28, 1990.

"Veto soviétique pour les baltes." *Le Monde*, November 21, 1990.

"Vremya trebuyet Novogo Myshleniya. Zapis besedy M. S. Gorbacheva s uchastnikami Issyk-Kulskogo foruma." *Literaturnaia Gazeta*, November 5, 1986.

"World Federation of Free Latvians Asks Reagan for Representation at the May 1985 Human Rights Meeting in Ottawa." *Baltic Bulletin*, May 1985.

"XIX Vsesoyuznaya konferentsiya KPSS: Vneshnaya Politika i Diplomatiya." *Pravda*, July 26, 1988.

"Ya—soldat, a ne myasnik." *Rosbalt*, November 12, 2016.

"Zurück zum Stalinismus." *Frankfurter Allgemeine Zeitung*, January 15, 1991.

Anderson, Bill. "Ford Is Urged to Cut Baltic Ties." *Chicago Tribune*, March 15, 1975.

Anderson, Bill. "New Stress over the Baltic Lands." *Chicago Tribune*, March 19, 1975.

Caumont, Hervé. "L'URSS: langue de fer pour les Baltes." *Quotidien de Paris*, August 28, 1989.

Cohen, Bernard. "Moscou menace les Pays baltes." *Libération*, August 29, 1989.

Conradi, Peter. "Lithuania Waits for Moscow to Show Its Hand." *Reuters News*, April 16, 1990.

Copin, Noël. "Toujours le stalinisme." *La Croix*, January 15, 1991.

Dobbs, Michael. "Baltic States Link in Protest 'So Our Children Can Be Free'." *Washington Post*, August 24, 1989.

Editorial. "Captive Nations." *Washington Post*, August 27, 1989.

Editorial. "For Now Mr. Bush Sets Right Tone." *St. Petersburg Times*, March 30, 1990.

Editorial. "Gorbymania R.I.P." *Los Angeles Daily News*, January 15, 1991.

Editorial. "The Lithuanian Alternative." *Washington Post*, March 28, 1990.

Editorial. "Lithuanian and Soviet Disunion." *St. Louis Post Dispatch*, March 23, 1990.

Editorial, "No New Iron Curtain." *The Times*, January 15, 1991.

Elsner, Alan. "Baker Soothes Baltic Ministers Side-lined at Summit." *Reuters News*, November 18, 1990.

Fein, Esther B. "Baltic Citizens Link Hands to Demand Independence." *New York Times*, August 24, 1989.

Fein, Esther B. "Gorbachev Said to Have Backed Attack on Baltic Movements." *New York Times*, August 30, 1989.

Friedman, Thomas L. "Baker, Outlining World View, Assesses Plan for Soviet Bloc." *New York Times*, March 28, 1989.

Gelb, Leslie H. "Behind the Lithuania Crisis." *New York Times*, March 23, 1990.

Gorbachev, Mikhail. "Obrashenie Prezidenta CCP k narody Litovskogo CCP." *Pravda*, April 1, 1990.

Gorbachev, Mikhail. "Verkhovnyy Sovet Litovskoy SSR Sovet Ministrov Litovskoy SSR." *Pravda*, April 14, 1990.

Gumbel, Peter. "Besieged Baltics: Lithuania Crackdown Signals a Bloody End to Era of Perestroika." *Wall Street Journal*, January 14, 1991.

Handelman, Stephen. "East Meets West This Week to Draft Plans for a New Europe." *Toronto Star*, November 18, 1990.

Hoffman, David, and Ann Devory. "U.S. Quietly Encouraged Initiative." *Washington Post*, April 28, 1990.

Hulen, Bertram D. "US Lashes Soviet for Baltic Seizure." *New York Times*, July 24, 1940.

Jackson, Harold. "George Kennan." *The Guardian*, March 18, 2005. https://www.theguardian.com/news/2005/mar/18/guardianobituaries.usa.

Jauce, Andra. "Apsveikumu es nesaņēmu, bet laba vēlējumus sev un tautai—gan." *Latvijas Jaunatne*, January 7, 1991.

Jerumanis, Aivars. "We Are Latvians and That Sacred Land by the Baltic Sea Is Ours." *Baltic Bulletin*, March 1988.

Katell, Andrew. "Baltics Call Soviet Annexation a 'Crime,' Equate Hitler, Stalin." *Associated Press*, August 22, 1989.

Khavkin, Boris. "Byl li u Sovetskogo Soyuza tretiy put'. Dokumenty 1939–1941 godov i preodoleniye proshlogo." *Nezavisimaya gazeta*, September 24, 2020. https://nvo.ng.ru/history/2020-09-24/1_1110_path.html.

Kivinen, Olli. "Kuka yrittää sammuttaa liekin?" *Helsingin Sanomat*, January 14, 1991.

Kļavis, Aivars, and Guntars Laganovskis. "Patiesība par leģendu." *Latvijas Vēstnesis*, January 1, 2004, https://www.vestnesis.lv/ta/id/83250.

Lewis, Anthony. "Abroad and at Home. The Power of History." *New York Times*, August 27, 1989.

McGrory, Mary. "When Diplomacy Slept." *Washington Post*, January 20, 1991.

McIntyre, Colin. "Baltic Republics Kicked Out of CSCE summit." *Reuters News*, November 19, 1990.

McQuillan, Lawrence. "US Refrains from Recognizing Lithuania." *Reuters News*, March 12, 1990.

Mekas, Jonas. "No, My Friend, We Won't Go Slow." *New York Times*, March 29, 1990.

Miłosz, Czesław. "Lituanie le grand mensonge." *Le Monde*, January 23, 1991.

Neef, Christian. "Secret Papers Reveal Truth behind Soviet Collapse." *Der Spiegel*, August 11, 2011, https://www.spiegel.de/international/europe/the-gorbachev-files-secret-papers-reveal-truth-behind-soviet-collapse-a-779277.html.

Oakes, John B. "Lean on the Lithuanians." *New York Times*, April 21, 1990.

Oberdorfer, Don. "Moscow Warned on Baltic Repression." *Washington Post*, January 18, 1991.

Remnick, David. "Gorbachev Shows His Tough Side; Nationalist Movements Are Learning His Tolerance Has Limits." *Washington Post*, August 30, 1989.

Riding, Alan. "Baltic Assaults Lead Europeans to Hold Off Aid." *New York Times*, January 23, 1991.

Riding, Alan. "Soviet Crackdown; Europeans Warn Soviet about Aid." *New York Times*, January 14, 1991.

Rosenthal, A. M. "How to Desert a Friend." *New York Times*, April 15, 1990.

Rosenthal, A. M. "The New World Order Dies." *New York Times*, January 15, 1991.

Roush, Matt. "TV Commentary: On the Air, Doom, Gloom and Optimism." *USA Today*, January 14, 1991.

Safire, William. "Essay: Baltic to Baghdad." *New York Times*, March 30, 1990.

Safire, William. "Gorbachev's 'Bloody Sunday.'" *New York Times*, January 17, 1991.

Safire, William. "World to Vilnius: Suffer." *New York Times*, April 23, 1990.

Sarraute, Claude. "Ces ne sont pas les Koweitens les Baltes!" *Le Monde*, November 22, 1990.

Savill, Annika. "The CSCE Summit—Inside File—Thaw Leaves Baltics Out in the Cold." *The Independent*, November 21, 1990.

Schmemann, Serge. "Summit in Europe: Reporter's Notebook." *New York Times*, November 20, 1990.

Sergi, Sergio. "Il Baltico in rivolta. Erano un milione, mano nella mano." *L'Unità*, August 24, 1989.

Thom, Françoise. "Le honteux lâchage des Baltes." *Quotidien de Paris*, November 11, 1990.

Vernet, Daniel "Coup de grâce pour la perestroïka." *Le Monde*, January 15, 1991.

Warren, Marcus. "Putin Lets NATO 'Recruit' in Baltic." *The Telegraph*, June 25, 2002.

UNPUBLISHED DISSERTATIONS AND PAPERS

Bergmane, Una. "French and US Reactions Facing the Disintegration of the USSR: The Case of the Baltic States (1989–1991)." PhD diss., Sciences Po Paris, 2016.

Bošs, Edijs. "Aligning with the Unipole: Security Policies of Estonia, Latvia, and Lithuania, 1988–1998." PhD diss., University of Cambridge, 2011.

L'Hommedieu, Jonathan. "Exiles and Constituents: Baltic Refugees and American Cold War Politics, 1948–1960." PhD diss., Turku University, 2011.

Pettai, Vello Andreas. "Framing the Past as Future: The Power of Legal Restorationism In Estonia." PhD diss., Columbia University, 2004.

Saharov, Juhan. "From Economic Independence to Political Sovereignty: Inventing 'Self-Management' in the Estonian SSR." PhD diss., University of Tartu, 2021.

Whittington, Anna. "Contested Privilege: Ethnic Russians and the Unmaking of the Soviet Union." Article accepted by *Journal of Modern History*.

PRESENTATIONS AT CONFERENCES AND SEMINARS

Piirimäe, Kaarel. " 'Estonia Has Not Time': Perceptions of the Post–Cold War as a Window of Opportunity." Paper presented at the Conference "Post–Cold War. Change and Continuity in the Making of a New World Order at the Turn of the 1990s." University of Minnesota, October 27–28, 2016.

Radchenko, Sergey. Presentation at the LSE International History Department Cold War Research Cluster Seminar, May 9, 2019.

Ramonaitė, Ainė. "Explaining the Birth of Sąjūdis: The Networking Power of Alternative Society in Soviet Lithuania." Paper prepared for the 10th Conference on Baltic Studies in Europe "Cultures, Crises, Consolidations in the Baltic World." Tallinn University, June 16–19, 2013.

INDEX

For the benefit of digital users, indexed terms that span two pages (e.g., 52–53) may, on occasion, appear on only one of those pages.